D0998657

St. Louis Community College

Forest Park
Florissant Valley
Meramec

Instructional Resources
St. Louis, Missouri

10/92

THE PEOPLE
WHO DISCOVERED
COLUMBUS

The Ripley P. Bullen Series
Florida Museum of Natural History
University of Florida

St. Louis Community College
at Meramec
Library

Florida Museum of Natural History
Ripley P. Bullen Series
Jerald T. Milanich, General Editor

Tacachale: Essays on the Indians of Florida and Southeastern Georgia during the Historic Period, edited by Jerald T. Milanich and Samuel Proctor (1978).

Aboriginal Subsistence Technology on the Southeastern Coastal Plain during the Late Prehistoric Period, by Lewis H. Larson (1980).

Cemochechobee: Archaeology of a Mississippian Ceremonial Center on the Chatta-hoochee River, by Frank T. Schnell, Vernon J. Knight, Jr., and Gail S. Schnell (1981).

Fort Center: An Archaeological Site in the Lake Okeechobee Basin, by William H. Sears, with contributions by Elsie O'R. Sears and Karl T. Steinen (1982).

Perspectives on Gulf Coast Prehistory, edited by Dave D. Davis (1984).

Archaeology of Aboriginal Culture Change in the Interior Southeast: Depopulation during the Early Historic Period, by Marvin T. Smith (1987).

Apalachee: The Land between the Rivers, by John H. Hann (1988).

Key Marco's Buried Treasure: Archaeology and Adventure in the Nineteenth Century, by Marion Spjut Gilliland (1989).

First Encounters: Spanish Explorations in the Caribbean and the United States, 1492–1570, edited by Jerald T. Milanich and Susan Milbrath (1989).

Missions to the Calusa, edited by John H. Hann, with Introduction by William H. Marquardt (1991).

Excavations on the Franciscan Frontier: Archaeology at the Fig Springs Mission, by Brent Richards Weisman (1992).

The People Who Discovered Columbus: The Prehistory of the Bahamas, by William F. Keegan (1992).

THE PEOPLE
WHO DISCOVERED
COLUMBUS

THE PREHISTORY

OF THE BAHAMAS

WILLIAM F. KEEGAN

University Press of Florida

Gainesville / Tallahassee / Tampa / Boca Raton
Pensacola / Orlando / Miami / Jacksonville

Columbus Quincentenary Series

Copyright 1992 by the Board of Regents of the State of Florida

Printed in the United States of America on acid-free, recycled paper

All rights reserved

The University Press of Florida is the scholarly publishing agency for the State University System of Florida, comprised of Florida A & M University, Florida Atlantic University, Florida International University, Florida State University, University of Central Florida, University of Florida, University of North Florida, University of South Florida, and University of West Florida.

University Press of Florida
15 Northwest 15th Street
Gainesville, FL 32611

Library of Congress Cataloging in Publication Data can be found on the last printed page of the book.

FOR LORIE

CONTENTS

1. Before the Beginning: Native Peoples of the West Indies   1

The Ethnohistory of the Guanahatabeys or Guanahacabibes. The Archaeology of the Guanahatabeys. The Genesis of the Guanahatabeys. Island Caribs. The Archaeology of the Island Caribs. The Tainos. The Saladoid Expansion, 2100 B.C.–A.D. 600. The Ostionoid Expansion, A.D. 600–1200. The Development of the Tainos in the Greater Antilles.

2. Introduction to the Geology, Geography, Climate, and Ecology of the Pre-Columbian Bahamas   20

Geology. Geography. Climate and Vegetation. Terrestrial Fauna. Coastal Environments. Marine Environments. Summary and Conclusions.

3. The Taino Colonization of the Bahamas   48

Taino Navigation. The First Settlement in the Bahamas. Motives for Colonizing the Bahamas.

4. Settlement and Settlers: Lucayan Settlement Patterns   65

Ideal Distributions: Steady-State and Weighted. Archaeological Surveys

FIGURES

MAPS

TABLES

PREFACE

 A re you still doing that archaeology stuff?"

That question started a phone call from Richard Nordstrom. It was the fall of 1977, and Rich and I were both at the University of Connecticut. He was completing his master's degree in marine biology (he is now president of ORCA Industries) and I my BA in anthropology. We shared a mutual interest in SCUBA diving and had worked together in a variety of capacities. Prior to that phone call we had last spoken six months earlier when I was president of the UCONN SCUBA Club and he was our diving instructor.

During those six months Rich had become involved in the fledgling Foundation for the Protection of Reefs and Islands from Degradation and Exploitation (PRIDE) on Pine Cay in the Turks and Caicos Islands. In those days PRIDE was more dream than reality, the offspring of Chuck Hesse and Kathy Orr. It was founded as a not-for-profit scientific and educational foundation that would actively work to educate the local and tourist publics and to protect and preserve the natural resources of the islands. PRIDE has been successful beyond all but Chuck's expectations.

PRIDE had arranged to offer a summer field school in conjunction with the UCONN School of Education. Dr. Thomas Goodkind was by then well known for his field schools in which present and prospective teachers were immersed in a "foreign" lifeway (although one of his field schools was held in the western United States, the setting was foreign to his typical student). The purpose was to bring new meaning to their role as teachers by bringing new meaning to their own educational milieu.

Rich had called because they wanted an archaeologist as one of the instructors for the course entitled "Field Study in Caribbean Island Environments," which was to be held on Pine Cay in July 1978. There was an archaeologist working on Middle Caicos at the time, but he was planning to leave in January and could not return in time for the course. I jumped at the opportunity. I was told that I needed to meet and get the approval of both Goodkind and the director of the PRIDE Foundation, Chuck Hesse. Goodkind was across campus, Hesse on Pine Cay. So less than a month after that momentous phone call I was on a plane for Pine Cay.

I had gone to Jamaica in 1973, in 1974 the Bahamas and Puerto Rico, in 1975 the Bahamas again, and in 1976 the Bay Islands, Honduras. Yet I was totally unprepared for what I was about to see. The twin-propeller plane took over three hours to reach Grand Turk from Miami. I then boarded a nine-seat island hopper, and we proceeded from Grand Turk to Middle Caicos to North Caicos and finally to Pine Cay. As the plane made its approach to the small coral runway I wondered what had happened to all the trees. Apparently, the Caicos were still recovering from Hurricane Donna, which struck the islands in 1960. Some say Pine Cay, highest elevation 25 feet, was completely under water. On none of the islands, except the settled areas of North and Middle Caicos, did the vegetation exceed six feet. You couldn't buy a piece of shade.

That night I met with Chuck, Kathy, and PRIDE's patron Bill Cowles and it was decided that I should meet the archaeologist. The archaeologist was Shaun Sullivan, then a Ph.D. candidate at the University of Illinois.

The next morning they woke me at 7:00 A.M. and put me on a Cessna headed for Middle Caicos. I was deposited at the Conch Bar airstrip (a dirt runway whose terminal was a 6-by-10-foot shed) and managed to arrange "trans" to the settlement of Bambara, the location of Sullivan's base camp. It took an hour to go the ten miles to Bambara. I arrived to find that Sullivan had not yet returned for the day from the field, but his assistant, Barbara Macnider, thought Shaun would have no objections to my staying and helping out for a few days. Shaun arrived about an hour later and all was settled; I would work with them for the next five days.

The days were spent profitably. There was a rainy day during which I coaxed from Shaun a day-long lecture on Caribbean prehistory. Two days were spent surveying with Barbara on North Caicos. We were led from plantation site to plantation site ("where the olden-time people lived") by a local guide who swore that he knew the locations of prehistoric sites. He was trusted because he had worked for Shaun on Middle Caicos. Our survey covered more than 30 miles yet produced no sites (most of our time being spent in the interior).

The most memorable day was spent at site MC-6 with Shaun and Grethe Seim. As I will discuss later, site MC-6 is a ceremonial/trading center—a Classic Taino outpost that was probably established after A.D. 1200 to manage access to a salt-producing pond and to facilitate the collection of marine resources on the Caicos Bank (notably queen conch).

MC-6 was a four-kilometer walk from Bambara along a true "Bahamian trail." Most trails in the Bahamas make parsimonious use of machete cuts and instead take full advantage of natural breaks in the vegetation. It is therefore difficult for the uninitiated to be certain that they are really on a trail. The trail wound along ridge tops through the dense brush of the interior and deposited us in a cactus forest on the northern margin of Armstrong Pond. On that day Armstrong Pond was a muddy brown color, but when I returned in the summer of 1984 it was all a white crust of crystalline salt. Sullivan found 18 sites around the margin of the pond; common sense tells us that the pond is the reason people settled there. Salt is the only logical motive.

We progressed along the margin of the pond until we reached the mile-long aboriginal road that led to the site (an irrefutable confirmation of the association between the site and pond). We left the dense closed-canopy (but only 10 feet high) hardwood coppice at the end of the road and stepped onto a grass-covered field. The field is the first permanently dry land above the seasonally flooded salina that today extends 4 kilometers to the sea. As we stepped out of the forest we were immediately engulfed in mosquitoes, my arms turning black before my eyes. Though they respected the power of Cutter's repellant, their incessant buzzing made me willing to offer my blood in return for silence, a deal that I knew was impossible since there were more of them than rations of my blood. Somehow you manage to ignore both the noise and their occasional forays into eyes, mouth, and ears.

MC-6 was spectacular. The site is a planned community of houses arranged around two plazas. The house locations are marked by stone foundations and depressions in a meter-high midden ridge. The larger plaza has a central court on which limestone rocks have been aligned. At first this court was thought to be a ballcourt, the scene of the Taino's *batey*. But when Sullivan completed the analysis of the detailed map he made he found that the stones were aligned with the rising and setting of certain stars and with the summer solstice. An on-the-ground observatory, the court is a unique Bahamian artifact of Taino culture. Sullivan's

(1981) research is testimony to the importance of detailed topographic mapping as well as to a broad-based knowledge of circum-Caribbean societies (for instance, ancient astronomy; Aveni and Urton 1982).

The day after my first visit to MC-6 I spent the entire afternoon waiting for a plane that I was never completely convinced would arrive. The nine-seat plane was filled with local women returning from a shopping trip to Grand Turk. Each take-off and landing, not to mention turbulence, was filled with entreaty and blessing ("Praise Jesus," "Thank you, Jesus"). The 250-pound woman who sat next to me took great solace in my presence; as the plane rose and descended her grip strengthened to flatten biceps into bone. Despite temporary disfunction in my right hand, I returned to Pine Cay safely, made arrangements for my part of the summer field school, and then read everything I could find on Caribbean archaeology. To borrow a line from Kurt Vonnegut, "So it goes."

From that day forth there has been no looking back. Certainly there were times when I thought it would soon end, but those were thankfully overcome. Early on I decided that I would one day write a paleoethnography of the Lucayans. My concept of what constitutes a paleoethnography has changed substantially from those days in the Caicos. Nonetheless, what follows is my present view of what should constitute a culture history in which archaeological methods are used to further anthropological goals.

In writing this book I have tried to reach two audiences. One is those people with a scholarly interest in questions concerning the Bahamas specifically, the West Indies in general, or, even more generally, small-island biogeography. There is a glaring lack of synthetic studies of Caribbean archaeology on all levels. My emphasis, of course, is on the Bahama archipelago. At the same time scholarly syntheses are lacking, there are even fewer sources available to the general audience. I have therefore sought to present this study in language that is easily understood by readers unacquainted with the jargon of anthropologists.

Outline of the Book

The book is organized to provide a historical depiction of the movement of peoples into the Bahamas, a portrait of the characteristics of the islands themselves during the early days of Taino settlement, and descriptions of how the Lucayans made their settlements, what they ate, how they organized themselves in social groups, and how their population grew to settle all of the archipelago, ending with the arrival of the Spanish and the Lucayans' untimely demise.

In the first chapter I take us "before the beginning" to glimpse the movement of peoples through the Antilles to the point from which they embarked for the Bahamas. I also introduce the native West Indians at contact and discuss their importance in Bahama prehistory. I describe the physical and biological worlds in the Bahamas in chapter 2 to set the stage. In chapter 3, I evaluate alternative models for the colonization of the Bahama archipelago with regard to their ability to account for observed patterns in the archaeological record.

Having established a first colony on Great Inagua, I next examine where the Lucayans chose to live and how determining those choices allows us to retrodict the way in which the islands were settled. In other words, I follow the Lucayans as they colonize all of the islands in the archipelago. The models used to explain how the islands were settled proved incomplete without a consideration of Lucayan social organization. I discuss in chapter 5 how the Lucayans were organized, where they resided in relation to family, and how their system of inheritance operated. In this discussion the missing pieces of the colonization puzzle are supplied, and the model of population expansion is completed.

Having peopled the islands, I turn next to the diet that sustained the colonists and that pulled them northward onto unoccupied islands (chapter 6). The final aspects of Lucayan society that I consider are reproduction, population growth, and the size of the Lucayan population at contact (chapter 7).

With chapter 8 we commence the beginning of the end. The arrival of Christopher Columbus, Columbus's search for the "City of Gold," the failure of the colonial enterprise, and the practice of overexploiting human resources in the absence of material counterparts are all considered. The arrival of Columbus and the reconstruction of his route through the Bahamas are discussed in chapter 8; the effects of the conquest are then examined (chapter 9). I also examine in chapter 9 the wholesale export of Lucayans to Hispaniola and, in the closing years, from there to the pearl beds off Venezuela. The Lucayans were the first people to be contacted, and the first to disappear from the face of the earth. By 1520, a Lucayan population of perhaps 80,000 had declined to, at most, a few refugees. The book concludes with a reflection on the methodology of archaeological anthropology and a short overview of the Lucayans on the eve of contact (chapter 10).

Each chapter includes information drawn from a variety of sources. These sources include historic reports (in the Bahamas limited essentially to the *diario* of Columbus's first voyage), ethnohistoric interpretations of those reports, ethnographic accounts of modern populations who are living in tropical forest and small-island settings similar to the Bahamas, ethnological interpretations of the general patterns of human culture, and, finally, the results of archaeological investigations. Although archaeology is typically presented last in the sequence, I have tried to avoid the error of placing too much weight on historic documents. Such reliance on the written word of the Spanish chroniclers has caused significant misinterpretations of the prehistoric record (Keegan 1989b; Davis and Goodwin 1990). The documents need to be treated as suspect until archaeological or other confirmation is established.

ACKNOWLEDGEMENTS

It goes without saying that I owe a debt to a great many people. A number of people had profound and long-lasting effects on my development as an archaeologist. Of special note are Nick Bellantoni, Nick Blurton Jones, Tim Earle, Julian Granberry, Marvin Harris, Allen Johnson, Jerry Kennedy, Pat Kirch, Kevin McBride, Charlie McNutt, Bob Preucel, Bill Sears, Shaun Sullivan, and John Terrell.

It has also been my great fortune to have collaborated with some truly excellent scholars, including Brian Butler, Michael DeNiro, Jared Diamond, and Morgan Maclachlan. They will recognize something of themselves in the chapters that follow. Dara and Eric Silverberg helped with first draft transcriptions. Tony Lyons assisted with the preparation of the bibliography. George Anthony Aarons, Judith Fandrich, and Geoffrey Senior read drafts and offered extensive comments. Dave Davis and Sam Wilson provided insightful reviews that improved the content and flow of the book.

More than a decade of archaeological fieldwork has been brought to bear on the questions that are addressed in this book. The work would not have been so professionally or personally satisfying without the help of Ellen Bethel, Tom Goodkind, Jim Kelley, David Knowles, Charles Misick, Rich Nordstrom, Kathy Orr, Grethe Seim, Dennis Williams, and the people at AUTEC on Andros. I owe a special debt to Bill and Ginny Cowles (formerly of Pine Cay) and to Chuck Hesse for supporting my first efforts. Neil Sealey has been a valued friend, colleague, and unending source of knowledge about all aspects of the Bahamas.

Fieldwork in the Bahamas would not have been possible without three remarkable people. Over the 10 years Corbett Torrence has worked with me on archaeological surveys covering almost 1000 km. His assistance has been invaluable. Between 1982 and 1987 Steven Mitchell and I seemed to be constant companions. Although differences in our professions have taken us down different paths, Mitchell deserves credit for his diligence in introducing geo(archaeo)logical approaches in the Bahamas and for conducting fieldwork on the most difficult of islands. Lastly, Gail Saunders has been a continuous source of encouragement and support. It is through her efforts that government permission for our research was obtained.

Funding for research reported in this book has been provided by William and Virginia Cowles, the PRIDE Foundation, EARTHWATCH, the Caribbean Research Foundation, UCLA Graduate School, UCLA Department of Anthropology, UCLA Friends of Archaeology, University of South Carolina Department of Anthropology, University of Florida Division of Sponsored Research, and the Wallace Groves Aquaculture Foundation.

The true catalyst behind this work is Loretta Cox Keegan. Instead of complaining about the long hours and months in the field, her present concern is, what will the *next* book be about? This book is for Lorie; she knows why. But, as with everything else these days, she will have to share it with Daniel, Lindsay, and Caroline.

1

Before the Beginning: Native Peoples of the West Indies

Most written descriptions of the Caribbean at the time of Columbus record the presence of only three cultures, usually called Ciboney, Arawak, and Carib (Rouse 1948). Even people with only the most rudimentary knowledge of Caribbean prehistory today know of the "peaceful Arawaks," "Carib cannibals," and "cave-dwelling Ciboney" (map 1.1). These names were lifted from the historic reports of the early contact period. What historic descriptions failed to record, archaeological speculation has supplied. In the process, accurate information was often the first victim. The names themselves not only are misleading and inaccurate but also mask the wide range of variability in language and customs that the Spanish chroniclers recorded. In addition, the names have come to assume temporal, spatial, and cultural dimensions.

The traditional outline of Caribbean prehistory reads as follows: The Ciboney were the last in a line of people who lived by hunting, gathering, and fishing whose ancestors arrived in the Greater Antilles at least 9,000 years ago (Veloz and Vega 1982). By the time of Spanish contact they had been pushed into peripheral locations in the extreme western provinces of Cuba and southwest Haiti. They lacked agriculture, pottery, houses (they lived in caves), and their language and religion were different from

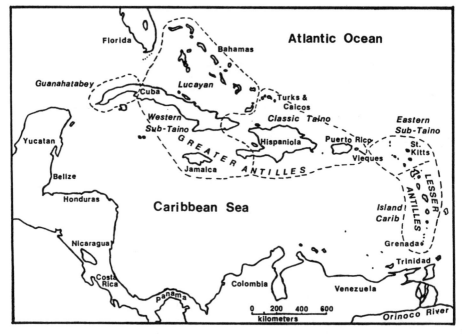

M AP 1.1. West Indian cultural geography at contact, after Rouse, 1986.

the other peoples who occupied the West Indies at Spanish contact. They were the losers in confrontations with the expanding Arawaks, and they disappeared from the historic record soon after contact.

The Ciboney were followed by at least one migration of Arawakan-speaking peoples who entered the West Indies at the time of Christ. The Island Arawaks colonized all of the Greater Antilles (except western Cuba), the Lesser Antilles, and the Bahama Islands. Their staple crop was manioc, which was made into cassava bread, they lived in large villages, they spoke a single language, and they shared a common religion. In eastern Cuba, Hispaniola, and Puerto Rico there developed a complex culture called by the Spanish Taino, which glosses as noble or good in their language. The Island Arawaks were the victims of the Spanish conquest. Their population declined from one million in 1492 to a few hundred by 1540.

Beginning just before the Spanish conquest, the Island Arawaks in the Lesser Antilles were hunted down and consumed by Caribs who entered the West Indies from the coast of the Guianas. The Island Caribs were cannibals who ate Island Arawak men and took Island Arawak women as their wives. By the time the Spanish arrived they had established a foothold in eastern Puerto Rico. The approach of the marauding Island Caribs, among other things, led to the colonization of the Bahamas as the Arawaks fled from their path. Island Carib militarism helped them to hold the Europeans at bay until the eighteenth century, by which time a large "Black Carib" population had developed in the Windward Islands through the joined forces of escaped slaves and native peoples.

Recent archaeological, ethnohistorical, and linguistic studies have demonstrated that most of the foregoing conventional history is inaccurate. Those conventional views are modern myths or "just so" stories created by scientists, avocationalists, and the public in their efforts to understand a complex history from a limited and biased ethnohistorical data base. In this chapter I seek to correct some of those misconceptions and in the process to introduce the peoples whose lives did leave, or are thought to have left, some imprint in the Bahamas.

In the present context only a very brief outline of West Indian prehistory is possible. To achieve detailed coverage this broad topic would itself require book-length treatment (see Rouse 1986; Siegel 1989; Wilson 1990a). The present discussion will focus first on the Guanahatabey (formerly called Ciboney). Although there is presently no evidence that these peoples ever occupied the Bahamas, it was at one time thought that they came from Florida, possibly along a route that passed through the Bahamas (Loven 1935), and it remains a possibility that they did settle in, or at least exploited the resources of, the Bahamas (B.A.T. 1984).

The Island Caribs are next. Although the Island Caribs never actually settled in the Bahamas, they are sometimes credited with forcing the Island Arawak colonization of these islands (Craton 1986). Moreover, the Island Caribs were the victims of a very successful slander. They deserve to have a more balanced view presented (Myers 1984; Allaire 1980, 1987; Davis and Goodwin 1990).

This chapter concludes with a brief discussion of the Island Arawak expansion through the Antilles, to set the stage for the movement of these peoples into the Bahamas. It should be noted that the culture history (or histories) of the peoples the Spanish called Tainos is extremely complex. The general nature of the following review does not allow this complexity to be expressed (see Rouse 1986; Wilson 1990a).

The Ethnohistory of the Guanahatabeys or
Guanahacabibes

The Guanahatabeys, formerly called Ciboney, were first described by Diego Velázquez de Cuellar (the man who initiated the Cuban entrada in 1511) in his letter to the king dated April 1, 1514: "The life of these people is of the manner of savages, for they have neither houses nor village quarters, nor fields, nor do they eat anything else than the flesh they take in the montes [mountains] and turtles and fish" (quoted in Sauer 1966:184). That report is supplemented by Bartolomé de Las Casas who wrote, "Indians at the Cape of Cuba [Cabo San Antonio] who are like savages, have no relations whatever with others of the island, nor do they have houses, but they live in caves, except when they go out to fish, and are called Guanahacabibes" (quoted in Sauer 1966:184).

Las Casas also provided an accounting of the natives of Cuba. In his 1516 memorial to Cardinal Francisco Jiménez de Cisneros, he described four native groups who needed to be salvaged: those of the Jardines or cays off both north and south Cuba; the Guanahacabibes of the Cape of Cuba; the Ciboneys, who were the same as those of the Jardines, but were kept as servants by the other Cuban Indians; and any left on the Lucayan islands who are described as of the same nature and ways as those of the Jardines (Sauer 1966:185). From this account it is evident that Las Casas had two classificatory groups in mind: the Guanahatabeys (i.e., the Guanahacabibes) and the peoples who have come to be called the Sub-Tainos (i.e., the Ciboney, the Lucayans, and the people of the Jardines).

Although both Las Casas and Velázquez lived in Cuba for some time, Loven (1935) has concluded that the discoverers and conquerors of this island never visited western Cuba and thus lacked firsthand knowledge of the Guanahatabey. Furthermore, when Pánfilo de Narváez entered the province of Habana he found caciques (chiefs) and conditions that were similar to those of eastern Cuba (Sauer 1966). In addition, five provinces or "chieftainships" have been identified in western Cuba from the reports of Velázquez and Narváez. These provinces bear the Taino names (from west to east): Guanahacabibes, Guaniguanico, Marien, Habana, and Hanabana (Rouse 1948:501).

In sum, both Velázquez and Las Casas reported that the people of western Cuba were different from those in the remainder of the northern West Indies, that these people lacked houses and lived in caves, lacked agricultural fields, and survived by hunting and fishing. Those reports apparently were not substantiated by firsthand observations.

The Archaeology of the Guanahatabeys

In 1935, Sven Loven presented a reasoned accounting of the evidence for the people he called "Guanahatabeyes" or "Siboneyes." First, Loven quoted the above passages from Velázquez and Las Casas. He then went on to identify the Guanahatabeyes with the aceramic cultural remains that had been uncovered in western Cuba by Harrington (1921) and Cosculluela (1946). It was concluded that the aceramic archaeological deposits of Cuba must be the remnants of the Guanahatabeyes, and that these people persisted from a migration that preceded the arrival of the Tainos.

But Loven was also a careful reviewer. He recognized that Las Casas had never observed the Guanahatabeyes, and that the assertion of Las Casas that they lived in caves "must not be taken as in complete harmony with reality" (1935:22). Furthermore, because reports of the Guanahatabeyes were not based on firsthand observations Loven reasoned that they must have been provided by the Tainos (1935:4): "The information obtained from the Cuban Tainos about the general cultural standpoint of this race, does not harmonize with their proper characteristics as established by the conclusions to which Cosculluela and Harrington came, through their excavations of the Cuban dwelling-sites." Finally, Loven concluded that, notwithstanding local traditions of "Wild Indians" killing the cattle of the seventeenth-century colonists and other reports as late as the mid-nineteenth century, it had not been established that "primitive people still lived in the most western part of Cuba at the time of the Conquest" (1935:4).

Within seven years the reasoned opinions of Loven were replaced by a less critical attitude. In the report of his investigations of the "Ciboney Culture of Cayo Redondo, Cuba," Cornelius Osgood (1942:50) stated: "Traditionally there lived in Cuba a primitive people distinguished in language and culture from the Arawak and Carib who dominated the West Indies in the time of the Spanish conquistadors. Apparently many of them had been made slaves or had been put into an inferior caste when the Arawaks moved into the east of Cuba, but those in the extreme west remained as before and in early historic times came to be known as the

Guanahacabibes or Ciboney, a group of semi-mythical cave dwellers, who
were finally shot down like predatory animals for killing the cattle which
wandered away from the early haciendas. There can be little doubt that
the dwellers on Cayo Redondo belonged to this same group of Ciboney."

The cultural synthesis that has served as the basis of most studies in
West Indian prehistory is Rouse's (1948) contribution to the *Handbook of
South American Indians*. Rouse reported that the Ciboney were the original inhabitants of the West Indies, as indicated by their peripheral position during historic times; that it was commonly assumed that they
originated in Florida; that most sites were coastal shell heaps; and that
their cultural characteristics were best understood in apposition to the
Tainos. In other words, they were nonagricultural hunter-fisher-gatherers
who lived in caves or used windbreaks in the open, wore breechcloths or
girdles made of vegetable fiber, did not deform their foreheads, lacked
pottery, lived in small social groups, held property in common, and possessed a non-Taino religion.

In Rouse's (1948) report it was assumed that the Ciboney survived in
western Cuba until contact, and that isolated groups of Ciboney-like Indians also survived until contact on the Guaicayarima peninsula in southwestern Haiti. The Haitian Ciboney were first reported by Gonzalo Fernández de Oviedo prior to his arrival on Hispaniola. Loven (1935) cites
Las Casas, who lived in southwestern Haiti, as contradicting Oviedo, and
recent archaeological investigations by Clark Moore (Rouse and Moore
1985) support Las Casas's observation that the Guaicayarima peninsula
was occupied by Tainos at contact. It seems that Oviedo simply confused
the peninsula names Guanahacabibe (Cuba) and Guaicayarima (Haiti)
while repeating the Velázquez account. Alternatively, Oviedo may have
known that western Cuba had not been visited at that time and therefore
moved these peoples to a similar sounding location that had been explored.

The final category of evidence that has been used to support the assumption that the Guanahatabey survived until contact is radiocarbon
dates (Rouse and Allaire 1978). Of these dates the most recent is A.D.
990–1650. This date does not, however, inspire confidence since it was
obtained from 1.25 centimeters (0.5 inches) below surface in a limestone
cave and was thus in close proximity to potential contaminants. Furthermore, the standard deviation of 200 years gives it equal probability of
predating European contact by centuries. Next in the sequence is an un-

calibrated date of A.D. 1030, which predates European contact by almost 500 years. At this time radiocarbon dates do not support the assumed survival until contact.

The Genesis of the Guanahatabeys

Whether or not they actually existed at contact, the modern creation of a Guanahatabey culture follows an obvious sequence. First, in 1514 one of the leaders of the Cuban entrada reported the presence of a savage people in a region of Cuba that had most likely not been visited by the date of his report. There is no reason to accept the veracity of that account. In fact, given the conquistadores' propensity for identifying strange people and places in the New World (Milbrath 1989) it should be discounted. A similar case involves Christopher Columbus who transferred the legend of a land inhabited entirely by women ("Amazons") to the Taino's mythical island of Matinino (Stevens-Arroyo 1988). Columbus also reported the presence of two races in Cuba—one born with tails and the other without hair (Sauer 1966:23). The Spanish were not the best ethnographers, especially when they lacked firsthand knowledge of the subject about which they wrote.

The Guanahatabeyes received additional life in what were probably retellings of the Velázquez account by both Las Casas and Oviedo. All three accounts are so similar as to support the interpretation that they derive from a single source. The major modifications are Oviedo's misplacement of the Guanahatabey in southwestern Haiti, and the embellishment in Las Casas's report that the Guanahatabey "live in caves, except when they go out to fish" (Sauer 1966:184). The Las Casas account seems to be at least partially inspired by Taino mythology, in which caves figure prominently (Alegría 1986). The myth about cave-dwelling men who were turned into trees when they left their cave to go fishing (Fewkes 1907; Stevens-Arroyo 1988) sounds too similar to the Las Casas account to be ignored. In this regard Osgood (1942:50) was correct when he called the Guanahatabey (Ciboney) "semi-mythical."

Unlike humans with tails and unlike Amazons, the Guanahatabey have achieved immortality at the hands of archaeologists. The discovery of an aceramic material culture that pre-dated the arrival of the Tainos came immediately to be associated with the name Guanahatabey (Ciboney), and it was correspondingly assumed that these people survived in western Cuba until contact (Harrington 1921; Loven 1935; Osgood 1942; Rouse 1948, 1986; Tabio and Rey 1979).

The notion of hunter-gatherer societies being pushed into marginal locations by expanding agriculturalists is a primary element of the diffusion models that have characterized West Indian archaeology. Further, the idea that the archaic hunter-gatherers in the West Indies survived until European contact is appealing from a commonsense point of view. First, such a survival provides continuity from the initial colonization of the West Indies until European contact. Second, the Guanahatabey provide a buffer between the Mayas in the Yucatan and the Tainos of Hispaniola, thus explaining the lack of evidence for any movement of artifacts between these societies. Third, their survival accounts for the apparent absence of Taino remains in western Cuba. Finally, it provides a name for the aceramic cultures of the West Indies, thus simplifying discussion of them.

But common sense and convenience are not enough. We presently lack sufficient evidence to support the belief that such a population survived in western Cuba until Spanish contact. The weight of the evidence suggests that the Guanahatabey were a creation of the Spanish or the Taino imagination, or both, that has been given life by modern investigators eager to add substance to a prehistoric material culture. In sum we must dispense with the Guanahatabey until more conclusive archaeological evidence for their existence is uncovered, and we must explain the aceramic remains found throughout the Antilles solely on the basis of material evidence.

Island Caribs

For years, the Island Caribs have served as the great villains of West Indian prehistory (Michener 1988), a pejorative attitude that is maintained today through our use of their name as a synonym for anthropophagy, the consumption of human flesh. The Island Caribs are reputed to have been cannibals who, during their northward migration from the coast of the Guianas into the Lesser Antilles, preyed upon the peaceful Island Arawaks —eating the men and taking the women as wives (Taylor and Rouse 1955). Recently, Island Caribs have been used to explain everything from being the stimulus or motivation for the Island Arawak expansion through the West Indies (i.e., they fled from the advancing Caribs) to being the warriors who Columbus reported were raiding the Lucayans (Craton 1986).

The question of who the Island Caribs were remains with us today (Allaire 1977, 1980). Oral traditions that were collected among the Island Caribs in the seventeenth and eighteenth centuries included a story of their origins that identified a homeland in the area today known as the Guianas. Armed with this origin myth, archaeologists have sought material remains that would document a late prehistoric or early protohistoric migration of Caribs into the Lesser Antilles from South America.

Actually, there are at least five different kinds of Caribs whose identities are frequently confused: the Caribes of Taino mythology, the semimythical Caniba who Columbus believed were the people of the Grand Khan, the generic cannibals who were any peoples that the Spanish chose to enslave, the Cariban-speaking peoples of the South American mainland, and the Island Caribs who occupied the Windward Islands of the Lesser Antilles. Only cannibals and Island Caribs will receive further consideration here.

The so-called cannibals are a legacy of the Spanish (Sued-Badillo 1978; Myers 1984; Davis and Goodwin 1990). On the one hand the Tainos were easily subjugated by the Spanish because they often attempted compromise and accommodation rather than warfare; they were thus considered peaceful. On the other, native peoples in the Lesser Antilles adopted more aggressive postures toward the Spanish, French, English, Dutch, and anyone else who threatened their sovereignty (Wilson 1990b). It is interesting to note that the Island Caribs' response proved the more successful since they survived unconquered into the eighteenth century.

The Spanish distinction of peaceful and warlike was not completely without self-interest. From the outset, Columbus seems to have had in mind the development of a slave trade similar to the one being operated by Portugal in Africa. Those peoples whom Columbus believed could be transformed into holiness through conversion to Christianity came to be known as the "peaceful Arawaks," while those who resisted were pagans who deserved harsh treatment and use as slaves. In fact, the agitation against slave taking by the priests who managed Spain's missionary efforts in the Greater Antilles caused the Crown to forbid slave taking among Indians who were friendly to the Spanish. But in response to economic interests, Queen Isabel in 1503 excluded from this ban all "cannibals." These "cannibals" were legally defined as "barbaric people, enemies of the Christian, those who refuse conversion, and those who eat human flesh" (Sauer 1966). In practice, this distinction broke down, and the effort was made to enslave all native West Indians (Sued-Badillo 1978; Davis and Goodwin 1990).

The Archaeology of the Island Caribs

After two decades of archaeological and linguistic research into the origins of the Island Caribs it is now clear that these people were not warlike invaders from South America but rather the product of cultural evolution in the Windward Islands of the Lesser Antilles (Allaire 1977, 1980; Sued-Badillo 1978; Davis and Goodwin 1990; Wilson 1990b). The Island Caribs spoke several languages and used an Arawakan language on a daily basis. Previously they were associated with Suazoid series pottery (Bullen 1964), but Allaire (1984, 1991) has demonstrated that the people who manufactured Suazoid series pottery were not the historic Island Caribs.

During the early historic period the Island Caribs interacted with both Cariban and Arawakan speakers on the mainland, which involved, depending on the circumstances, trade, raiding, alliance, intermarriage, and even ceremonial gift exchange with enemies (Boomert 1986). Since they were restricted to the Windward Islands, from Martinique southward, it is unlikely they exerted a significant influence over the Taino chiefdoms in the Greater Antilles. They certainly played no role in stimulating Taino expansion nor in the interisland raiding reported in the Bahamas.

The Island Caribs are an interesting case because they have been used to provide simple answers to complicated questions. Present opinions have maintained the Spanish dichotomy of peaceful Indians (Tainos) and warlike Indians (Caribs) that was used to balance competing and contradictory religious and economic interests. It will be shown that the Tainos, including the Lucayans of the Bahamas, are not so deserving of their peaceful reputation.

The Tainos

The name Arawak has also been identified as a misnomer that resulted from confusing the name of a language family with the name of an ethnic group (Rouse 1987). The historical documents indicate that the people who called themselves "Arawaks" were restricted in their distribution to the lands around the mouth of the Orinoco River including the island of Trinidad (Glazier 1978; Rouse 1986). The people who colonized the West Indies spoke a different language and were culturally distinct from these South American Arawaks. At a more general level the languages of the Tainos and the Arawaks share enough similarities to be classified as members of the Arawakan language family. The differences between these languages were substantial. Consider, for example, the differences between two more closely related members of the Indo-European language family, English and German. Irving Rouse (1987) has suggested that the commonly used name *Arawaks* be replaced with the name *Tainos* when discussing native West Indians at contact. *Taino*, which glosses as "noble" or "good" in the Taino language, was used by the Spanish to distinguish these people from the Island Caribs.

As discussed with regard to the name *Ciboney*, the Tainos also used other names to distinguish various subgroupings (e.g., *Ciguayo, Macorix*). The Tainos in the Bahamas have come to be known as the Lucayans, which is an anglicized form of the Spanish name *Lucayos*. The name may ultimately come from the Taino words *Lukku-Cairi*, which glosses as "island men." For simplicity, the name *Taino* will be used in reference to the peoples of the Greater Antilles at contact, *Island Arawaks* or the names of pottery series will be used for earlier time periods because no better alternative exists, and the name *Lucayan* will denote the peoples of the Bahama archipelago as a way of recognizing cultural differences.

The Saladoid Expansion, 2100 b.c.-a.d. 600

The origins of the Tainos are conveniently traced to the banks of the Orinoco River in Venezuela (Rouse 1989a). As early as 2100 b.c. villages of horticulturalists who used pottery vessels to cook their food had been established along the Middle Orinoco. During the ensuing two millennia their population increased and they expanded downriver and outward along the Orinoco's tributaries (Lathrap 1977, 1987; Roosevelt 1980; Sanoja and Vargas 1983).

One path of expansion led these people to the coast of the Guianas. From the Guianas the opening of the West Indies awaited only the discovery of Grenada, which is separated from Trinidad by the widest gap in the chain of islands leading to Puerto Rico. Once this 120-kilometer water gap was breached, every island in the Lesser Antilles was visible from the island that preceded it (Sleight 1965).

The movement of these people down the Orinoco River and through the Lesser Antilles to Puerto Rico is well documented (Roosevelt 1980; Sanoja and Vargas 1983; Zucchi, Tarble, and Vaz 1984; Rouse 1986). The migration is easily traced because these people manufactured a characteristic type of pottery known as Saladoid, named after the archaeological site of Saladero at which it was first described (Rouse and Cruxent 1959). In particular, the use of white-on-red painted decorations has facilitated the identification of the path along which this population expanded. Another indicator of migration is the presence of certain animals in the island's archaeological remains (Goodwin 1979).

It should be noted that pottery styles subsumed by the Saladoid series are often of restricted distribution. One possibility is that these restricted styles represent distinct social groups who entered the West Indies independently (Chanlatte Baik and Narganes 1980; Chanlatte Baik 1991; Haviser 1991). Alternatively the styles may represent localized ritual activities (Rouse 1986). Whatever the case, the underlying diversity within the Saladoid series requires additional attention (Roe 1989).

Since we are unable to learn the names that these peoples had for themselves, the name assigned to their pottery series has been expanded to include the peoples who manufactured and used the pottery. Thus, we refer to these colonists as the Saladoid peoples.

The expansion of Saladoid peoples into the Antilles occurred at a rapid pace. The earliest ceramic age settlements in the West Indies date to circa 400 B.C. (Haviser 1991; Rouse 1989b). Saladoid settlements appear almost instantaneously on Puerto Rico and the islands of the Lesser Antilles (Rouse 1989b). Given what is known of human reproductive potential and the time that elapsed between their departure from the mainland and their colonization of Puerto Rico, the inescapable conclusion is that the Saladoid peoples settled only the very best locations on a few of the Lesser Antilles at this time. The most likely scenario is that most islands were settled temporarily and were then abandoned in favor of more abundant resources on other islands. Only those few locations with superior resource concentrations were settled for a period that could be considered permanent (Watters 1982; Keegan and Diamond 1987; Haviser 1990).

This practice of establishing temporary settlements that were moved in response to resource availability is typical of extensive horticultural-ists. Extensive horticulture is a type of farming that involves the cultiva-tion of a wide variety of crops in a single garden. Following two or three years of cultivation, the garden is left fallow for at least ten years, but sometimes for more than twice that long, to allow the forest to regener-ate. Extensive horticulture, which is also know as swidden, slash-and-burn, and casual cultivation, is highly productive in tropical climates and is common throughout the tropics even today (Conklin 1968; Ruddle 1974; Johnson 1983; Keegan 1986b).

The Saladoid peoples are believed to have been extensive horticul-turalists. Paleobotanical studies have only recently been attempted. Based on later plant use (Sturtevant 1961), on evidence from South America (e.g., Roosevelt 1980), and on the presence of certain food-processing arti-facts, it has been proposed that Saladoid horticulturalists grew manioc (cassava), cocoyams, sweet potatoes, and a variety of other food crops. Their gardens also contained vegetable dyes, fibers, and medicinal plants. Saladoid peoples lived in small villages. The earliest known villages in the Lesser Antilles follow the riverine settlement pattern of the main-land. On Grenada, Antigua, St. Martin, Vieques, St. Croix, and St. Kitts, these villages were located inland on river terraces that provided access to the best setting for gardens (Haviser 1990). The shifting, extensive character of their gardening practices is evident from the absence of deeply stratified sites and from settlement patterns in which different components are arranged in horizontal and sometimes overlapping rela-tionships (Watters 1982).

Shortly after the initial colonization of the Antilles there was a rapid and almost complete shift from inland to coastal settlement locations. However, it must be kept in mind that on such small islands the distinc-tion between inland and coastal is often blurred. Although horticulture continued as the primary source of foodstuffs, the change in settlement patterns was accompanied by a shift from terrestrial to marine sources of animal protein. At the earliest sites, the remains of land crabs predomi-nate in archaeological deposits. However, following the shift to coastal villages, the shells of marine mollusks and bones of marine fishes are the main components of archaeological deposits (Carbone 1980a; Goodwin 1980; Jones 1985; deFrance 1988; Keegan 1989d).

Two explanations have been suggested to account for this shift from an emphasis on land resources to an emphasis on marine resources. The first proposes that a growing human population soon depleted the availability of land resources, which forced a shift to marine resources. For this proposition to be correct we should observe evidence of a growing human population along with evidence that it was economically more efficient to focus on land, rather than sea, resources. Archaeological studies have demonstrated that both of these conditions prevailed. Furthermore, the speed with which Saladoid peoples expanded through the Lesser Antilles supports the notion that these islands offered somewhat limited terrestrial resources. As long as land animals were the most efficiently exploited source of protein they were the focus of food-getting activities. But when a focus on obtaining marine resources came to provide a more efficient protein source (perhaps owing to the decline in the availability of land animals), the shift to marine food sources was rapid (Goodwin 1979; Keegan 1989d).

The second explanation for this shift proposes that changes in climate resulted in drier conditions that acted to reduce the population densities of the humidity-sensitive land crabs (Carbone 1980b). Land crabs occupy burrows that must possess moist soil at the bottom, so the onset of drier conditions would limit the availability of suitable burrow locations. If this proposal is correct, we would expect the shift from terrestrial to marine animals to occur at about the same time on each island. Since the timing of this shift was different on each island, it would seem that the overuse of land crabs by the Saladoid people was at least as important, if not more important than any possible changes in climate.

Finally, population growth and expansion merit consideration. It can be demonstrated with simple equations from population biology that the Saladoid colonists probably maintained exponential growth rates during periods of expansion and that the majority of the Lesser Antilles may have been bypassed or settled only temporarily during the initial Saladoid expansion. If one extends Roosevelt's (1980) analysis of Saladoid peoples on the Orinoco River out onto the Lesser Antilles a remarkable coincidence occurs. The estimated population growth rate in Parmana, the region of study on the Middle Orinoco, is exactly the same as the rate estimated for St. Kitts (Goodwin 1979). This coincidence suggests the question: Since Roosevelt observed a shift in protein sources when the population density doubled from about 1.5 to 3.0 persons per square kilometer in Parmana, did anything similar happen on St. Kitts? In Parmana the shift in protein source involved a dramatic increase in maize in the diet (Roosevelt 1980; van der Merwe, Roosevelt, and Vogel 1981); on St. Kitts it has been estimated that the shift from land crabs to marine mollusks occurred at an equivalent doubling point.

Obviously such back-of-the-envelope estimates require a heavy dose of all else being equal. Nonetheless, this coincidence suggests that it would be worth investigating economic continuity during the Saladoid (i.e., the return rates are the same, only the food-resource options are different), along with taking yet another look at the interisland contemporaneity of the crab/shell transition, this time with contemporaneity defined in terms of population densities rather than of absolute dates.

In sum, Saladoid peoples expanded rapidly from northeastern Venezuela and the coast of the Guianas through the Lesser Antilles and Puerto Rico to establish frontiers in eastern Hispaniola. The initial migration through the Lesser Antilles to Puerto Rico took place over about four centuries, a period that was insufficient for the establishment of permanent communities on every island in the Lesser Antilles. It must therefore be the case that most of these islands were not occupied during this initial migration. One stimulus to this rapid expansion was the small size of these islands and their limited terrestrial resource bases (D. Harris 1965). These constraints are apparent in the rapid and almost complete shift from terrestrial to marine sources of animal protein that accompanied the shift to the coastal settlement locations that provided ready access to the marine environment. The completion of this transformation of a riverine people to an island people was the foundation for the next major episode of expansion.

The Ostionoid Expansion, A.D. 600-1200

Irving Rouse (1986) has suggested that the Saladoid advance was halted in eastern Hispaniola by the presence of a large and well-established population of hunter-gatherers known as the Courian Casimiroids. With their forward progress barred, the Saladoid population behind the frontier continued to grow, and their adaptation to island life was further refined. The shifts from inland riverine settlement locations to coastal locations and from terrestrial to marine protein sources have already been discussed. With regard to material culture, the most obvious change was a simplification in pottery decorations. In fact, the earliest pottery on the frontier was almost completely undecorated, with only red slip and the simplest modeling retained from the Saladoid series. These simplified designs have been classified as comprising the Ostionoid series. This name comes from the archaeological site of Ostiones in Puerto Rico, and it is here generalized to denote the peoples who completed the colonization of the West Indies.

By A.D. 600 the Ostionoid peoples had resumed the advance of their Saladoid ancestors and had begun to expand along both coasts. Expansion along the southern coast of Hispaniola led to the colonization of Jamaica, while movement through the northern valleys led to the colonization of the eastern tip of Cuba. At this point, Rouse (1986) has identified another frontier boundary. In this area the mountains of eastern Cuba or the presence of another well-established population of hunter-gatherers, acting singly or in concert, slowed the Ostionoid advance.

Behind the frontier, the use of rectilinear parallel-line incision came into fashion as the characteristic decoration on pottery vessels. Pottery that has this type of decoration has been classified as a subseries of Ostionoid known as Meillacan. This subseries is named for the archaeological site of Meillac in Haiti (Rouse 1939). The initial development of a distinctive Meillacan style has been dated to about A.D. 800. Because the earliest pottery at archaeological sites in Cuba is of the Meillacan style, the final advance into central Cuba is dated to between A.D. 800 and 1200 (Rouse and Allaire 1978).

The Development of the Tainos in the Greater Antilles

The expansion of the Island Arawaks through the Antilles can be viewed as a series of waves whose rate of advance increased every time a frontier was breached. The earliest advance in the Greater Antilles, which is represented by the spread of Saladoid series pottery from Puerto Rico to Hispaniola, covered about 150 kilometers (90 miles) in about 500 years. The next advance, represented by the distribution of Ostionoid series pottery across Hispaniola and into Jamaica and eastern Cuba, covered about 600 kilometers (360 miles, excluding water gaps) in less than 300 years. Finally, the distribution of Meillacan subseries pottery in Jamaica and central Cuba reflects expansion over 300 kilometers (180 miles) in less than 100 years.

A group of archaeological sites in the Yuma Province, Dominican Republic, illustrates a sequence of local developments during the colonization of the Greater Antilles that appears to characterize the developmental sequence throughout Hispaniola and possibly Puerto Rico. The discussion that follows summarizes and interprets information from the *Arqueologia de Yuma (República Dominicána),* by Marcio Veloz Maggiolo, Iraida Vargas, Mario Sanoja O., and Fernando Luna Calderón (1976).

The first phase, called Musiépedro, began about A.D. 350. The pottery in this phase is mostly "simple" and "ordinary," which reflects the transition from Saladoid series to Ostionoid series pottery. The archaeological sites are small middens that probably reflect temporary camps.

In the South American lowlands today, the year is often divided into a period of extensive horticulture and a period of hunting-gathering "treks" over large ranges (Werner 1983). This type of subsistence strategy could account for the rapid movement of the Saladoid peoples through the Lesser Antilles and their somewhat slower progress through the much larger island of Puerto Rico and could explain why an established hunter-gatherer population in Hispaniola, the Courian Casimiroids, were able to halt their progress. In effect, the hunting and gathering part of the Saladoid subsistence strategy was the domain of the Courian Casimiroids in Hispaniola. These overlapping subsistence strategies would have resulted in what ecologists call resource depression (MacArthur 1972). Resource depression makes it more difficult to obtain the shared resource, thus making food procurement more expensive. It can be suggested that it was not until an alternate strategy was developed to replace treking that a further advance became possible.

About A.D. 800–840, the Atajadizo phase began. At this time the village sites show evidence of a greater permanence of settlement, although there continue to be signs of periodic abandonment and reoccupation. In contrast to the Musiépedro phase sites, which were part of an annual cycle, the Atajadizo phase villages were probably tied to longer-term horticultural cycles.

For example, horticulturalists in the tropical forest of South America will today move their villages when the best lands are in fallow (Johnson and Baksh 1987). On average, villages are moved about every three to five years, while garden lands are left fallow for ten or more years. Villages are frequently moved very short distances, sometimes less than a mile. The moves are made because it is easier to move the village than it is to walk each day to distant gardens. Furthermore, the houses themselves have often been allowed to deteriorate to the point at which they need to be replaced. Any time after the period of fallow is over, the vicinity of the old village could be reoccupied. The old village continues to be attractive because it offers ready-made clearings for houses, and the fruit trees that were planted in the old gardens and trash heaps often still produce a usable crop.

The Atajadizo subsistence strategy was one of extensive horticulture. Large, flat, ceramic griddles (burens) used for baking cassava bread became more common at this time. This increased use of cassava bread is characteristic of an intensification of food production that would have been associated with the increase in local population densities. Collected and hunted foods continued to be important, and the reliance on fish and shellfish increased to a level that was maintained in subsequent phases.

It was during the Atajadizo phase that the greatest diversity of pottery styles in the West Indies occurred. Such diversity appears to reflect a more localized orientation of the population. On the one hand, the loss of opportunities for further expansion along the coasts required the accommodation of the growing population in already settled areas. One result was that similar pottery styles came to be associated with the water passages that provided the easiest avenues of transportation (Rouse 1986). In this regard, the pottery styles of western Hispaniola more closely resembled those of eastern Cuba than those of eastern Hispaniola. On the other hand, the population densities in each of these regions were at this time too small to support the rise of chiefs who could unite larger regions.

The Atajadizo phase thus represents an intermediate stage of intra-regional development. During earlier phases the rapid expansion of population at low densities promoted continued communication between neighboring groups throughout the Antilles. During later phases the rise of chiefdoms acted to break down regional cultural boundaries and to promote a unification of the material culture that was manifested as the Classic Taino culture.

One of the regional styles that developed at this time is the Meillacan subseries of the Ostionoid series. Veloz Maggiolo, Ortega, and Caba Fuentes (1981) have equated the development of this subseries with explosive changes in the economy. They proposed that an intensive system of cultivation along the river terraces of Hispaniola was initiated at this time. In effect, the peoples had come full circle from their initial riverine emphasis on the mainland through a focus on marine sources of animal protein to a reemphasis of agricultural production on the large rivers of Hispaniola. The Atajadizo phase reflects an intensification of food production in concert with a growing population that could no longer be relieved through outward expansion.

The final phase in the Yuma sequence, known as Guayabal, began about A.D. 950. At the Yuma sites the earliest manifestations of the cultural practices that would spread across the Greater Antilles about A.D. 1200 were observed. The development of these cultural practices culminated in the Classic Taino chiefdoms that the Spanish encountered when they arrived in the New World.

During the Guayabal phase the specialized use of space becomes apparent. Villages change from small, loose aggregations of residences to the planned arrangement of houses around central plazas. These oval or rectangular plazas were the locations for various ceremonies. In at least two cases the plazas served as astronomical observatories, and in others they were the places at which the native West Indian form of the ball game was played (Alegría 1983). In addition to the specialized use of space, the villages also grew in size to an average of 500 to 1,000 people.

By A.D. 1492, the largest villages were reportedly occupied by more than 3,000 people (Dunn and Kelley 1989). The Classic Taino settlements were hierarchically ordered. At the lowest level were the villages of lineage headmen or chiefs. At the second level were district chiefs to whom the headmen owed allegiance. A paramount chief ruled a large region with district chiefs and lineage headmen allied beneath him.

Agricultural practices during the Guayabal phase show a further intensification of food production. The starch yields from manioc plants were increased by emphasizing bitter varieties, and the yield of tubers was increased by planting the manioc in low mounds of fertile soil. The yields from corn plants were increased by the development of irrigation systems. In conjunction with the intensification of agricultural production was a broad-spectrum emphasis on the capture of animal protein. Specialized fishing and collecting strategies emerged, and domesticated animals (dog, agouti, and possibly the cat-sized rodent, hutia) also were kept.

The stage is set for the expansion of the Tainos into the Bahama archipelago.

2

Introduction to the Geology, Geography, Climate, and Ecology of the Pre-Columbian Bahamas

The Bahama archipelago is today comprised of the politically indepen-dent Commonwealth of the Bahamas and the Turks and Caicos Islands (map 2.1). Modern political considerations aside, the islands form a single archipelago with common geological, ecological, and cultural roots. I use the names *Bahamas* and *Bahama Islands* as generic terms for the archi-pelago as a whole.

Geology

The Bahama Islands did not exist 200 million years ago. Never a part of the North American continent, the Bahamas developed on a limestone platform created with the initial separation of the continents and the opening of the North Atlantic Ocean. It seems appropriate that the is-lands whose platform was created with the separation of the Old and New Worlds should also be the location of the events that would lead to their reunification.

During most of the 200 million years that followed the opening of the North Atlantic, the Bahamas was a vast shallow bank (platform) on which marine sediments accumulated. The Earth's crust beneath the Bahamas platform was stretched thin during the separation of the continents. This

M AP 2.1. The Bahama archipelago.

thinning resulted in what may be described as a race between the rate at which new sediments could accumulate and the rate at which the weight of these sediments caused the platform to sink. Bore holes drilled deeply into the tectonically stable Bahamas platform reveal that at least 6,100 meters (20,000 feet) of limestone sediments have accumulated on the Bahamas platform during the past 200 million years (Beach and Ginsburg 1980; Garrett and Gould 1984). All of this limestone was created in shallow water, with room for new sediments made available by the continuing subsidence of the Earth's crust.

About 80 million years ago a second major change occurred. At this time deep troughs and channels were created within and between the Little and Great Bahama Banks, the Bahamas was separated from Cuba and Florida, and the southeastern Bahamas and the Turks and Caicos Islands broke into a series of small banks surrounded by deep troughs and basins. In effect, each of the banks became an independent unit with their surrounding coral reefs acting to trap fine sediments. Without the raised margin provided by the coral reefs, the fine sediments on the banks would have been washed into the depths of the ocean. Geographer Neil Sealey (1985) has compared the growth of the Bahama Banks to a bucket in which the walls of the coral reef grow vertically and retain the fine sediments behind their retaining walls.

The islands themselves are products of the Pleistocene Ice Ages. For about 2 million years a series of glacial advances and retreats have occurred. Glacial activity exerted a profound influence on the Bahama platform even though glaciers did not reach the Bahamas. During periods of glacial advance much of the Earth's water was tied up in the ice caps and in glaciers. In the Bahamas, sea level fell by well over 120 meters (400 feet) during one glaciation, and by just under 120 meters during the final glaciation (map 2.2).

Those precipitous drops in sea level exposed all of the Bahama banks. The exposure of this large landmass modified local climate and produced extreme seasonal variations in temperature and rainfall. The prevailing easterly trade winds were also amplified. These winds moved the fine marine sediments into a series of high sand dunes that run perpendicular to

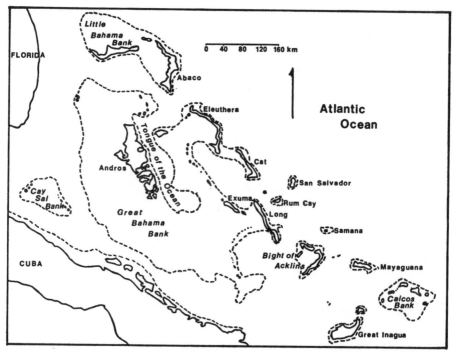

MAP 2.2. The Bahama Banks exposed at lowest Pleistocene sea levels. Courtesy of Neil E. Sealey.

wind direction. In addition, very fine clays, silts, and sands from the deserts of northern Africa were carried to the Bahamas on the trade winds and deposited during rain showers. These fine Saharan sands are the primary component of the red, iron-rich, "pineapple" soils.

The high sand dunes that were formed by the trade winds later hardened or lithified (turned to stone) into fossil sand dunes known as eolianites. These fossil dunes today form the backbones of most islands. Almost all elevations greater than 3 meters (10 feet) were formed in this way (Doran 1955). The locations of these ridges along the windward coasts have afforded different levels of protection to the lee shores. Small bays with sand beaches, large ponds, and tidal creeks have developed behind their protective barricade.

In general, lee shores have continued to build seaward through the gradual accretion of wave-transported sediments. After periods of quiet accretion, storm waves rework the sediments into dunes of up to 2 meters (7 feet) in height (Doran 1955). Through time, series of low dunes separated by narrow swales (troughs) have given a corrugated texture to the lee shores of many islands.

The narrow outlets (tidal creeks) of bays may become choked by the rapidly accumulating sediments and eventually closed into ponds. Wind-blown sediments and evaporation then work together to form periodically flooded swashes and salinas that in turn give rise to permanently dry land. Through these continuing processes of expansion, the lee shores have slowly emerged from behind ridges to create the characteristic pattern of a high windward coast backed by a low leeward plain (map 2.3).

Although the wind plays the dominant role in piling marine sediments into high dunes and in filling coastal ponds with sediments, the ocean was ultimately responsible for the creation of the Bahamas. Calcium carbonate in the forms of marine plant and animal structures and egg-shaped (oolitic) precipitates are the products of shallow marine banks. These solid forms of calcium carbonate are the sediments that are naturally cemented into limestone. Waves were responsible for the movement and accretion of these sediments and were thus a creative force in the emergence of the islands. Waves also removed some of what they had helped to create through the erosion of headlands and the reshaping of existing landforms.

A final factor is the manner in which changes in sea level influenced the growth of coral reefs. The significance of coral reefs in the creation of

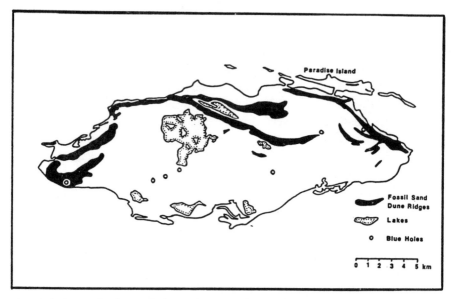

MAP 2.3. Typical ridge and plain physiography (New Providence Island). Courtesy of Neil E. Sealey.

these islands cannot be overstated and is most apparent in the southern Bahamas, especially on the islands of Great Inagua and Mayaguana. Mayaguana Island has the appearance of a coral atoll, with a coastline comprised almost entirely of fossil coral reef and a low interior of permanently or seasonally flooded zones and now-dry Pleistocene-age tidal creeks (tidal creeks are similar to estuaries but lack a freshwater inflow; Sealey 1985:58). Here, on a small scale, the coral reef "bucket" is visible up close (fig. 2.1).

In sum, the Bahama Islands are the products of geological processes extending back over 200 million years. The islands were formed through the actions of winds and waves on the marine sediments produced in a shallow sea that was first exposed during the lowered sea levels of the Pleistocene Ice Ages. Although this broad time scale may not seem particularly relevant for this study of the people who first occupied the Bahamas only 1300 years ago, the geology of these islands exerts a profound influence over their ecology, and the geological processes that began over 200 million years ago when the Bahama platform was created continue to play important roles today.

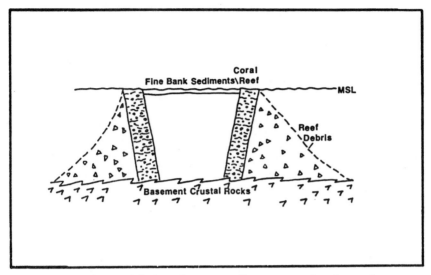

FIGURE 2.1. Bucket model of a Bahamian atoll. Courtesy of Neil E. Sealey.

Geography

In 1864, Governor Rawson W. Rawson commissioned an inventory of Bahamian landforms. A total of 29 islands, 661 cays, and 2,387 rocks were counted. Islands and cays (pronounced *keys*) have been distinguished primarily by their size; the name cay being applied to small islands or islets following the Spanish transliteration of the Taino word for island. It has been suggested that a minimal distance of 25 kilometers (15 miles) in some direction is sufficient to distinguish islands from cays (Sullivan 1981). However, common usage sometimes violates this arbitrary 25-kilo-meter cutoff (Rum Cay, for example) (table 2.1).

Of primary importance in this study are the 19 largest islands. All of the known Lucayan settlements are either on these islands or on cays that are less than 1 kilometer (0.6 miles) from an island. These islands are: Grand Bahama, Great and Little Abaco, Andros, New Providence, Cat, Eleuthera, Long, Great and Little Exuma, San Salvador, Rum Cay, Samana Cay, Crooked, Acklins, Mayaguana, Great Inagua, Providenciales, North Caicos, Middle Caicos, and East Caicos.

The Bahamas extends over 1,000 kilometers (600 miles) in a southeast-erly direction from Grand Bahama Island (27° N latitude) to within 150

TABLE 2.1 Island Areas, Elevations, and Hurricane Crossings

Island	Area (sq km)	Highest elevation	Hurricanes (1871–1963)
Abaco	1681	37 m	8
Grand Bahama	1373	21 m	16
New Providence	207	38 m	10
Berry Islands	31	24 m	NA
Bimini Islands	23	6 m	NA
Andros	5957	22 m	9
Eleuthera	518	51 m	NA
Cat Island	389	63 m	NA
San Salvador	163	38 m	NA
Rum Cay	78	30 m	NA
Conception	10	20 m	NA
Long Island	448	54 m	7
Exuma Islands	104	38 m	5
Crooked Island	238	47 m	9
Acklins Island	389	43 m	9
Samana Cay	39	24 m	NA
Mayaguana	285	40 m	5
Great Inagua	1544	33 m	3
North Caicos	107	24 m	NA
Middle Caicos	120	26	NA
East Caicos	47	48 m	NA
Providenciales	59	48 m	NA
South Caicos	18	46 m	NA
Grand Turk	20	32 m	NA

Source: Bahamas Ministry of Education 1985.

kilometers (90 miles) of the Dominican Republic (21° N latitude) at Grand Turk, their extreme southeastern end (map 2.1). The islands are north and east of a line connecting Florida and the Dominican Republic between 71° and 79° W longitude. The Bahamas is separated from the North American continent by about 100 kilometers (60 miles), between Grand Bahama Island and West Palm Beach, Florida. The shortest distances to the islands' southern neighbors are the 90-kilometer (54 mile) and 110-kilometer (66 mile) water gaps that separate Great Inagua Island from Cuba and Haiti, respectively. Water passages within the Bahamas range from a few meters in the Caicos Islands to 120 kilometers (72 miles) between Great Inagua and Acklins Island. The average distance between islands, excluding water gaps of less than 10 kilometers (6 miles), is 48 kilometers (29 miles).

Climate and Vegetation

The Bahamas has a marine tropical climate characterized by persistent easterly trade winds, with warm wetter summers and cool drier winters. The low elevations preclude orographic rainfall, and no rain shadows occur. Summer convective rainfall is often localized, with wind direction and the configuration of the shallow banks causing higher levels of rainfall to the west and northwest. Winter rainfall is less localized and corresponds to atmospheric depressions associated with cold fronts.

An example of localized summer rainfall is the behavior of the island cloud, a narrow ribbon of clouds formed by air heated over shallow banks and landmasses. In the Caicos Islands, the cloud ranges between Providenciales and North Caicos. Within this 30-kilometer range, daily rainfall typically is limited to a 1.6- to 3.2-kilometer-wide area. The result is that the western Caicos receive on average 300 millimeters more rainfall per year than the eastern Caicos (Sullivan 1981). This island cloud effect is especially pronounced on islands that occupy small isolated banks (i.e., Great Inagua, Mayaguana, the Caicos Islands).

The persistent trade winds exert a major influence on climate and vegetation. The winds are predominantly from the east (51 percent and 29 percent of the year for Grand Turk and Nassau airports respectively), from the southeast (25 percent and 18 percent), and from the northeast (14 percent and 16 percent) (Doran 1955:2; Halkitis, Smith, and Rigg 1980). An average of only 8 percent or 29 days per year were recorded as "calm" at the Nassau Airport (Halkitis, Smith, and Rigg 1980:7) (fig. 2.2).

Wind speeds average 4–10 knots for 50 percent of the year and exceed 21 knots only 1 percent of the year in Nassau. At the PRIDE Foundation field station on Pine Cay, Caicos Islands, wind speeds averaged 14 miles per hour from 1980–83. The entire archipelago lies within the North Atlantic hurricane belt, with hurricane season between August and October (Little et al. 1977). The number of hurricanes crossing each island between 1871 and 1963 is presented in table 2.1. The frequency with which hurricanes cross an island increases from south to north.

Temperature, rainfall, and potential evapotranspiration covary from south to north. Their interrelationship produces recognizable ecological climatic "life-zones" that are roughly coterminous with the 800-millimeter and 1,200-millimeter rainfall isohyets (map 2.4). Characteristic rainfall values for each island are presented in table 2.1. The formation types (i.e.,

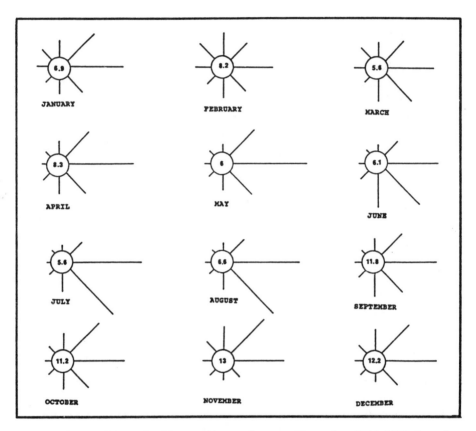

FIGURE 2.2. Wind roses for Nassau Airport, January–December 1964–1970. Length of each spoke gives percentage of winds from that direction (1 mm = 1 percent), and numbers are days recorded as calm. Courtesy of Neil E. Sealey.

plant communities) associated with these subareas represent potential vegetation cover and are used to retrodict the vegetation during the time the islands were occupied by the Lucayans. Deforestation since the eighteenth century has left a degraded environment on all islands (tables 2.2, 2.3).

Northern Subarea: Subtropical Moist Forest

The islands of New Providence, Great and Little Abaco, Grand Bahama, the Berry Islands, and the northern half of Andros are located in this subarea. Its southern boundary is marked by the 1,200-millimeter

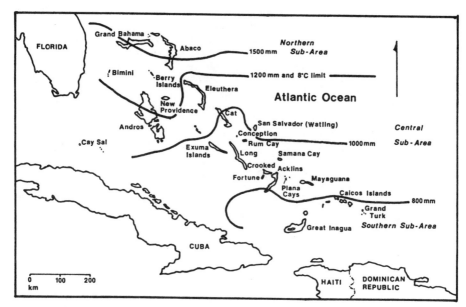

M AP 2.4. Ecological subareas as defined by rainfall isohyets.

rainfall isohyet and the limit of winter temperature minimums at or below 8°C (Sears and Sullivan 1978). This minimum temperature places these islands in the subtropics. Rainfall and potential evapotranspiration are approximately equal.

Yellow pine (*Pinus caribaea* v. *bahamensis*) forests dominate the interiors of the northern islands. They grow in dense stands, with a maximum canopy height of 21 to 24 meters and diameters that may exceed one meter, on soily rock plains, on rough, slightly elevated ground, and on minor ridges (Little et al. 1977: chapter 4). Hardwood shrubs and trees, with a maximum canopy height of 3 meters, may occur as underbrush. The pines are replaced by those hardwoods on high ridges and along the coast. Pine forests occur on a variety of lithofacies (limestone types) and soil types. The agricultural potential of these lands depends on rock debris and soil type, which includes dark leaf mold and other organic/residual soils and brown or red lateritic soils (Little et al. 1977:65). On Great Abaco, the Owens-Illinois Company cleared, bulldozed, and fertilized 7,200 hectares in the 1960s. The land was planted in sugar cane and produced 19,000 tons of raw sugar in its second year (Albury 1975:253–254).

With the exception of Pine Cay, Caicos Islands, yellow-pine stands are

TABLE 2.2 Areas of Land Cleared by the Loyalists (ca. 1800)

Island		White male heads of families	Planters with 10 or more slaves	No. of slaves	Hectares cultivated	Hectares per family head plus slaves
Nassau	B	131	2	1024	102	0.09
	N	165	27	1264	1224	0.86
Exuma	B	11	4	75	141.6	1.65
	N	26	19	679	1036.4	1.47
Long I.	B	63[a]	12	306	612	1.66
	N	29	19	476	952	1.89
Cat I.	B	12	—	16	100	3.57
	N	28	16	442	698.8	1.49
Andros	B	4	3	56	116	1.93
	N	22	7	132	325.2	2.11

Source: Saunders 1983:4–5.
Note: Loyalists also settled on Eleuthera, Crooked Island, Abaco, the Caicos, and Grand Turk, but figures are not available.
[a]Includes 21 families of "Colour."
B = land cleared before 1788.
N = land cleared after 1788.

TABLE 2.3 Exports of Hardwoods by the Loyalists (ca. 1800)

Year	Lignum Vitae (in tons)	Mahogany (in feet)	Braziletto (in tons)
1794	52.5	25,700	.5
1795	458	4,220	.5
1796	756	7,724	.25
1797	277	5,380	.75
1798	1,188	700	0
1799	120	8,306	0
1800	898	1,040	0
1801	673	2,000	1.5
1802	301	0	0
1803	147.25	500	0
1804	427	0	.5
1805	267	12,000	0
Total	5,564.75	67,570	4

Source: Saunders 1985:table 5.

restricted to the northern subarea. The exception is probably the result of the extensive freshwater lakes and the well-developed freshwater lens on Pine Cay. Henry (1974) has suggested that the best pinelands are islands with high water tables. In addition, pines are a type of secondary climax vegetation. Thus islands with a dominant pine vegetation may reflect the more intensive removal of hardwood competitors.

Sears and Sullivan (1978) have suggested that the subtropical temperatures of the northern subarea exerted a major influence on Lucayan population expansion. They assumed that bitter manioc was the staple crop in the Lucayan subsistence economy, and that environmental conditions that precluded bitter manioc's efficient growth would likewise preclude human settlement. Studies of bitter manioc growth in Africa indicate that the plant stops growing at 10°C (50°F) and that the leaves and upper branches will die at 8°C (46.4°F) (W.O. Jones 1959; Sears and Sullivan 1978:19). Varieties of sweet manioc are more cold resistant and are grown on these islands today. Moreover, tropical cultivators usually grow both sweet and bitter varieties or cultivate only sweet manioc (Murphy and Murphy 1974; Johnson 1983).

Sears and Sullivan's conclusion that the northern islands were never permanently settled has been disproved by recent archaeological surveys (Keegan 1985, Keegan and Sealey 1988). These recent findings raise the question of whether the identification of bitter manioc as the staple crop was inaccurate or whether climatic changes have occurred. For now, the answer appears to be both.

Victor Carbone (1980a, b) has examined minor climatic oscillations during the Holocene with reference to cultural development in the Caribbean islands. He reports a "warm though variable" trend commencing about A.D. 1100 which became a "little climatic optimum" that ended with a cooling trend about A.D. 1400 (Carbone 1980b: figure 7). The difference in mean temperatures in A.D. 1100 and A.D. 1400 amounted to about 1.5°C (2.7°F). Temperature data reported for the modern Bahamas were collected during the cooling trend that began in the 1950s, and an interpolation of isotherms indicates a 0.5°C (0.9°F) decline in mean annual temperatures from 1961–70 over similar records for the period 1931–60 (Carbone 1980b:212–213).

The small magnitude of these temperature differences and their expression as estimated annual averages are not sufficient to conclude that temperatures never reached the critical minimum for bitter manioc growth. However, they do suggest that the settlement of the northern islands was

less precarious than Sears and Sullivan (1978) suggest, especially if bitter
manioc was but one cultigen in a diversified horticultural regime.

Central Subarea: Tropical Moist Forest

Eleuthera, Cat Island, Great and Little Exuma, the Exuma Cays, Long
Island, Rum Cay, San Salvador, Samana Cay, Crooked Island, Mayaguana,
the southern half of Andros, all but the southern tip of Acklins Island,
and northwestern North Caicos comprise the coppice islands of the central subarea. Rainfall decreases from north to south (1,200–800 millimeters) and increasingly is exceeded by potential evapotranspiration.
Temperature minimums occasionally fall below 10°C but never reach
8°C.

The modern coppice vegetation is characterized by low (2–3 meter)
tropical hardwoods. However, human interference has reduced the canopy height and has also reduced the number of species present (Gillis
1977). The major episode of plant and animal colonization took place
when the archipelago's shallow banks were exposed during the Pleistocene glaciations. As a result, the floristic composition is fairly homogeneous, although every island has a different set of dominant species
that reflects localized climatic differences and proximity to the source
areas of Cuba, Hispaniola, Florida, Puerto Rico, and the Yucatan Peninsula
(Gillis 1977). A number of species are of recent European introduction, of
which coconut palms (Cocos nucifera) and Australian pine (Casuarina litorea) have had the greatest impact on the landscape. Both occur along
sandy coasts and frequently are associated with archaeological sites.

The physical environment that existed before the arrival of Europeans
can be reconstructed from evidence contained in early historic accounts
and in studies of the modern ecology. The first written descriptions were
made by Christopher Columbus, who described the islands as luxuriant
with many green groves (Dunn and Kelley 1989). Columbus's descriptions
have been a source of confusion because they do not reflect present-day
conditions. The lack of conformity between past and modern conditions
results from five centuries of forest removal. Beginning shortly after Columbus's first voyage, Europeans began harvesting the tropical forests of
the circum-Caribbean. Among the most valuable wood was brazilwood
because of the red dye it produces. By 1725, hardwoods already were
scarce on some islands (McKinnen 1804; Riley 1983:81). It is safe to as-

sume that this scarcity was not limited to particular land grants. Illegal logging is reported for some islands and adjacent cays. The types and sizes of the most frequently mentioned trees are listed in table 2.4.

Sandra Riley (1983:98) has suggested that the pre-Loyalist settlers were so stubbornly fixed on the sea that only the threat of starvation would force them to cultivate crops. This would appear to explain why soil erosion was initially insignificant. However, on closer examination, and with the exception of the primarily commercial settlement of Nassau, it turns out that "old inhabitants" (pre-1783) cultivated as much land per capita as those who arrived after 1783 (Saunders 1983). The difference is in the total area of land under cultivation after the arrival of the Loyalists. These figures are important because they provide a means for evaluating the impact of Lucayan land-clearance practices. For instance, if the Lucayans cultivated as much land as did the Loyalists, then a similar rate of sedimentation should be observed in coastal ponds.

The clearance of land and the export of hardwoods during the Loyalist period (circa A.D. 1783–1805) was responsible for the degradation of the tropical forest to its present state. The Loyalists cleared extensive tracts on which they planted cotton and sisal. Because these tracts exposed the soil to the direct effects of wind and rainfall, erosion removed much of the islands' topsoil. Finally, when their cotton crop failed, the Loyalists turned to lumbering (Albury 1975).

The removal of large trees began in earnest with the resettlement of

TABLE 2.4 Common Hardwoods with Their Maximum Heights

Scientific name	Common name	Maximum height (m)
Swietenia mahagoni	Mahogany	6–15
Tabebuia bahamensis	Chicken toe	6–15
Lysiloma sabicu	Horseflesh	6–15
Exothea paniculata	Inkwood	6–15
Lysiloma latisiliquum	Wild tamarind	6–15
Bursera simaruba	Gum elemi	6–15
Piscidia piscipula	Dogwood	6–15
Metopium toxiferum	Poison wood	6–15
Pinus Caribaea	Yellow pine	6–24
Krugiodendron ferreum	Ironwood	5–9
Cedrela odorata	Spanish cedar	3–8
Caesalpinia vesicaria	Brasiletto	3–8
Guaiacum sanctum	Lignum vitae	3–6

Source: Patterson and Stevenson 1977.

the Bahamas in the late seventeenth century. In fact, one of the original endowments to Harvard University (then Harvard College) was 10 tons of brazilwood from Eleuthera (Miller 1945). Although it is located in the northern subarea, a description of Great Abaco in 1783 is instructive: "The island abounds with Timber, Fir, Madeira Wood, Mahogany, Fustich, Lignum Vitae, Braseleto, Logwood, and Sundry Woods fit for dying" (Riley 1983:137). The Betsy Bay Settlement on Mayaguana, at the southern extreme of the central subarea, was described in 1857: "The timber is of large size, and among the Varieties I saw, may mention the tamarind, Madeira, horseflesh, green and black ebony, stopper, cassada and lignumvitae, and much ship timber, knees, etc. Where the settlers had cleared, the ground was literally covered with peas, potatoes, eddoes, corn, etc. . . . and the produce is certainly as luxuriant as in any island in the Bahamas" (Dalleo 1979:17).

The continuation of slash-and-burn cultivation to the present has maintained a degraded forest. Moreover, the almost complete removal of economically important hardwoods (e.g., mahogany, horseflesh, lignum vitae), combined with the submergence of the shallow banks, probably has prevented the natural reseeding of presently unexploited areas. Even the cessation of land clearance would not be sufficient to reverse these processes. The forests can never return to their original condition because of the absence of seed trees and the modification of the soil matrix.

Sediment samples from pond cores dated to the period before the arrival of the Loyalists reflect a slow, constant rate of sediment accumulation (Mitchell 1984). All of the Lucayan period is included in these sediment samples, and there is no indication that Lucayan land-clearance practices produced a substantial increase in soil erosion. In contrast, there is a dramatic rise in sedimentation as a result of erosion and evidence for increasingly drier conditions commencing with the arrival of the Loyalists.

Today, the central subarea is characterized by tropical broadleaf woodlands (e.g., Brazilian cerrada) to the north, which grade into thornwoods dominated by members of the pea family (Leguminosae) (see Whittaker 1975:138–139). These types of vegetation are typical of the dry, xeric conditions on limestone islands, but they appear also to be the result of a truncated successional sequence.

The aboriginal forest was probably a tropical seasonal forest grading into tropical broadleaf woodlands to the south. While present rainfall levels are below those for modern seasonal forests, the vegetation developed during a period of higher rainfall and the islands' high water tables would have provided moisture in excess of that received through rainfall. This distinction is made because the seasonal forest would have provided a higher level of soil fertility and protection from the desiccating effects of the constant trade winds. The degradation of the environment during historic development would have had an effect similar to that described for shifting from a forest-fallow to a bush-fallow agricultural regime (see Boserup 1965).

In summary, the environment encountered by the Lucayans was a tropical seasonal forest with well-developed organic/residual soils and a soil climate more favorable to cultivation. The forest canopy reached 15 meters in the north with a slight reduction in the southern islands of the central subarea. Rainfall may have been somewhat higher and the mean annual temperature slightly warmer.

Southern Subarea: Tropical Very Dry Forest

Great and Little Inagua, the Turks and Caicos Islands (except North Caicos), Ragged Island, and the southern tip of Acklins Island are situated in the southern subarea. The boundary between subareas is along the 800-millimeter-rainfall isohyet. In contrast to the northern islands, with their distinct wet (May/June to October) and dry seasons, there is a pronounced drier break (July to August) in the April/May to October/November rainy season (Little et al. 1977:9). October is the wettest month.

In the southern islands the constant trade winds exert a pervasive influence on life zones (see Klingel 1961). While long-term records are not available, wind speeds recorded during the testing of a wind-electric generator on Pine Cay averaged 14 miles per hour for a three-year period. This average wind speed is somewhat higher than the average for the northern islands (see Halkitis, Smith, and Rigg 1980). Doran (1955) reports that tropical storms occur at an average of about one every four years.

The wind affects the environment by increasing evaporation and transpiration. The early settlers of the Turks and Caicos Islands recognized the significance of evaporation for the production of salt, but their reasoning was faulty; they believed that trees attracted rain, and that the removal of trees would increase the yields from solar distillation (Sadler 1972). In fact, the removal of trees increased the air flow above the salt pans, which increased the rate of evaporation.

The effects of transpiration are more difficult to specify because they are a function of climatic conditions in conjunction with the plant's morphology and physiology (Wilson, Loomis, and Steeves 1971:194–200). The wind affects transpiration rates in two ways. First, wind moving over the leaves removes water, which reduces the relative humidity. The concentration of water vapor in the leaves remains much higher than that in the atmosphere, and the plant continues to lose water. The second effect is the cooling of the leaf by the removal of radiant heat.

On Great Inagua, potential evapotranspiration is 2.5 times higher than average rainfall (Little et al. 1977). For plants, especially those with stomata adapted to xeric conditions, that difference is significant only when an alternative source of water is not available (e.g., groundwater). All of the southern islands presently lack well-developed groundwater resources, although localized freshwater lenses do occur. Groundwater levels were probably significantly higher prior to human colonization.

The best evidence for higher groundwater tables comes from Pine Cay, Caicos Islands, which has the only standing freshwater ponds in this subarea (Nordstrom 1979). There are presently seven ponds on the cay, but an eighteenth-century French navigation manual reported the presence of a large "lagoon" with enough freshwater for fifty ships' crews (Bellin 1768). The dissection of this lagoon reflects modern construction activities and increased aridity from land clearance.

Although groundwater can supplement rainfall, land clearance also affects soil fertility. The forest cover limits nutrient leaching, diffuses raindrops, maintains cooler soil temperatures, provides litter faster than it decays, and acts to neutralize the alkaline carbonate matrix (Webster and Wilson 1966). Deforestation reverses those processes and exposes the soil to direct insolation and rainfall that further reduce the amounts and availability of plant nutrients (Roosevelt 1980).

Previous attempts to correlate prehistoric occupations with environmental variables have given primary attention to the arid character of the modern environment. Sears and Sullivan (1978), for example, cite the occurrence of ponds that produce salt through solar distillation. However, it should be noted that solar salt production was not limited to the southern subarea. Commercial salt production was conducted on Long Island, Rum Cay, Little Exuma, Eleuthera, Cat Island, and San Salvador in the central subarea; and on New Providence, the Berry Islands, and several small cays in the northern subarea (Bahamas Department of Archives, 1980).

Agricultural land in the southern islands (and Mayaguana should be included in this discussion) is limited to the western shores. Vegetation along the eastern windward shores tends to be stunted, xerophytic, and salt tolerant. Higher average wind speeds have contributed to the development of a low (about one meter) vegetation that is visibly bent by the wind. As Gilbert Klingel (1961:178) expressed it: "Life flowed all in one direction."

With the Atlantic Ocean as a potential fetch, ocean swells break on the near shore reefs in a cascade of spray. This salt spray is carried on the winds and at times produces the effect of rainfall on shore. The wind also creates a chop on the sea between the reef and the shore.

Since rainfall is, for the most part, limited to summer convective showers, the windward coasts receive less rainfall. Convection cells are generated over sun-heated landmasses and shallow banks. When the heated air penetrates cooler levels of the atmosphere, cumulus clouds are formed. Rainfall would be evenly distributed if these clouds were stationary, but the trade winds, which are at their strongest in the summer, form the clouds into a narrow band ("island cloud") and direct them to the west-northwest (Little et al. 1977; Sullivan 1981). Since these islands are preceded by deep open water, cloud formation usually is limited to the atmosphere above the island; an exception is Mayaguana, which does receive clouds generated over the Caicos Islands. The resulting rainfall distribution is biased to the west-northwest.

The modern settlements on Great Inagua, Mayaguana, and the Turks and Caicos Islands are restricted to the western sides of these islands. Swidden agriculture is the foundation of the economy in those settlements, although this is being replaced by modern industry. Two settlements are exceptions to this pattern, but these, on South Caicos and Grand Turk, were founded to maintain access to salt-producing pans and deep-water anchorages. Both of these settlements import almost all of their food, and fresh water is only available from rainwater catchments or desalination.

Paleoecological and geological evidence point to higher levels of rainfall and deeper soils in the past (see Carbone 1980a). The best example is found in Conch Bar Cave on Middle Caicos where solution features in the cave were produced when acidic water dissolved the limestone walls of this enormous cavern. A higher level of rainfall would have been required to produce the observed effect, and a deeper soil layer was necessary to neutralize the carbonate matrix and to acidify the water that passed through the soil.

Even though higher rainfall levels and greater soil fertility probably maintained a more verdant vegetation, a clinal variation from east to west would, even then, have characterized the environment. The windward shore would have supported low, stunted tropical woodland and thornbrush with cacti and other succulents. Moving to the west, canopy height would have increased with woodland vegetation dominating thornbrush.

Terrestrial Fauna

The modern terrestrial fauna is dominated by feral species of European introduction that today inhabit islands with relatively inaccessible interiors: dogs, cats, goats, hogs, cattle, horses, and donkeys. In addition, black or Norway rats arrived as stowaway passengers on ships from Europe (Deagan 1988).

The pre-European fauna was characterized by far less diversity. Mammals were limited to hutia (*Geocapromys* sp.) and bats. The bones of both have been recovered from archaeological sites, although bat bones are found only in cave deposits, where they probably died natural deaths. Hutia were introduced from Cuba at a date sufficient to permit speciation. At one time they were distributed throughout the Bahamas, but they are today limited to a natural colony on the Plana Cays (between Mayaguana and Acklins Island) and to a transplanted colony in the Exuma Cays.

Clough's (1972) study of the Plana Cays colony indicates that hutia are nocturnal, occupy natural shelters in caves and crevices during the day, and are facile climbers. They consume leaves, small twigs, bark, and fruit from six plant species. The body weights were measured in 1967–68 and averaged 906 grams (two pounds). The animals were easily captured by hand and with the aid of small nets. They adapted well to short-term captivity (four days) and tolerated high densities without increased aggression. In the wild, Clough estimates a population density of seven hutia per acre. Fecal pellet counts indicated that they were evenly distributed over the cays during activity periods.

The hutia may have been domesticated as a food source by the Island Arawak. Domestication would explain their occurrence in the Bahamas while similar small mammals from the Greater Antilles are absent. However, the apparently minor contribution of hutia to the Lucayan diet argues against this hypothesis.

Reptiles are today the major type of animal life on the islands (Bahamas National Trust, n.d.b; Ostrander 1982). Of these, anole (*Anolis* sp.) and curly tail (*Leiocephelus* sp.) lizards as well as the pygmy boa (*Epicrates* sp.) have been identified as very minor components of archaeological faunal samples (Sullivan 1981). Of greater importance to the Lucayans was the rock iguana (*Cyclura carinata*). All of the reptiles once enjoyed ubiquitous distributions, but human interference has restricted the modern range of the rock iguana.

As with the hutia, natural populations of iguana do not adapt well to human company. In fact, Iverson's (1979) scientific study of the Pine Cay population proved fatal for that colony. In addition, studies have indicated that high densities may be necessary for reproductive success (Campbell 1978). Therefore, overexploitation would seriously affect the long-term viability of rock iguana populations. Iguana are typically herbivores, although they are reported to consume dead fish that wash ashore. Adults may achieve lengths of one to two meters. Undisturbed populations achieve high densities (see Ostrander 1982), with a standing biomass estimated at 15 kilograms per hectare (82.5 pounds per acre) (Iverson 1979).

A rich and varied bird life includes both permanent and seasonal residents. Bird species and their habitats are reviewed by Campbell (1978) and Sullivan (1981). Archaeological faunal samples typically contain very few bird bones, and birds comprised less than 0.5 percent of the diet (Wing 1987). Although birds were not of dietary importance, Columbus reports that the Tainos used bird feathers for a variety of decorative purposes. Parrot feathers were especially prized for their beautiful colors.

One bird worthy of special note is the West Indian flamingo (*Phoenicopterus ruber*). The last remaining Bahamian colony of flamingos is located on Great Inagua, but historic nesting colonies were reported as far north as Great Abaco (Campbell 1978:78). Historic hunting reduced the population to near extinction. Today about 25,000 birds occupy Great Inagua and about 4,000 nests are constructed annually. Flamingo nests are clearly visible on the mud flats of Lake Windsor, where they would have provided easy prey. Flamingos are available from March to August, after which they return to salinas in Hispaniola and Cuba. Although there are no faunal samples from archaeological sites in the vicinity of flamingo ponds, the possible prehistoric use of these birds cannot be excluded.

A final animal was introduced by the Lucayans. During his first voyage Columbus reported seeing dogs (*Canis familiaris*). Recently dog bones were recovered from a prehistoric context during the excavation of site MC-12 on Middle Caicos. Dogs may have been used for hunting hutia, iguana, and flamingo, and they would have removed feces and other refuse from the villages (Gregor 1977). It is possible that they were used as food, although this practice is not reported in documents from the contact period, and only one dog has been identified in faunal samples.

During the initial period of colonization, terrestrial animals would have been at their highest densities and would have comprised a major component of the diet. Their minor contribution to identified biomass in prehistoric faunal samples suggests that their availability declined rapidly during Lucayan times, or that their availabilities were somehow restricted in ways that limited their importance in Lucayan diets.

Coastal Environments

The edge of the sea is an environment of continuous change. Lands that were once submerged are exposed, and vice versa. These landforms are not strictly land or sea but instead possess characteristics of both. Recent landforms include sand beaches and salinas (fig. 2.3). The beaches are composed of carbonate sands that support a vegetation that is dominated by pioneer species, such as the sea grapes, grasses, and purslane that dominate the Bahamas "whitelands." Since their introduction during historic times, the Australian pine (Casuarina litorea) and coconut palm (Cocos nucifera) have proved to be successful colonists of new beaches. Where Casuarina occur, archaeological sites are usually at least 30 meters from the beach, which reflects the seaward growth of the coast. Numerous archaeological sites have also been found in coastal coconut groves.

Salinas and marls are smooth plains with scant vegetation that create a border between marine tidal flats and the mainland (Sullivan 1981:81). They are often called tidal flats because they flood during extreme high tides, but they are here called salinas to avoid confusion with permanently submerged marine tidal flats. It should also be noted that commercial salt pans are often called salinas, as well, although these represent a special case that is not important to the present study. Salinas are composed of sand or marl accumulations that were leveled by shallow-water tidal action. They occur along the lee shores of Great Abaco, Andros, Crooked and Acklins islands, and the Caicos Islands.

FIGURE 2.3. Salinas along the south coast of North Caicos, Turks and Caicos Islands.

Older coastal habitats are composed of eolianites or beach rock. Eolianites are lithified (hardened, solidified) windblown sediments that formed during the Pleistocene epoch. They range from smooth to highly eroded depending upon local wave action. Highly eroded eolianite beaches have shallow pockets and fissures with numerous small, sharp pinnacles covering their surface.

Beach rock is formed beneath coastal sand dunes. Pressure from sand deposits, alternate wetting and drying of the dune by the tide, and heat from the sun combine to produce a type of rock that is exposed when the dune is removed by storm waves. Beach rock is a sandstone formed through the hardening of consolidated beach sands. It breaks into regular and rectangular shaped blocks, which caused Columbus to comment on its possible use as a building material and more recent suggestions that submerged beach-rock formations near Bimini are part of the Atlantis road (Richards 1988). The age of beach rock can be estimated from color, texture, and degree of cementation. Certain fossil beach rock formations attest to higher eustatic sea levels (prior to 35,000 years ago), and these may extend into relatively deep water. Recent formations have incorporated modern artifacts such as nails and bottle caps.

While the tidal movement of littoral sands prevents the development of plant and animal communities, conditions are significantly different on eolianites and beach rock. The rock substrate provides a firm place of attachment for marine alga, which are fed upon by a variety of mollusks that are stratified according to environmental tolerances. Mollusks that were eaten by the Lucayans include nerites (*Nerita* sp.), chitons (*Chiton* sp.), and West Indian top shells (*Cittarium pica*).

Marine Environments

From the shore, the marine environment follows a regular sequence of change in relation to depth (fig. 2.4). The near-shore zone is characterized by bare sand that is maintained by wave action. The stable substrate be-

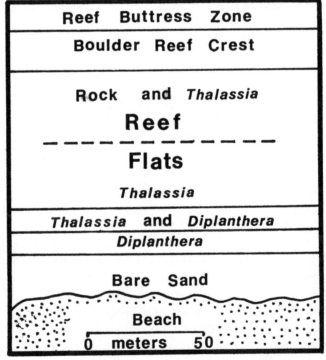

FIGURE 2.4. The marine environment from beach to deep water.

neath these shifting sands may support mollusks in low frequencies. Such bare-sand mollusks include tellins (*Tellina* sp.), which were consumed by the Lucayans, of which the sunrise tellin (*Tellina radiata*) is most familiar to shell collectors.

On both lee and windward shores the bare-sand zone is replaced by a zone of marine spermatophytes (*Thalassia testudinum, Syringodium filiforme*). These sea grasses stabilize the substrate and support a rich and varied bottom-dwelling marine life, including the economically significant mollusks: *Strombus gigas* (queen conch), *Strombus costatus, Xancus angulatus, Cassis* sp. (Helmet), *Codakia orbicularis, Tellina* sp., and others (Jackson 1972, 1973; Keegan 1982a).

During the day the tidal flats also support a low density of adult carnivorous fishes (bonefish, *Albula vulpes*; porgy, *Gerres* sp.; mojarra, *Eugerres* sp.), along with juvenile representatives of reef associated species. At night, adult carnivores (grunts, *Haemulon* sp.; snappers, *Lutjanus* sp.) and omnivores (parrotfish, Scaridae; surgeonfish, *Acanthurus* sp.), which spend their days in protective schools around coral-reef refuges, disperse over the tidal flats to feed (Randall 1965; Ehrlich 1975; Wing and Reitz 1982).

The shallow grass-flat banks of the Bahama archipelago have also supported marine turtles and monk seals and were occasionally visited by marine mammals. These animals may have been encountered by the Lucayans during fishing expeditions on the banks, but turtles and seals could have been more easily captured when they came ashore to nest and breed. Porpoises would have been available on shore following accidental beachings.

Marine turtles were once abundant throughout the Caribbean. Their prehistoric use is well documented in faunal samples (Wing and Reitz 1982), and they provided an important source of food and small but important amounts of money during historic times (Nietschmann 1981). The intensity of human predation, especially after the European introduction of large mesh nets and metal harpoons, has reduced modern populations to the level of endangered species, and, despite the intensification of scientific research, the behavioral ecology of marine turtles is not thoroughly understood (Carr 1981). A major gap in this knowledge is the natural population densities of these animals (Meylan 1981b).

Three genera of marine turtles are common in the Caribbean. Loggerhead turtles, *Caretta caretta*, are carnivores that typically weigh 90 to 225 kilograms, but that may reach a length of three meters and a weight of 450 kilograms. These turtles have not attracted human predators because their meat is considered distasteful and their shells are of little economic value (Campbell 1978). No loggerhead bones are reported from archaeological sites. Hawksbill turtles, *Eretmochelys imbricata*, are carnivores that weigh up to 135 kilograms (Campbell 1978). They are less common than other marine turtles and are today captured primarily for their shell. Hawksbill bones are recorded for archaeological sites in south Florida and St. Lucia (Wing and Reitz 1982). Green turtles, *Chelonia mydas*, are principal herbivores that were once abundant on the shallow banks, where they graze on sea grasses. They achieve a weight of 126 kilograms and were once an important source of food (Campbell 1978; Bjorndal 1981; Nietschmann 1981). Green turtles are reported from archaeological sites throughout the Caribbean (Wing and Reitz 1982).

It is probable that Lucayans who lived near turtle-nesting beaches took advantage of their seasonal access to turtles. These beaches are characterized by surf-built sand berms that exceed the zone of flooding (Carr 1981), a beach form that is more typical of windward shores, which were less frequently settled by the Lucayans. Since faunal samples are not presently available from sites that are located near beaches with the appropriate characteristics, the intensity of predation cannot be judged.

Historically, the hunting of marine mammals was an important component of the Bahamian economy. At one time, the Bahamas supported a thriving whaling industry, and monk seals were captured when they came ashore to breed. Hunting has all but eliminated marine mammals from Bahamian waters.

The prehistoric importance of whales and of the other common cetacean, the porpoise, *Tursiops truncatus*, was probably limited to the relatively rare incidents of accidental beaching. The frequency of such accidents cannot be specified. However, one illustrative case occurred in December 1979, when 25 porpoises were stranded on Pine Cay, Caicos Islands. These cetaceans would have provided a fabulous bounty for the Lucayans. Their presence at a low frequency in archaeological sites on Middle Caicos, Florida, and Trinidad has been reported (Wing and Reitz 1982).

A more actively sought marine mammal would have been the monk seal, *Monachus tropicalis*. This carnivore once fed on fish and squid over the shallow Bahama Banks (Campbell 1978:28-31). Females are reported to have reached weights of 270 kilograms, which makes them the largest animal to regularly come ashore in the Bahamas. During historic times, seals were captured throughout the islands. It is reported that bellowing herds could be heard for miles, and that hunters could kill up to 100 seals in a single night. Monk seals were especially vulnerable during the winter when they came ashore to give birth. For a period of about six weeks centered in December, females remained ashore to give birth and nurse their young. The typical form of historic capture was to club the sleeping seals at night. This practice led to the destruction of entire colonies and contributed to their regional extinction.

Archaeological evidence for monk seal capture is limited to a single bone from MC-6 that cannot be positively identified. However, faunal samples are not presently available from the Exuma Sound area, reported to have supported the largest herds in historic times.

Returning to the succession of marine environments, as one progresses from the shore the next major habitat is the patch-reef zone, which ends at the barrier coral reef. Coral-reef zones have either not developed along lee shores, or they are a significant distance from shore. Shallow tidal flats along these shores can extend as huge banks for over 100 kilometers (e.g., the Bight of Acklins, the Caicos Bank, the marls of Great Abaco).

Along ocean-facing windward coasts, the reef flat grades through zones of mixed sea grass/coral rock/patch reef as water depth increases to over 10 meters at the fringing barrier reefs. The barrier coral reef is located at distances ranging from several kilometers from shore to contact with fossil reefs that now comprise portions of the shore. Reefs provide narrow barriers that protect the shore from ocean swells. They are highly productive in terms of animal biomass and support dense populations of fishes (Glynn 1973; Ehrlich 1975; Randall 1965).

The sea floor drops to depths in excess of 200 meters beyond the reef. Whales and pelagic fishes migrate through these waters (Wing and Reitz 1982; Wing and Scudder 1983). Columbus recorded the presence of whales on his arrival in the Bahamas during his first voyage (Dunn and Kelley 1989).

Summary and Conclusions

The physical environments of the Lucayans were in many respects different from the ones encountered today. The islands and their diverse fauna and flora have been modified by physical and historical-cultural processes during the past 500 years. On a general level, temperature probably averaged several degrees warmer and rainfall levels would have been slightly higher. When combined with a lusher climax vegetation, the milder climate would have improved soil fertility throughout the archipelago and mitigated the impact of winter temperature minimums in the northern subarea. Subsurface groundwater lenses would have been fully charged, and standing fresh water would have been more common. Terrestrial and marine resources were at their highest densities, and species that were overexploited by historic populations would have had wider distributions (e.g., marine turtles, monk seals, flamingos, hutia).

The milder climate was not, however, sufficient to override subareal differences. Although conditions in the southern subarea would have been more favorable, probably supporting a tropical woodland climax vegetation, the tradewinds and convective rainfall would have acted to maintain the degraded character of eastern shores. Topographic, ecological, and archaeological evidence suggests that about 42 percent of Mayaguana, 84 percent of Great Inagua, and nearly 100 percent of Grand Turk, South Caicos, and eastern East Caicos were not suited for permanent prehistoric settlement. These exceptions are subject to future revisions, as shown by the recent discovery of archaeological sites on Grand Turk. Nevertheless, the sites on Grand Turk appear to have been temporary habitations.

The central subarea would have supported tropical seasonal forest with tropical woodlands in the drier southern islands. The forest canopy would have reached at least 15 meters (60 feet). Interior lateritic and black loam soils were probably deeper, although the most significant improvement would have been the humic enrichment and neutralization of alkaline sandy soils.

The absence of evidence for soil erosion indicates that a forest-fallow system of swidden cultivation was practiced (see Boserup 1965). This practice would have maintained soil fertility, and the growth of root crops would have promoted a conservative use of land (Carneiro 1961). The more favorable conditions in these central islands would have supported higher population densities than was possible in the southern islands for the same level of investment.

When the prehistoric environments of the Bahamas archipelago and the Greater Antilles are compared from the perspective of the Taino colonists, the Bahamas appear as an attractive alternative to subsistence intensification on Hispaniola. Root crops provide high yields in relatively poor soils, and the more pronounced dry season of the southern Bahamas may have promoted even higher yields of manioc per hectare than those obtained along the north coast of Hispaniola (see Roosevelt 1980). Humic-enriched sandy soils provide the best medium for planting root crops because they promote efficient root growth and because soil preparation and weeding is less difficult than on other soils.

In terms of animal capture, high densities of land crabs, hutia, and rock iguana would have been encountered. The extensive shallow banks would have supported larger populations of marine animals than the significantly smaller tidal-flat habitats of northern Hispaniola. This difference is apparent in the level of historic queen conch (*Strombus gigas*) exports from the Turks and Caicos Islands to Haiti (Doran 1958; Hesse and Hesse 1977). In addition to queen conch, the shallow banks supported seasonal aggregations of monk seals and green turtles. It is possible that the seasonal exploitation of the rich marine and terrestrial animal resources in the southern Bahamas was the reason for the Tainos' initial familiarity with the archipelago.

At this point it can be concluded that, contrary to their present degraded character in relation to the Greater Antilles, the Bahama Islands circa A.D. 600 presented attractive, even inviting, places to live. Although production in these small limestone islands could not be intensified to the levels possible in the larger volcanic islands of the Greater Antilles, the initial consideration would have been their potential productivity with regard to the colonists' economy. From this perspective the Bahamas provided an attractive location for population expansion.

3

The Taino Colonization
of the Bahamas

The Bahama archipelago was first settled during the Ostionoid expansion that began about A.D. 600 and ended about A.D. 1200. Opinions vary concerning when during this period colonization first took place. The majority opinion states that the Bahamas was colonized after A.D. 800, coincident with the development of Meillacan pottery and the expansion of the Tainos into central Cuba. The minority opinion, which I favor, dates the timing of initial colonization to at least a century earlier. Efforts to identify the first settlement in the Bahamas afford the opportunity for some archaeological detective work.

It should be noted that the study of origins is fraught with difficulties. It is almost impossible to demonstrate that the earliest example of something has been found. When dealing with settlements, the very small number of early settlements (only one at the very beginning) tend to be swamped by the larger number of later sites. An additional complication is that natural and cultural modifications of the landscape often destroy or mask the presence of prehistoric sites. In other areas of the Caribbean, coastal sites that were occupied before sea level reached its present height have been submerged; other sites have been buried by volcanic ash or have been eroded into the sea, and still others have been destroyed by modern construction activities (Watters 1982).

In the Bahamas, the greatest impact has come from the erosion and accretion of sand in coastal zones. In addition, the historic excavation of cave earth for fertilizer destroyed most cave sites, and construction on the developed islands, especially on New Providence and Grand Bahama, has destroyed other sites (Mitchell and Keegan 1987).

Such constraints do not make the study of the initial colonization of the Bahamas impossible. Rather, they require that this event be examined as part of a logical process (Keegan and Diamond 1987). The simple discovery and dating of archaeological deposits is not sufficient (see Rouse and Allaire 1978). Instead, a logical scenario must be employed, one that includes the investigator's categories of means, motive, and opportunity.

Taino Navigation

When the Spanish arrived in the West Indies, they observed the Tainos using dugout canoes. Canoes are of great antiquity in the Caribbean basin (McKusick 1960; Glazier 1991). Their manufacture and use probably began along the large rivers of lowland South and Central America where they would have provided an efficient means of transportation. Even today, rivers are the avenues of choice because the dense vegetation and difficult terrain of the tropical forest make overland journeys extremely difficult. Dugout canoes can be made with only fire and a tool that can be used to knock away the charred wood. A final requirement is patience because an entire year may be needed to complete the canoe using such simple tools (Wilbert 1977).

The expansion of the Island Arawaks from the South American mainland into the Antilles was made possible by enlarging the canoe that was already in use in the Orinoco River and its tributaries. Smaller versions of the dugout described for the Taino still enjoy widespread use in the tropical islands.

The Spanish described Taino dugouts as having been hollowed from a single large tree trunk (fig. 3.1). Recently, however, Steven Glazier (1991) suggested that their sides were built up with planks. The canoes were sleek, fast, and could easily be righted and bailed when overturned (Dunn and Kelley 1989:69). A paddle shaped like a baker's peel was described in Columbus's diario. One was also recovered from a cave near Great Abaco (DeBooy 1913). Columbus observed canoes in the Bahamas that could carry up to 50 people, and even larger dugouts were reported among the Cuban Tainos. In Cuba, finely crafted and elaborately decorated canoes

FIGURE 3.1. Taino canoe. After Oviedo 1547.

belonging to the chiefs were housed in special buildings that were maintained on the beach.

It is reasonable to assume that dugout canoes provided an efficient means of transportation that facilitated the colonization of the Bahamas. The major change that accompanied migration into the Antilles was an increase in vessel size to accommodate people and their belongings during interisland moves. It is likely that other types of canoes were also developed for use in other, more specialized activities, such as fishing and local transport.

The best way to justify the conclusion that movement over water was not a serious constraint is to examine the Island Arawak record of seafaring. During the Saladoid expansion the 120-kilometer (72 miles) water gap between Trinidad and Grenada was breached. Communication between the islands and the mainland was maintained throughout prehistory (Boomert 1987). During the Ostionoid expansion, Cuba (80 kilometers, 48 miles) and Jamaica (200 kilometers, 120 miles) were reached first. The subsequent appearance of Meillacan pottery decorations in Cuba and Jamaica is evidence for additional contacts across those distances. Finally, Columbus reported that trading expeditions were regularly conducted between Long Island in the central Bahamas and Cuba (Daggett 1980). Such expeditions crossed at least 260 kilometers (156 miles) of open sea, which is the longest water passage between adjacent islands anywhere in the West Indies. When one compares the distances between islands in the West Indies with those that were crossed in the world's other oceans, the West Indian distances are inconsequential (Nicholson 1976; Keegan and Diamond 1987).

The First Settlement in the Bahamas

Three different islands have been identified as the location of the first Taino settlement in the Bahamas. Two of these proposals identify Hispaniola as the source of colonists, but they differ over whether the Caicos Islands or Great Inagua was the first to be settled; the third identifies Cuba as the source area and Long Island as the first colony (map 3.1).

Cuba to Long Island

Perhaps the earliest opinion regarding the colonization of the Bahamas was that the colonists came from Cuba and settled first in the central Ba-

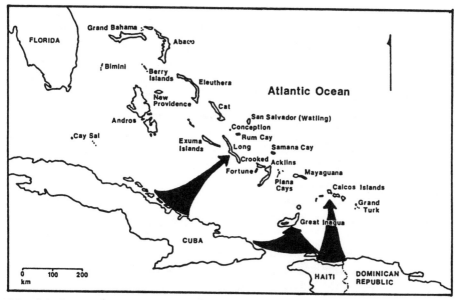

MAP 3.1. Proposed migration routes for Taino expansion into the Bahamas.

hamas. This proposal has evolved into what can be called the Cuba to Long Island hypothesis (Winter et al. 1985), first suggested before archaeological research had been conducted in the central and southern Bahamas.

At the time, it was felt that the Tainos were severely restricted in their movements by limited seafaring abilities. It was therefore proposed that because the shallow banks between Cuba and Long Island offered the easiest passage, this crossing was the first to be breached. Columbus's report that trading expeditions were being conducted between Long Island and Cuba was taken as additional support for this hypothesis. It was reasoned that exchange practices at the time of contact were a reflection of relationships that were first established when the Bahamas were colonized.

The distribution of pottery types has been used to support all three colonization proposals. Two general categories of pottery are found in Bahamian archaeological sites. The most common type was made in the Bahamas from red clay soils and shell temper. This pottery is known as Palmetto Ware (Hoffman 1967; Sears and Sullivan 1978; Mann 1986). The second category is sand-tempered pottery, which must have originated outside the limestone Bahamas. The closest source is the Greater Antilles. The petrographic analysis of quartz sand-tempered pottery recovered from Bahamian sites has shown that some of the sherds are of Cuban origin (Winter, Granberry, and Leibold 1985). However, it is not certain when this pottery arrived in the Bahamas.

The majority of Palmetto Ware pottery sherds are undecorated. The little decoration that does occur is restricted to a narrow band near the vessel rim and is executed in the Meillacan style (Sears and Sullivan 1978). Stylistic similarities have been interpreted as evidence that Palmetto Ware developed out of the Meillacan subseries. Because this subseries is associated with population expansion into central Cuba, by extension it has come to be associated with the initial settlement of the Bahamas.

At present, the Cuba to Long Island proponents have been able to demonstrate only that pottery was traded between these islands, and that certain Meillacan stylistic elements were adopted for use on Palmetto Ware. Exchange between Cuba and Long Island was reported by Columbus, which may explain all of the material evidence that is currently available. Because there is no indication as to when this commerce began, it does not provide any clue to the location of the first Lucayan settlement. In fact, if the colonists originated in central Cuba, then the Bahamas could not have been colonized before A.D. 1000–1200, the time at which central Cuba was itself colonized.

Hispaniola to the Caicos Islands

A consideration of the physical and cultural geographies of the northern Caribbean during Ostionoid times reveals that the earliest and closest possible source of Bahamian colonists was Hispaniola. In terms of distance, Hispaniola is much closer to the southeastern Bahamas than Cuba is to the central Bahamas. Moreover, western Hispaniola was settled several centuries before central Cuba.

The earliest scientific archaeology in the southern Bahamas was conducted by Shaun Sullivan in the mid-1970s (1976, 1980, 1981). Sullivan's discoveries on Middle Caicos led him to suggest that the weight of the evidence strongly supported the Caicos Islands as the first to be settled. Support for that conclusion was drawn from three sources: settlement patterns, pottery analysis, and ecological factors (Sullivan 1981).

First, Sullivan classified prehistoric open-air sites as either inland or coastal. By his accounting, all of the inland sites were in the Caicos Islands, while all but one of the coastal sites were on Bahama islands to the north and west. Because a shift from inland to coastal settlement locations had already been established as the sequence during Saladoid expansion, it was assumed that a similar shift had occurred in the Bahamas. The presumed emphasis on the interior was interpreted as proof that the Caicos sites were the oldest.

Second, a number of sites were discovered in which only imported pottery was found. As stated previously, imported pottery was manufactured from materials that do not occur naturally in the Bahamas, most notably quartz sand. Only after the Bahamas were colonized was pottery made from local materials, primarily red loam soil and burned *Strombus* shell. Because shell-tempered pottery was invented after the Bahamas was colonized, the first settlements in the Bahamas should contain only imported pottery. The import-only sites in the Caicos were unique in the Bahamas at the time.

Finally, the majority of his sites were positioned along the margin of Armstrong Pond. Armstrong Pond is important because it produces enormous quantities of crystalline salt every summer. Salt is known to have been an important trade item well into prehistory, so Sullivan suggested that access to salt was the motivating factor in the initial colonization of the Bahamas. Furthermore, the largest of the Armstrong Pond sites, MC-6, has a community plan that is more typical of Classic Taino than of Lucayan settlements (fig. 3.2). (The significance of this and other plaza sites will be discussed in later chapters.)

Sullivan's (1981) colonization model can be summarized as follows. Beginning about A.D. 800, people from Hispaniola began to visit the Caicos Islands. The purpose of their visits was the collection of salt and of other locally abundant marine resources. At first these visits were seasonal, timed to coincide with the natural production of salt through solar distillation. Archaeological sites during this Antillean period were primarily small scatters that contained only imported pottery and were located in the interior (Sullivan 1980, 1981). The Antillean period lasted less than two centuries. By A.D. 1000, more permanent settlements had been established, Palmetto Ware pottery had been invented, and a population adapted to life on these small islands was emerging. The emergence of the Lucayan culture is signaled by a shift from inland to coastal settlement locations, which reflects their maritime economy, and by the use of Palmetto Ware pottery. The maritime emphasis of the Lucayans then led to their northward expansion into the other Bahama islands.

At the time, Sullivan's model seemed both reasonable and logical. It

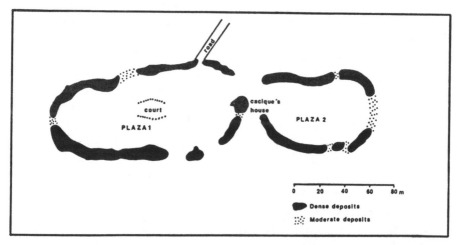

FIGURE 3.2. The two-plaza community plan of site MC-6. Black areas are dense concentrations of artifacts and structural remains, stippled areas are moderate concentrations. After Sullivan, 1981.

has not held up, however, in light of more recent discoveries or under close scrutiny. The first problem concerns the classification of sites as either coastal or inland. Sullivan reported that all 30 of the open-air sites on Middle Caicos were at inland locations (map 3.2). Twenty-three of these sites are in the interior, but they are small scatters of pottery, each with less than 12 potsherds, that contain no evidence for habitation. Instead of these being interpreted as evidence for settlements, they should be viewed as activity areas away from habitations. Moreover, it has not been demonstrated that these special-purpose sites were created by the initial colonists, so it is inappropriate to compare their location with those of the permanent villages in the rest of the Bahamas. Recent archaeological surveys have located special-purpose sites at inland locations in other Bahama islands (Keegan and Mitchell 1986; Keegan 1991b).

The remaining seven sites can be interpreted as permanent villages. Three of these are located on margins of tidal creeks that have outlets to the sea. At the time of Sullivan's research, no other settlements on tidal creeks were known. More recently, surveys have shown that Lucayan settlements are commonly found on tidal creeks, especially on windward coasts where tidal creeks provide protected bays (Keegan 1991b). Thus, even though a site may appear to be inland, the tidal creek is actually an extension of the coast. In addition, one of the seven sites is clearly coastal; a one-lane road is all that separates the site from the beach.

The last three villages are located in an unusual setting, along the margin of the periodically flooded salina that forms the south coast of Middle Caicos. The primary factor motivating settlement in this location was access to Armstrong Pond. Thus, these three villages, along with the 12 small pottery scatters, are better viewed as reflecting attempts to maintain access to salt than as examples of an initial emphasis on interior settlement locations.

In the Lesser Antilles the initial interior settlements were established to gain access to prime agricultural lands along river drainages (Haviser 1990). Similar conditions do not prevail in the Bahamas. Thus, even though these sites are almost 6 kilometers (4 miles) from the tide line of the Caicos Bank, they are located on the first stretch of permanently dry land; the land that separates them from the sea is not suited for permanent habitation. In other words, they are located as close to the coast as is possible. Finally, given that these islands are building along their south coasts, it is possible that most of the salina was underwater at the time

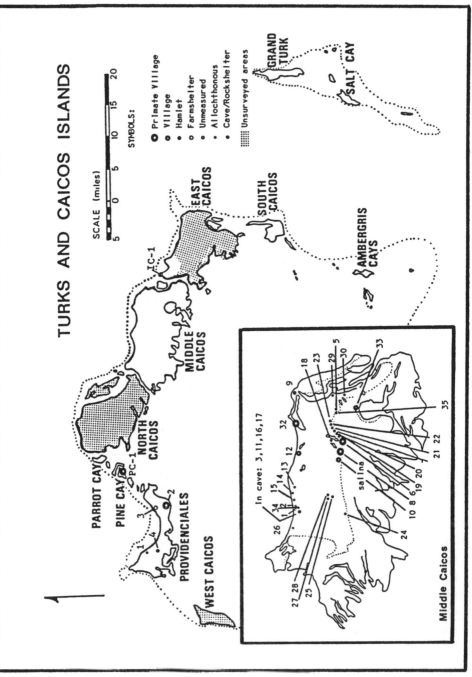

MAP 3.2. Lucayan sites on Middle Caicos, Turks, and Caicos Islands.

these sites were occupied. In this case, their inland location would reflect changes in coastal geomorphology rather than a conscious decision to establish interior settlements.

The consideration of site locations on Middle Caicos indicates that the inland/coastal dichotomy is not particularly useful. It is clear that a variety of factors provides better explanations for the apparent inland locations than does the colonization hypothesis.

The second problem is with Sullivan's pottery analysis. Sullivan classified the imported pottery into four classes defined according to differences in the minerals that were included as temper. He next employed the archaeological technique known as seriation to order his sites from earliest to latest and used cross dating with sites in the Greater Antilles to assign dates. This procedure involved first identifying the types of temper in imported pottery that was found in association with Palmetto Ware. These types were taken as the most recent imports. Next, he arranged the frequency of his pottery classes: the class that was most abundant during the earliest time period was superceded when another class became more popular, and so on until his final class was associated with Palmetto Ware.

Aside from the problem of very small sample sizes (some sites have only one or two sherds), this technique is based on the assumption that each site received an equal contribution of all of the pottery classes that were being manufactured during a given time period and that the pottery came from an area in which the sequence of change actually occurred. Neither of these assumptions is reasonable for the Middle Caicos sites. In fact, a more reasonable interpretation is that Sullivan's different imported-pottery classes reflect trade with different locations in the Greater Antilles. For example, his earliest class of temper is ferromagnesian minerals. Pottery with this type of temper has recently been shown to be quite common at Lucayan sites in the central Bahamas where it occurs in association with Palmetto Ware. One explanation is that imported pottery with ferromagnesian or biotite temper was manufactured in Cuba, a possibility that Sullivan acknowledged.

The final problem concerns the dating of sites associated with the salt trade. The largest site, MC-6, has what may be house foundations arranged around two plazas (fig. 3.2). On the larger plaza, rocks are aligned to coincide with astronomical events, and on the edge of the plaza there is what has been identified as the foundations of a chief's house. Site

MC-6 is duplicated almost exactly by villages in the Greater Antilles (Castellanos 1981; Alegría 1983). As previously discussed, these plaza communities are associated with the rise of the Classic Taino chiefdoms beginning after A. D. 1200.

Since plaza communities are a late development, Middle Caicos may actually have been colonized after A.D. 1200 as a Classic Taino outpost or gateway community. In this scenario, Sullivan's identification of salt and marine-resource availability as the motivating factors is reasonable. However, it is unlikely that the salt trade was the motivating factor for the initial colonization of the Bahamas. There is no evidence that access to salt was an important consideration in the location of settlements until the rise of the Classic Taino chiefdoms. Furthermore, all of the sites on Middle Caicos can be interpreted as the product of a late intrusion by Tainos from Hispaniola.

Hispaniola to Great Inagua

The evidence for the Cuba-Long Island and Hispaniola-Caicos hypotheses is better explained as a reflection of exchange relationships that postdate initial colonization. Even though this explanation does not account for the initial colonization of the Bahamas, the southern Bahamas are still the most likely location for the first colony and Hispaniola the most likely source of colonists. A third hypothesis, favored by the author, states that the Tainos entered the Bahamas through Great Inagua during the Ostionoid expansion into Cuba.

According to Rouse (1986), the Ostionoid expansion across northern Hispaniola to Cuba stalled on the Cuban frontier. The result was a growing population in western Hispaniola that was ready to avail itself of the Bahamian outlet only 90 kilometers (54 miles) to the north. In fact, the frontier that Rouse has identified in this area is unnecessary given the reclassification of pottery styles. If Palmetto Ware developed directly out of an Ostionan Ostionoid tradition, then the colonization of the Bahamas could date to before the development of Meillacan Ostionoid pottery around A.D. 800.

Taino expansion along the north coast of Hispaniola and onto Cuba was obviously the key to the colonization of the Bahamas. The problem became finding archaeological evidence that matched what was expected of the first colony. The archaeological survey of Great Inagua provided such a breakthrough. Great Inagua had been ignored previously because the architects of an earlier colonization model did not have time to survey the island. Therefore, in their summary of Bahamas prehistory, William Sears and Shaun Sullivan (1978) simply concluded that Great Inagua must have been too dry to have ever supported permanent settlement.

Great Inagua is a better candidate for the first colony than is the Caicos for several reasons. Inagua is larger and is closer to both Hispaniola and Cuba. Furthermore, if salt were the motive behind colonizing these islands (Sullivan 1981), Great Inagua has more substantial salt-producing ponds. When the southern and western shores of Great Inagua were finally surveyed, 10 prehistoric sites were identified (Keegan 1985). However, simply finding sites on Great Inagua did not provide a complete solution to the problem.

One method for evaluating which island was the most likely first landfall is to calculate which island had the greatest chance of being contacted from Hispaniola (map 3.3). Two factors are of immediate impor-

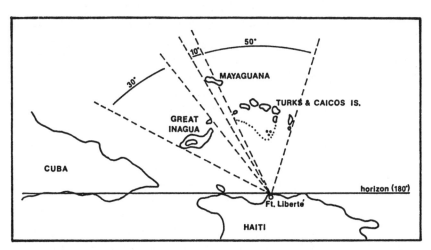

M AP 3.3. Configuration of islands in the southern Bahama archipelago illustrates the "target effect." Using Ft. Liberté, Haiti, as the embarkation point, the horizon is divided into arc segments that define the probabilities for contact with those islands when the direction of travel is selected at random and when winds and currents are not considered. Under these conditions, the Turks and Caicos Islands present a unified target that subtends 50° of the 180° horizon, which gives a 20 percent probability for contact. Similarly, Great Inagua presents a target of 30° (16 percent probability), and Mayaguana presents a target of less than 10° (6 percent probability). When winds and currents are also considered, Great Inagua is the most accessible target.

tance. The first is distance and the second is maritime conditions that influence travel over that distance (wind, waves, and currents).

With regard to distance, none of the southern Bahama Islands are visible from the north coast of Hispaniola. However, signs of these islands in the form of weather patterns and bird migrations (especially flamingos) would indicate the presence of islands to those who knew how to interpret the signs (Keegan and Diamond 1987). In terms of measured distance, Great Inagua is the closest Bahama island to the Greater Antilles, being only about 10 kilometers (6 miles) farther from Hispaniola than is Cuba (80 kilometers, 48 miles).

Maritime conditions can be divided into the categories of wind direction, wind intensity, and ocean currents. The net effect of these three factors is to favor voyaging from east to west. The primary factor is the easterly trade winds, which are dominant about two-thirds of the year. These winds are complemented by the northwesterly trending Antilles Current, which flows through the islands at between 0.5 and 0.9 knots. These winds and currents today move a variety of floating objects onto beaches in the southern Bahamas. On the windward beaches of Great Inagua and Mayaguana, the author has observed wooden statues and spoons, dugout canoes, and a canoe paddle of apparent Haitian origin. A Haitian source has been proved in one case: rocks trapped in the root system of a palm tree that washed ashore on Great Inagua have been shown to match the unique geologic assemblage in the vicinity of Cap Haitien (Keegan and Mitchell 1986) (fig. 3.3). If the Tainos simply let the winds and currents take them where they would, they would have drifted to Great Inagua.

It is, however, more likely that the Bahamas were colonized during purposeful voyages. To determine where such purposeful voyages are most likely to have ended, the effects of wind intensity must be considered. Wind speeds recorded at Nassau Airport average 4 to 10 knots about half of the year, exceed 21 knots only 1 percent of the year, and are recorded as calm on only about 29 days (about 8 percent of the year). It has been estimated that Taino dugouts could have maintained speeds of 4 to 6 knots. Although seagoing canoes would have been designed to counter the effects of the wind, the wind speed equaled or exceeded vessel speed for about 75 percent of the year.

Human-powered vessels cannot be expected to maintain high speeds on long-distance voyages, especially in the face of contrary winds. Furth-

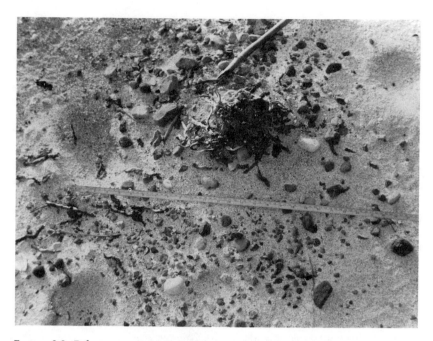

FIGURE 3.3. Palm root containing rocks on the beach at Southeast Point, Great Inagua. The palm root originated near Cap Haitien, Haiti.

ermore, the height, speed, and intensity of waves, which are direct functions of the wind, would also exert an influence. Shallow-draft vessels like the Taino canoes would have encountered great difficulty in maintaining a direction of travel parallel to wave direction. With the wind and waves coming from the same direction, travel between islands could be significantly impeded.

Wind, waves, and ocean currents interact either to favor passage between islands by pushing the craft along its intended course, or to impede travel by blowing from some angle to the direction of travel, thereby deflecting the canoe from its intended course. If voyages from Hispaniola to the southern Bahamas were timed to coincide with favorable marine conditions, travel to Great Inagua would have been favored about 281 days per year, while travel to the Caicos Islands would have been favored on about 91 days per year. Great Inagua was an easier target than the Caicos Islands because it is both closer and more accessible. Great Inagua is the logical first colony, but logic is not by itself sufficient proof.

Because Palmetto Ware was invented after the Bahamas was colonized, the earliest site(s) should contain only the pottery that the immigrants brought with them. It is expected that sites containing only imported pottery will be found on the first island colonized. This expectation is met on Great Inagua. Almost all of the archaeological sites on Great In-agua contain an abundance of imported pottery. In addition, a one-acre village site having only imported pottery on its surface was found. The site also contained the food remains that occur on permanent settle-ments (e.g., molluscan shell and animal bones). The presence of such refuse is the basis for calling the site a village. Further research at this site is needed to determine whether Palmetto Ware is truly absent or whether it was simply not observed during surface collections. A collec-tion of samples to date the site must also be made.

Motives for Colonizing the Bahamas

At first glance, it seems difficult to explain why anyone would choose to leave the very large islands of the Greater Antilles to settle on the small, dry islands of the southern Bahamas. Previous explanations have therefore emphasized stimuli that would make such a move attractive to us: the islands of the Greater Antilles near the Bahamas had filled to capac-ity, and colonists were literally pushed into the Bahamas (Sears and Sul-livan 1978), the Island Caribs were raiding the Greater Antilles so people moved to the Bahamas to escape from them (Craton 1986), or the pres-ence of an abundant source of a valuable trade good (salt) attracted colo-nists (Sullivan 1981). None of these explanations is satisfactory.

In the first place, the population in the Greater Antilles at the time the Bahamas was colonized was probably quite small. That the popula-tion seems to have grown at an exponential rate until Spanish contact contradicts the filled-to-capacity explanation. Second, the Island Caribs never expanded beyond the Windward Islands of the Lesser Antilles, and their development occurred many centuries after the Bahamas was colo-nized. Furthermore, as the Spanish learned, the Tainos were quite capable of defending themselves against Carib incursions. Finally, although salt may have been a major trade good during Classic Taino times, its impor-tance and stimulating influence would not have been felt until several centuries after the Bahamas was colonized.

Despite their smaller size and drier climate, the southern Bahamas would have been very attractive from the perspective of Ostionoid horticulturalists. When modern differences in the environment of the Bahamas and Hispaniola are the sole consideration, the Bahamas do appear to be a poor choice. However, when the prehistoric environments are interpreted in terms of food-getting strategies, the Bahamas would have provided an excellent location for population expansion.

As discussed in chapter 2, the prehistoric vegetation of the Bahamas would have been characterized by lush tropical woodlands or tropical forest. Even if rainfall was not appreciably greater, the taller tropical vegetation would have acted to retain water and make the islands significantly less dry. The soil would also have been richer given almost two million years of undisturbed development, and the sandy soils would have been well suited for the type of root-crop cultivation that was practiced by Ostionoid peoples. With regard to the first arrivals, the easily hunted land animals would have occurred in high density as a result of the absence of predators and competitors. Seasonal aggregations of monk seals and green turtles would have also provided an abundant food source that was easily harvested. Finally, the smaller size of the Bahamas is actually an advantage for people who rely on the sea for a substantial portion of their food. Marine animals of all types would have been more abundant and more readily accessible than they were on north-coast locations in the Greater Antilles.

The abundance of marine and terrestrial resources in the Bahamas combined with the more favorable climate and vegetation provide strong support for the conclusion that the Bahamas were an attractive location during the period of Ostionoid expansion. It will be shown below that by viewing access to Bahamian resources as the primary motive for their colonization, one can explain the rapid spread of population through the Bahamas that followed initial colonization. This conclusion provides a much better explanation for our archaeological observations than do any of the alternative explanations.

Further support for the southern Bahamas as the first area colonized is found when the distribution of populations throughout the archipelago is examined. When other factors are held constant, we would expect the area that was colonized first to have achieved the largest population size. This expectation is based on the recognition that the first area to be colonized has the longest period of time during which the population can increase in numbers. Archaeological surveys have demonstrated a steady decline in population density to the north of Acklins Island. This decline can be interpreted as a weighting of the distribution that resulted from differences in the timing of island settlements. Thus, as the population expanded to the north, each new island colony had a somewhat shorter period of population growth, and the islands to the south achieved the largest populations.

4

Settlements and Settlers:
Lucayan Settlement Patterns

Where and with whom people live tells us a great deal about their lives. Archaeologists have recognized that fact for at least fifty years, and a proliferation of regional, spatial, and geographical approaches have been proposed (Willey 1953; Chang 1968; Hodder and Orton 1976; Earle and Preucel 1987). Most studies of prehistoric settlement patterns have simply described spatial relations between and among communities. In the course of empirical studies, resource distributions, technology, population parameters, social structure, political organization and constraints imposed by other settlements have been identified as important factors whose multivariate interactions create settlement systems. The manner in which these factors produced Lucayan settlement patterns is the subject of the chapters that follow. Included are the results of archaeological surveys conducted over a ten-year period. Although some areas of the Bahamas have not been examined completely, enough of the islands have been covered to suggest that there are no major surprises waiting to be found.

Ideal Distributions: Steady-State and Weighted

Because the factors just listed suggest a potentially infinite list of characteristics that could be recorded for archaeological sites, it is necessary to restrict descriptions to that set of variables most relevant to the purposes of this study. The main issue is the manner in which the Bahama archipelago was colonized, so the following discussion emphasizes spatial relations that characterize migrations.

When environmental influences are constant (as in the central subarea of the Bahamas), the major determinants of settlement density distributions are the variables population growth and timing of settlement. Furthermore, if population growth occurs at a constant rate, then two distinct and mutually exclusive density distributions can occur, a steady-state distribution and a weighted distribution. For simplicity these models can be described as pull and push, respectively. In the steady-state case colonists are pulled to new islands by an abundance of resources. In the case of weighted distributions the colonists are pushed out of the area they occupy. (The economic relations that produce these distributions are discussed in chapter 6, and their demographic counterparts are considered in chapter 7.)

A steady-state distribution occurs when the ratio of humans to some common denominator is equal over a specified area. It is produced by the rapid expansion of population at low and equal densities and is favored by both productive and reproductive factors. In terms of production, efforts to maximize access to resources will result in rapid expansion at low densities. Under these conditions a new island will be colonized when the colonizing group's numbers produce a human per land-unit ratio that is lower than or equal to that on the occupied island.

With regard to reproduction, individuals should attempt to position themselves in a group of optimal size, with optimal defined by the maximization of some currency (E.A. Smith 1981). But individuals belong to groups, and groups face the problem of spacing in relation to other groups. The maximizing solution is the equal partitioning of the available territory, albeit equal partitioning can only be achieved for short periods of time (Sibley 1983). Finally, ecologists have suggested that there may be a reproductive value to dispersal "even when the local environment is not deteriorating and even when the process of dispersal itself incurs considerable mortality" (Horn 1978:423).

One complication that needs to be kept in mind is that people travel in groups. For estimation purposes it is assumed that the Bahamas were settled by household- to hamlet-sized groups of 30 to 50 people. For example, using 50 individuals as the size of a colonizing group, the group would settle an island of 100 square kilometers when the total population per land-area ratio of the island they occupied declined to 0.5 persons per square kilometer.

The weighted distribution is consistent with intuition concerning how people should move across a landscape. In addition, it reflects expectations derived from carrying-capacity and population-pressure models of cultural development and change (Ammerman and Cavalli-Sforza 1973). When the population on the first island grows to a density that exceeds that which could be achieved by settling a new island, the human per land-area ratios are unequal. The actual ratios are set by the timing and length of settlement, the period of population growth on every island in relation to other islands. In this way the density of settlement reflects the sequence in which the islands were colonized.

The economic logic of a weighted distribution comes from the "satisficing" model of economic behavior. In this case, the decision-making unit selects the first option that will satisfy its level of aspiration (Wright 1984:104–105). For example, if a group required 30 square kilometers to obtain a satisfactory level of production, then their position in relation to other groups would be the first location that provided them with 30 square kilometers. Dispersal would progress until all of the "satisfactory" locations were occupied, at which time the next island would be colonized. A maximizer would not stop at 30 square kilometers if more was available.

The weighted distribution characterizes traditional explanations for population expansion in the West Indies. Since every major island in the Lesser Antilles supported similar resource distributions, it seems logical to assume that each island was colonized in turn. In addition, the islands are of sufficient size to expect that each island supported more than one settlement during the initial period of population expansion. It has already been demonstrated that humans cannot reproduce fast enough to support that belief. The islands of the Lesser Antilles may even have been bypassed during the Saladoid expansion in favor of a direct jump to Puerto Rico. The optimization model provides a better explanation for Saladoid period dispersal.

A final note is that a weighted distribution will occur in linear archipelagos when the number of linear steps and the distribution of islands by size cause the first islands to become socially circumscribed. For example, by the time Eleuthera, which is at the northern limit of the central subarea, was settled, Acklins Island had been occupied for so long

its population density exceeded the initial density of the Eleuthera settlement. Continued growth at a constant rate would maintain this unequal relationship.

Archaeological Surveys in the Bahamas

The 1960s proved to be a watershed in Bahama archaeology. Prior to
1960 there were a number of spot surveys and informal investigations
that succeeded in identifying various isolated artifacts along with 61 prehistoric sites, 45 of which were in caves (Mason 1877; Maynard 1890,
1893, 1915; Fewkes 1907; Joyce 1907, 1919; DeBooy 1912, 1913; Goggin
1937, 1939, 1952; Granberry 1956, 1957, 1980).

Thorough archaeological surveys and excavations were initiated in the
late 1960s (Hoffman 1967, 1970; MacLaury 1968, 1970; Pratt 1974a, b; Sullivan 1974; Sears 1975, 1976; J. Winter 1978a, b, c, 1980, 1981, 1982). With
the exception of Sullivan's work in the Turks and Caicos Islands, these
surveys were restricted to single islands in the northern subarea and to
the northern islands of the central subarea. By the 1980s, what remained
to be surveyed was a series of large islands along the primary north-south
axis of the archipelago. Surveys of most of these islands have been conducted by the author since 1982 (Keegan 1983a, b, 1985, 1988; Keegan
and Mitchell 1984a, b; Keegan and Sealey 1988; Keegan, Williams, and
Seim 1990).

These surveys have identified a predominantly coastal orientation of
settlement. More specifically, Lucayan sites tend to be restricted to lee-
shore sand beaches adjacent to shallow marine grass flats. This location
provided access to marine mollusks and fishes, freshwater lenses beneath
coastal sand dunes, unobstructed canoe landings, and agricultural land
(Sears and Sullivan 1978). Because previous studies have shown that Lucayan settlements were usually restricted to coastal habitats, these locations have been the focus of most research efforts.

Interior habitation sites are known only for Middle Caicos. The unique
circumstances surrounding these sites were discussed in the previous
chapter. The only other interior Lucayan sites are small scatters of pottery on Eleuthera, Great Abaco, and San Salvador, all of which show evidence for short-term special-purpose functions (e.g., water or clay procurement). The Eleuthera and Great Abaco sites are associated with

freshwater sinkholes. In sum, permanent habitations were located in coastal settings.

I sought complete coverage of the coasts during my surveys for several reasons. First, coastal access is restricted along most coasts in the undeveloped southern Bahamas. Therefore, locations selected by random sampling might have been impossible to reach. Second, previous surveys indicated that settlements were restricted to lee-shore beaches and significant windward estuaries. Therefore, little would be achieved through restrictive random surveys. Finally, I tested backpacking along the coast during the first survey and found it a fast and efficient means for covering most of the desired shorelines. Given the choice between complete coverage and random sampling, I chose complete coverage (Flannery 1976; Sanders, Parsons, and Santley 1979; Watters 1980).

Adequate coverage of Eleuthera, Cat Island, San Salvador, and the Turks and Caicos Islands had been achieved during previous surveys (Hoffman 1967; MacLaury 1968; Sullivan 1974, 1976, 1981; J. Winter 1980, 1981, 1982; Winter and Stipp 1983). To obtain evidence that related to population expansion, surveys were concentrated along the main axis to the south: Long Island, Crooked Island, Acklins Island, Mayaguana, and Great Inagua (Keegan 1983a, b, 1988; Keegan and Mitchell 1984a, b). These surveys revealed the characteristics of areas that were chosen for sites as well as those that were rejected for some reason.

The information obtained from thorough surveys was used to structure spot surveys on Great and Little Exuma, islands that are peripheral to the main north-south axis. Spot surveys were also conducted on Grand Bahama and New Providence, islands which are severely disturbed by modern construction and which have also been investigated by others (J. Winter 1978a, 1981, 1982; Granberry 1980; Keegan 1982b; B.A.T. 1984). The spot surveys indicated that the site-location criteria had been accurately defined, even though these spot checks certainly missed small sites.

Finally, Great Abaco and Andros still await complete surveys. I made a one-day visit to the three known sites on Great Abaco (J. Winter 1982), and Ian Lothian reports having found at least 15 other sites since then (pers. com.). No formal studies have been made. On Andros, employees of the Atlantic Undersea Testing and Evaluation Center (AUTEC, a division of General Electric under contract with the U.S. Navy) have recently become interested in archaeology. With their assistance the first Lucayan site found on the island was excavated in 1988 (Keegan and Sealey 1988), and several other sites have since been found. The results of almost every archaeological survey conducted in the Bahamas archipelago are summarized in table 4.1, which also contains references to published reports. (I

TABLE 4.1 Archaeological Surveys in the Bahama Archipelago

Grand Bahama Island (Keegan 1982b, 1985)
    3 open-air, 1 rockshelter, 2 submerged cave burials
Cay Sal Bank (Granberry 1980)
    No sites
Bimini Cays (DeBooy 1913; Granberry 1957)
    No sites; stone pendant, coral zemi isolated finds
Berry Islands (Sears and Sullivan 1978)
    No sites
Great Abaco and Cays (DeBooy 1913; Rainey 1934; Keegan 1985)
    19 open-air, 1 cave (Mores Island), 1 burial cave (as many as 30 sites have recently
    been identified but published reports are not yet available)
Andros (Goggin 1939; Sears and Sullivan 1978; Keegan and Sealey 1988; Palmer 1989)
    3 open-air, 3 burial caves, 1 submerged cave burial (as many as 20 sites have re-
    cently been identified but published reports are not available)
New Providence (Granberry 1956; Winter 1978b; B.A.T. 1984; Keegan 1985)
    7 open-air, 10 caves, 1 rockshelter
Eleuthera (Rainey 1934; Sullivan 1974; Keegan 1985)
    17 open-air, 3 burial caves
Cat Island (MacLaury 1968; Keegan 1985)
    19 open-air sites
San Salvador (Rainey 1934; Hoffman 1967)
    23 open-air, 2 caves
Rum Cay (Keegan 1985)
    11 open air, 1 cave
Conception Island (Hoffman 1988)
    6 open-air sites
Long Island (Krieger 1937; Sears and Sullivan 1978; Keegan and Mitchell 1984b; Keegan
    1985; Hoffman 1987c)
    47 open-air, 4 caves
Great and Little Exuma (Keegan and Mitchell 1984a)
    12 open-air sites
Exuma Cays (Sears and Sullivan 1978)
    No sites
Crooked Island (Hoffman 1973b; Winter 1978c; Granberry 1978; Keegan 1983a, 1988)
    14 open-air, 3 caves
Fortune Island (Hoffman 1987a)
    2 open-air sites
Acklins Island (Keegan 1983a, 1988)
    29 open-air, 1 cave

(continued)

Table 4.1—*continued*

Samana Cay (Hoffman 1987a, 1988)
   11 open-air sites
Mayaguana (DeBooy 1913; Keegan 1983b, 1985)
   10 open-air sites, 1 effigy celt isolated find
Great Inagua (Krieger 1937; Keegan 1985)
   9 open-air, 1 cave
Turks and Caicos Islands (DeBooy 1912; Sullivan 1976, 1981; Keegan 1985; Keegan et al. 1990)
   43 open-air, 8 caves, 1 submerged cave burial

     Totals
     285 open-air sites, 40 cave sites, 4 submerged cave burials

---

excluded some informal surveys because I am not familiar with their results.)

Lucayan Site Types

In order to make meaningful comparisons of settlements on different islands it is necessary to ensure that like phenomena are being compared. For example, an island with ten villages is very different from an island with ten conch-processing stations, even though both might be reported in the literature as having ten sites. Working with a sample of more than 150 open-air sites, five categories of sites were defined (table 4.2). The longest linear dimension (henceforth, site length) was used to distinguish between these categories. The most important distinction is between sites at which people lived for extended periods and those at which a more limited range of activities was conducted.

TABLE 4.2 Lucayan Site Types

Site Type	Longest linear distance (m)
Village	>200
Hamlet	90–199
Household	20–89
Shelter	10–19
Allochthonous	<10
Caves and rockshelters	n/a

Size differences were used to distinguish three types of permanent settlement: villages (greater than 200 meters in length), hamlets (90 to 199 meters), and households (20 to 89 meters). These habitation sites have scatters containing pottery, marine mollusc shells, fish bones, small limestone (fire-cracked) rocks, and other materials. They are located on lee-shore sand beaches or windward tidal creeks, and their soil exhibits evidence of organic enrichment (Sullivan 1974; Keegan 1988). The kinds of remains found in these sites indicate that they were places at which people lived for extended periods of time. Size differences are viewed as reflecting the number of people who lived at a site.

Shelters and procurement areas are temporary activity areas created during the extraction of resources. Both are located away from typical habitation areas. Shelters are positioned to gain access to agricultural land, and procurement areas are located in relation to other discrete resource distributions (e.g., marine resources, fresh water, clay deposits). These sites are characterized by small surface scatters with few potsherds and few mollusc shells. In some cases, "Indian-opened" conch, which have a small hole rather than the modern slash in the spire, can be used to identify probable procurement areas in the absence of pottery (Keegan 1982a). Organically enriched soils are usually absent, and these sites lack deep subsurface deposits.

Some of these sites apparently were semipermanent or were occupied seasonally over a number of years. For example, small sites on the cliff overlooking the windward coast of northern Long Island are positioned to gain access to prime agricultural land and to a set of marine mollusks and fishes that are different from those available on the lee shore (Keegan and Mitchell 1984a). This type of shelter continues in use today, although it is disappearing as motor transport becomes increasingly available.

Allochthonous sites are named for the geological term meaning formed or originally occurring elsewhere. It is likely that a number of "sites" were created when pottery in Lucayan cave sites was removed with cave earth destined for agricultural fields (Keegan and Mitchell 1986). Historic cave earth excavations led to the first discoveries of Lucayan artifacts (Brooks 1888; DeBooy 1912, 1913), and a unique effigy vessel discovered beneath a house on Walker's Cay, Abaco, has been attributed to a cave earth excavation (Carr and Riley 1982; Riley 1983). Allochthonous sites are distinguished by the presence of a few similar potsherds, the absence of mollusc shells, and their location near historic fields and away from resource distributions.

A final category, caves and rockshelters, is self-explanatory. Most of these sites have been disturbed. Caves have yielded burials, wooden artifacts, and pottery. Their walls are occasionally decorated with carved designs known as petroglyphs (Hoffman 1973b; Maynard 1890). Caves and rockshelters were apparently used as short-term shelters (Granberry 1978), and the prominence of caves in Taino mythology suggests that they were important locations for ritual activities (DeBooy 1912; Granberry 1956, 1978; Hoffman 1973b; Keegan 1982b; Alegría 1986; Stevens-Arroyo 1988). They are not included in the present analysis because they were used mostly for special purposes. However, it should be noted that they typically are less than 2 kilometers from open-air sites. Thus, they provide evidence of possible open-air habitations in areas that have not been surveyed thoroughly and on islands that are severely disturbed by historic development.

The arbitrary division of site lengths into type categories was based on the frequency distribution of site lengths for all known sites (fig. 4.1). In most cases, site length was used because the typical settlement plan was houses aligned parallel to the beach. There are, however, several sites that conform to an oval distribution of houses around a central plaza, notably MC-6 and MC-12 on Middle Caicos (Sullivan 1981). The measurement of cross-plaza distances at MC-6 suggests that sites with a second dimension greater than 60 meters were probably plaza sites. Because

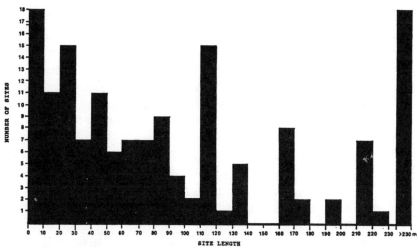

FIGURE 4.1. Histogram of Lucayan site sizes (in meters).

site measurements are being used as a proxy for population numbers, the longest linear dimension of plaza sites was doubled in the site-length calculation to account for houses on both sides of the plaza.

When the site lengths for all known sites are plotted, four primary and five smaller peaks are identified. The change in length between these modes and peaks averages 30 meters. It will be argued in chapter 7 that this interval reflects the addition of one house for every increase of 30 meters of site length.

Although the average change in length is 30 meters, the break between permanently occupied settlements and seasonal or short-term sites is made at a length of 20 meters because single houses would generate less lateral dispersion of materials. Households, which have a linear dimension of 20 to 89 meters, would have had one to three houses. The break between households and hamlets was made because there is a mode at the 100- to 109-meter interval and a peak at the 150- to 159-meter interval. Hamlets would have averaged four to eight houses. Finally, villages have site lengths greater than 200 meters. This length was selected because there is a break in the frequency distribution between 170–199 meters, and because these sites do not follow a regular pattern of linear increase. Sites of this type are the largest and least common on every island.

Settlement Timing and Contemporaneity

Archaeological surveys identified where the sites were located, and their classification into site types showed the main activities that the sites represent. The next question is when the sites were occupied. It should be noted at the outset that a chronology has not been established for Lucayan sites. None of the artifacts, except European objects, date strictly to a specific period, and very few radiocarbon dates have been obtained.

Because there are insufficient temporal controls to distinguish differences in the timing of settlements, it is assumed that all known Lucayan sites were occupied at the same time. Although this assumption is extended to all sites, it is less critical for obvious short-term sites (e.g., shelters), which serve only to document the intensity of land use in a particular area. If they were contemporaneous, then they indicate land-use intensity during a single time period; if they were used at different times, then they indicate temporal differences in land use. In either case, they provide evidence for interisland differences in land-use intensity.

More critical assumptions are that habitation sites were occupied at the same time and that settlement patterns throughout the archipelago represent a terminal-period distribution of the Lucayan population (post–A.D. 1200). No single source of evidence is available to support this assumed terminal-period contemporaneity. However, a variety of evidence can be cited in support of the assumption.

The first consideration is the relative impact of postdepositional influences on site visibility. All known sites were identified from surface scatters. Therefore, processes that have acted to increase or decrease site visibility have had a significant effect on survey results. The primary sources of postdepositional effects are geomorphic changes in shorelines and biotic disturbances of buried deposits. These processes exert relatively constant influences throughout the archipelago, and interisland settlement pattern differences cannot be attributed to their differential impact. Although these processes could act to reveal sites that were occupied during different time periods, their influence is sufficiently regular to conclude that similar temporal mixes would occur on every island. Therefore, settlement pattern differences would reveal differences in settlement intensity even if specific temporal differences were not distinguished.

Because geological and biotic disturbances had similar effects on site visibility, attention is next directed to the length of occupation—in other words, how long people lived at a site before it was abandoned. On islands and other circumscribed areas suitable settlement locations are limited. The effect is an increase in the length of time a village is occupied accompanied by an increase in the frequency with which special-purpose sites were used to relieve local pressures (Butt 1977). In the Greater Antilles, the permanence of terminal-period settlements is apparent in planned communities, investment in public works (e.g., ball courts), and the intensification of local agricultural production (e.g., mounds, irrigation works) (Veloz Maggiolo et al. 1976; Wilson 1990a). In the Bahamas, settlement permanence is indicated by the development of planned communities with major public works (MC-6, MC-12), midden accumulations of 45–110 centimeters, and radiocarbon dates from two sites that indicate about 200 years of continuous occupation. Unfortunately, comparable information is not available for more sites.

The relationship between population distributions and resource pro-

curement provides additional support. The initial distribution of population would have been at low densities with settlements located to take
advantage of high-ranked resources. These high-ranked resources were
easily depleted, which would have encouraged mobility, thus limiting the
buildup of site deposits. High mobility combined with the exploitation of
high-ranked resources would result in islands with habitats whose return
rates were equalized (see E. Smith 1983). Only a very limited record of the
initial period would remain intact.

The pattern of small-scale settlements in habitats that were abandoned
and later reoccupied is typical of the initial period in the Greater and
Lesser Antilles (Rainey 1934; Rouse 1941; Veloz Maggiolo et al. 1976;
Goodwin 1980; Watters 1982). Recent research at the Pigeon Creek site
and the Three Dog site, San Salvador, has revealed a deep cultural strata
that may reflect a distinct early component (Rose 1982, 1987; Mary Jane
Berman, per. com. 1986). The most compelling evidence for early period
sites would be Ostionan Ostionoid pottery. Yet pottery in this series has
not been confirmed in any Lucayan site (Hoffman 1967; Sullivan 1981).
This absence suggests that initial period settlements have not been preserved as surface scatters, that later settlements have covered these deposits, or both.

The localized depletion of high-ranked resources would have provided
the initial impetus for rapid expansion. After the average return rates for
habitats on an island were equalized, settlement locations would have
been established to provide access to the densest distributions of resources in the expanded optimal set. Since marine mollusks (*Strombus
gigas*) and certain fishes were within the initial optimal set, and since
their capture could only be increased through increased effort, the same
settlement locations would have been favored. The result would be the
occurrence of later sites atop earlier site deposits.

The rapid growth of population adds further support to the assumption
that settlements were contemporaneous. It is likely that initial settlements did not exceed 50 people, yet by the time of Spanish contact the
Lucayan population may have numbered 40,000 (Martyr 1970; Granberry
1979–81). The accuracy of this census is defended in chapter 7.

Studies of population growth have shown that a major increase in
population numbers will occur when a group reaches some threshold
level (Kirch 1984; Keegan, Johnson, and Earle 1985). This threshold would
have been reached toward the end of Lucayan autonomy and would have

produced a geometric increase in the number of terminal-period settlements. At a constant rate of growth, the total population of the prehistoric Bahamas would have doubled during the century before Spanish contact. The result would be a dramatic increase in the number and size of settlements. The majority of sites that ever existed were occupied during the terminal period.

That interpretation can be carried one step farther by calculating the number of individuals who occupied known sites. If the Lucayan population was 40,000, then every site identified, and more, would be required to account for that number. Since suitable coastal locations are limited, it is apparent that most locations with easy coastal access would have been occupied. In addition, Columbus reports seeing two or three settlements along the west coast of San Salvador (Dunn and Kelley 1989). His report corresponds to the number of settlements identified during archaeological surveys. The other settlements described by Columbus also were located during surface surveys (Keegan 1984a, 1989a; Keegan and Mitchell 1987), and Spanish pottery and other European objects have been found at several sites (Brill et al. 1987; Hoffman 1987a, b; Mitchell and Keegan 1987). The materials recovered from the surfaces of those sites look identical to what is present in other surface scatters.

A final consideration is pottery types. All Lucayan habitation sites contain locally manufactured Palmetto Ware pottery. At present, there are no modal differences that could be used to date the pottery. Other investigators have attempted to use imported pottery to date Lucayan sites (Granberry 1956; Hoffman 1967; Sears and Sullivan 1978; Sullivan 1981). However, these Ostionan, Meillacan, and Chican styles share motifs that blend together to the degree that they are now classified as components of a single Ostionoid series (Rouse 1986). These styles were manufactured for long periods of time without significant changes, and the Lucayans had continuous access to Meillacan pottery from Cuba and Haiti and to Chican pottery from the Dominican Republic from at least A.D. 1000–1500.

Imported pottery occurs in low frequencies (typically less than 1 percent of total pottery collections) and exhibits a regularity of distribution that suggests it derives from contemporaneous exchange relations. The analysis of pottery petrology may someday provide evidence for datable changes in pottery manufacture, but this technique is not sufficiently developed at this time (Mann 1986).

The evidence for site contemporaneity can be summarized as follows:

1. The relationship between population growth and resource supply is consistent with the assumption that known sites were occupied at the same time. The rapid growth of population during the terminal period would have produced a geometrical increase in both the number and size of sites. With expansion constrained to a limited coastal habitat, and the reoccupation of the best endowed habitats promoted by economic return rates, early-period sites would have been covered by terminal-period settlements.
2. The permanence of settlements increases the probability that sites were contemporaneous. The increased volume of materials generated by more permanent settlements would also promote their visibility.
3. Spanish estimates of Lucayan population size indicate that all of the known settlements, plus others that have not been discovered, must have been occupied at the time of contact. Therefore, it is reasonable to assume that known sites were occupied during the period just prior to the arrival of Columbus.
4. Pottery types do not yet provide an adequate framework for dating Lucayan sites, but there is a similar distribution of imported pottery types that suggests comparable exchange relations. The distribution of imported pottery provides weak support for the assumption that sites were contemporaneous.

The assumption that known Lucayan sites were occupied at the same time is a useful working hypothesis. More work, especially with regard to dating sites, needs to be completed. Nonetheless, if the assumption is not accurate we would expect to find empirical evidence that is not consistent or is contradictory to the expectations of the models. To date, all of the evidence has conformed to the predictions of the models, sometimes in counterintuitive ways.

Settlement Patterns

Thorough archaeological surveys in which both site size and spacing were recorded provide the primary sources of evidence in this section.

Great Inagua, Mayaguana, Acklins Island, Crooked Island, Long Island, Great and Little Exuma, Rum Cay, Cat Island, and Eleuthera serve as the main comparative base. The conclusions reached from the analysis of patterns on those islands receive additional support from the patterns on islands from which either site size or spacing data are incomplete. The peripheral islands are San Salvador, New Providence, Great Abaco, Grand Bahama, and the Caicos Islands.

Information on site size and spacing is used to examine whether Lucayan settlement patterns conform to a steady-state or weighted distribution, recognizing that these distributions are generated by different sets of conditions. Settlement spacing is largely a function of available resources and the size of the population exploiting those resources. Because resource distributions in the central Bahamas were relatively homogeneous, differences in settlement spacing reflect the length of time that an island has been occupied. Settlement densities are used in this analysis to ensure that equivalent units are compared. For example, a ratio of site length per coastline length allows the comparison of relative land use on islands of different lengths.

For settlement patterns to be more than a description of observations, the patterns must be linked to higher-order generalizations that specify the variables that generated the patterns. With regard to colonization studies, the settlement succession model proposed by John Hudson (1969) provides a useful analytical guide. Hudson's model assumes that agricultural activities are performed in a fine-grained (homogeneous) environment, and that agricultural decision making follows the prescriptions of microeconomic principles (Preucel 1982, 1985), assumptions consistent with the evidence and approach presented in this study.

Changes in settlement spacing are viewed as progressing through three stages. During the initial settlement of a region the settlement pattern exhibits a low density of randomly distributed sites. This pattern is replaced by a clustered distribution of settlements as population increases and fills the gaps between initial settlements. The final stage is characterized by intersettlement competition, which leads to the regular distribution of settlements across the landscape.

The two ideal distributions proposed to explain population expansion in the prehistoric Bahamas can be expressed in the terms used in Hudson's (1969) model. A steady-state distribution produces exactly the same settlement pattern on every island. Whether the pattern is random, clustered, or regular would depend on the population's stage in the successional sequence. The weighted distribution is the product of timing differences, with interisland settlement pattern differences maintained by a constant rate of population growth. The weighted distribution should match Hudson's (1969) succession with regular, clustered, and random distributions marking interisland differences in the direction(s) along which the colonists migrated.

The expectations derived from theory are related to empirical reality with two measurement techniques. First, the linear-nearest-neighbor statistic was calculated for every island. This statistic provided ambiguous results, so a second measure of settlement clustering was developed. The second measure involved calculating site-catchment associations to obtain an index of settlement densities. These associations provide a ratio of people per land area, thus facilitating the comparison of settlement densities on different islands.

As discussed above, Lucayan settlements are aligned along leeward and windward shores. Because the windward coasts have an irregular distribution of suitable settlement locations, the more regular lee-shore distributions were used to calculate the linear-nearest-neighbor values (Pinder and Witherick 1972, 1975). The statistic (LRn) is calculated by dividing the mean distance between nearest-neighbors ($Dobs$) by the average distance between randomly distributed nearest-neighbors: $LRn = Dobs \div 0.5(L/n-1)$, where L is line length and n the number of points. If LRn has a value of one, the observed conditions match those predicted for a random situation (Pinder and Witherick 1975:17). Values less than one suggest an element of clustering, and values greater than one suggest a regular pattern of spacing. Perfectly regular spacing is identified when LRn equals two.

The level of confidence for nonrandom patterns depends on the number of points per pattern. When only 10–20 points are used, LRn must exceed 1 ± 0.5 to achieve a 95 percent probability that the pattern is nonrandom (Pinder and Witherick 1975: figure 3). The number of Lucayan sites per island falls within this range of potential random matching.

A second consideration is the definition of line length. Lines that include end points frequently raise the mean distance between nearest neighbors to a level that would suggest regular spacing. However, this appearance of regularity may be the unjustified result of "boundary effects" (Hodder and Orton 1976). Boundary effects result from assuming that an end point's only neighbor would also be its nearest neighbor if it were not located in a terminal position. To avoid possible bias, boundary sites were included as the penultimate site's possible nearest neighbor but were otherwise excluded from the analysis.

When the linear-nearest-neighbor statistic was calculated for Lucayan sites, the LRn value for all islands, except Cat Island, fell within the range of random matching (table 4.3). Cat Island, with an LRn value of 0.5, has a 95 percent probability of clustering. The statistical evidence for a random distribution on the other islands could be the product of stochastic effects, for instance, the random distribution of suitable settlement locations, or the initial pattern of settlement in a region (Hudson 1969). However, an examination of the assumptions on which linear-nearest-neighbor analysis is based suggests that the random pattern is an artifact of the analysis.

In the equation, "the predicted random average is half the mean distance that would separate points if they were distributed with perfect regularity throughout the entire line length" (Pinder and Witherick 1975:17). While this definition may characterize most cases, it is possible for regularly spaced pairs of sites to produce a random value. In other words, when the number of clusters is equal to the number of regularly spaced pairs, an artificial random value will result. This appears to be the case with Lucayan sites.

When only the largest settlements on each island are considered, set-

T A B L E 4.3 Linear-Nearest-Neighbor Values

Island	Ribbon length (m)	Points	LRn (total)	LRn (w/out extremes)
Great Inagua	63.5	9	1.39	1.15
Mayaguana	59.7	10	1.43	0.97
Acklins Island	73.9	29	1.24	0.89
Crooked Island	29.4	10	1.29	1.14
Long Island	170.4	11	—	1.11
Exuma Islands	45.9	12	1.15	0.79
Rum Cay	46.7	11	—	0.86
Cat Island	122.3	18	1.49	0.50
Eleuthera	178.4	17	1.18	1.07

Note: Settlement spacing is random when LRn = 1, clustered when LRn is significantly less than 1, and regular when LRn is significantly greater than 1. The only significant value is 0.50 for Cat Island.

tlement spacing exhibits a roughly alternating pattern of clustering and
dispersion with a further tendency toward clustering (table 4.4). This pattern is apparent when the actual spacing of settlements is compared to an

TABLE 4.4 Spacing of Large Lucayan Sites

Island	Adjacent large sites	Spacing (km)	X–X̄
Long Island			X̄=5.8
	11–12	0.7	−5.1
	12–15	10.0	4.2
	15–16	2.0	−3.8
	16–27	7.2	1.4
	27– 9	3.7	·−2.1
	9–18	7.2	1.4
	18– 6	3.7	−2.1
Acklins Island			X̄=7.8
	1–27	9.3	1.5
	27– 6	4.0	−3.4
	6–10	10.8	3.0
	10–13	2.1	−5.7
	13–14	1.0	−6.7
	14–24	7.0	−0.8
	24– 9	13.0	5.2
Cat Island			X̄=15.3
	15–16	13.3	−2.0
	16–12	54.0	38.7
	12– 9	5.6	−9.7
	9–10	0.5	−14.8
	10– 3	14.0	−1.3
	3– 8	0.4	−14.9
	8– 7	2.1	−13.2
	7– 4	12.8	−2.5
	4– 2	20.0	4.7
Eleuthera Island			X̄=44
	15– 5	30.0	−14.0
	5–12	79.0	35.0
	14– 4	36.2	−8.2
	4– 1	23.3	−20.7
	1– 7	7.5	−36.5
Exuma Islands			X̄=6.6
	15–11	4.7	−1.9
	11–12	2.6	−4.0
	12–14	3.6	−3.0
	14–10	5.8	−0.8
	10– 5	13.9	7.3
	5– 4	2.3	−4.3

average value or to regular spacing. The value for regular spacing is calculated as the equal partitioning of total line length (total line length/$n-1$). The difference between actual spacing and regular spacing is positive for more dispersed sites and negative for more clustered sites.

Those calculations indicate that large settlements are not randomly distributed and that the overall pattern tends toward clustering. The clustering of sites can be explored further by considering the frequency of settlement pairs, which are sites that are situated within each other's catchment area. Studies of resource procurement indicate that a radius of 1.5–2.0 kilometers accurately characterizes the primary catchment areas of Lucayan settlements (Sullivan 1981; Wing and Scudder 1983). The more conservative value (1.5 kilometers) is used for the following comparisons.

Of 173 sites on 10 islands there are 71 sites separated by less than 1.5 kilometers. When sites at the end of linear distributions are eliminated to avoid boundary effects ($n=20$), and the number of sites associated as settlement pairs are summed, then 90 percent of all sites are less than 1.5 kilometers from another site. The site types associated as settlement pairs are summarized in table 4.5.

Such pairing may be attributed to social and economic factors. When sites of unknown type are eliminated ($n=35$), then 61 percent ($n=22$) of

TABLE 4.5 Settlement Pair Associations

Site types	Number of pairs
Village-hamlet	2
Village-household	2
Village-shelter	1
Village-unmeasured	1
Hamlet-hamlet	2
Hamlet-household	12
Hamlet-shelter	1
Hamlet-unmeasured	7
Household-household	4
Household-shelter	1
Household-allochthonous	6
Household-unmeasured	5
Shelter-shelter	4
Shelter-unmeasured	3
Unmeasured-unmeasured	18
Total	71

the pairs relate villages, hamlets, and households. These associations are similar to the settlement clusters of the Trobriand Islands (Powell 1960) and may reflect allied matrilineal moieties (chapter 5). This pairing of lineages was formalized in the dual plaza arrangement of settlements MC-6 and MC-12 on Middle Caicos and at similar plaza settlements in the Greater Antilles (Castellanos 1981; Sullivan 1981; Alegría 1983). Further evidence for an apparent moiety division is expressed by differential access to imported materials on opposite sides of plaza 1 at MC-6 (Sullivan 1981).

The remaining associations are between shelters (11 percent, $n=4$), the spacing of which may not reflect the catchment criteria of more permanent habitations; between habitations and allochthonous sites (19 percent, $n=7$), which may reflect specific procurement activities within the catchment or postdepositional disturbances of sites; and between habitations and shelters (8 percent, $n=3$), which provide an indication of the distribution of demand for land (see Berreman 1978).

Settlement pairs were produced by several mechanisms. If the identified associations hold for unmeasured sites, then 60 percent of the settlement pairs can be explained as communities paired by social relations. This assumption is reasonable because about half of the unmeasured sites were reported for San Salvador where a similar distribution of site types should obtain, and because the remaining sites were either disturbed or were located in areas that could not be surveyed properly.

The analysis of settlement-pair distributions is accomplished with an index of catchment associations. Two catchment indexes are presented. They measure the number of cases involving sites that are separated by less than 1.5 kilometers, and the number of cases involving sites whose catchment areas overlap (separated by less than 3 kilometers). The number of cases is used because some sites have more than one other site within their catchment. In the present analysis every case involves at least two sites. If each pair were counted as two sites, the multiple associations would produce artificially high values. When the number of cases is divided by the total number of sites, an index of catchment association is obtained for every island.

Catchment indexes for every island were compared by assigning a number (henceforth, step number) that corresponded to the island's position in the expansion sequence. The numbers were assigned to match the most likely sequence of island hopping from south to north. For the most part these numbers conform to an island's relative position on a north-south number line. Organized in this way there is a decline in the catchment indexes from Acklins Island to the north, and to the east and west from Long Island (table 4.6, fig. 4.2). San Salvador was excluded from this analysis because insufficient information was available.

TABLE 4.6 Catchment Indexes

Step number	Island	Sites within catchments	Sites with overlapping catchments
1	Great Inagua	0.22	0.33
2	Mayaguana	0.60	1.20
3	Acklins Island	1.34	3.34
4	Crooked Island	0.80	1.60
5	Long Island	0.75	1.58
6	Exuma Islands	0.67	1.17
7	Cat Island	0.61	1.17
8	Rum Cay	0.33	0.83
9	Eleuthera	0.35	0.53

Note: Catchment indexes are calculated by dividing the number of cases in which a site is within 1.5 km of another site by the total number of sites, and by dividing the number of sites whose 1.5 km catchments overlap by the total number of sites.

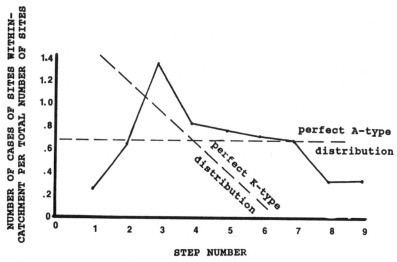

FIGURE 4.2. Plot of the ratio of the number of sites separated by less than 1.5 km divided by the total number of sites. Step numbers: 1, Great Inagua; 2, Mayaguana; 3, Acklins Island; 4, Crooked Island; 5, Long Island; 6, Great and Little Exuma Islands; 7, Cat Island; 8, Rum Cay; and 9, Eleuthera.

The index values indicate that settlement clustering conforms to the direction of population expansion. The decrease in values from south to north and along branches from the main axis corresponds to population density differences expected from progressive timing differences. In sum, the overall distribution of settlements in the archipelago is weighted. The weighted distribution is, however, made up of three additional but more restricted patterns.

First, the values for the southern islands (Great Inagua, Mayaguana) are lower than those for islands to the north. These lower values do not follow the expected pattern. The lower values can be explained as resulting from the much poorer environments in the southern subarea and may even reflect abandonment of the southern islands shortly after initial settlement.

Second, the index values indicate that differences in clustering in the central islands are not significant. The central islands have values that range from 0.61 to 0.80 (Crooked Island, Long Island, Cat Island, Great and Little Exuma). It appears that any timing differences were minor and that initial settlements were timed to coincide with the availability of equivalent island shore lengths.

Finally, there are large declines in the values for Eleuthera, which is the northernmost island in the study, and for Rum Cay on the eastern branch of the expansion network. The significance of these low values is reinforced by the absence of settlement pairs and sites with overlapping catchments on islands to the north (e.g., New Providence, Grand Bahama).

Three conclusions are indicated by the analysis of settlement spacing. First, catchment indexes document a steady decline in land-use intensity from Acklins Island to the north, and to the east of Long Island. The decline in these indexes matches the pattern expected for a weighted distribution with land-use intensity increasing as a direct function of the years an island was occupied. This pattern can be interpreted as evidence that the population expanded from south to north and along branches to the east and west in a regular sequence.

Second, the catchment indexes for the central islands are sufficiently similar to interpret the pattern as a steady-state distribution. This distribution would result from the colonization of each island when the person per land-unit ratio was equal to that on the occupied island. Moreover, the spacing of large settlements in the central subarea exhibits a pattern of regularly spaced settlement pairs with a tendency towards clustering. This distribution is similar to the spread stage, which occurs after coloni-

zation and before the competition stage in Hudson's (1969) model of settlement succession. This pattern supports the dating of settlements to a
postcolonization period.

Finally, settlements are more widely dispersed in the southernmost
islands than would be expected for either a steady-state or a weighted
distribution. This nonconformity indicates that some other variable(s) affected the distribution of settlements in the southern subarea. As previously suggested, environmental quality is probably responsible for the
more dispersed pattern.

Settlement Densities

A second measure of settlement distributions is obtained by calculating settlement densities. Settlement density is measured as the ratio of
site length per coastline length. These values emphasize site size rather
than site proximity and provide a better estimate of overall population
densities. Since different levels of thoroughness were achieved during
coastal surveys, only coastal segments that were thoroughly surveyed
were included in the study. The index denominator was measured as the
distance between boundary sites in kilometers. The numerator was calculated using the longest linear dimension (doubled for plaza sites) measured in meters. An additional problem involved accounting for sites of
unknown length. Sites of unknown length were ignored in the first analysis. In a second calculation of settlement density a value of 30 meters was
used for sites of unknown length. This value was selected because most
of these sites appeared to be small, even when they were also disturbed.
This value is used to overcome differences in the number of unknown
site lengths on different islands. Finally, it again is assumed that all
known sites were contemporaneous.

The comparison of site-length per coastline-length ratios is accomplished by sequencing the islands using the step numbers assigned above.
San Salvador was again excluded because site size information was not
available. The ratios are interpreted with reference to ideal steady-state
and weighted distributions. The former would result in a horizontal line
joining the values for every island, because the ideal would be equal settlement densities. The latter is represented by a steady decline from
south to north, which reflects the sequential expansion of the population.

The actual pattern does not exactly fit either ideal distribution (table

4.7, fig. 4.3). Great Inagua and Mayaguana again have values well below those expected for their position in the sequence. From Acklins Island to the north, and to the east from Long Island, there is a semiregular decline

TABLE 4.7 Site Length per Coastline Length Index

Step number and island	Coastline length (km)	Site length (m)	Site length per coastline length (m/km)
1. Great Inagua	63.55	940–1030	14.79–16.21
2. Mayaguana	59.70	632–662	10.59–11.09
3. Acklins Island	73.90	2115–2325	28.62–31.46
4. Crooked Island	29.40	628–688	21.36–23.40
5. Long Island	170.40	2715–3045	15.93–17.87
w/out south sites	100.40	2655–2980	26.44–29.73
6. Exuma Islands	45.90	1125	24.51
7. Cat Island	122.30	2540	20.77
8. Rum Cay	46.70	320–530	6.85–11.35
9. Eleuthera	178.40	1313–1373	7.36– 7.70

Note: A range is given for site length values to account for sites of unknown size. An arbitrary 30 meters was assigned to every unknown site for comparative purposes.

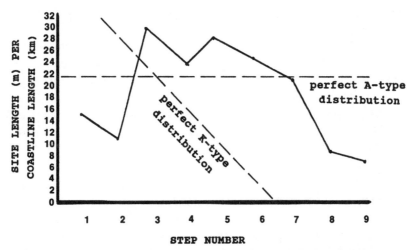

FIGURE 4.3. Plot of site length (m) per coastline length (km) ratios. Step numbers: 1, Great Inagua; 2, Mayaguana; 3, Acklins Island; 4, Crooked Island; 5, Long Island; 6, Great and Little Exuma Islands; 7, Cat Island; 8, Rum Cay; and 9, Eleuthera.

in settlement densities. Limited surveys on islands to the north of Eleuthera suggest that this trend continues to the north.

One exception to the otherwise regular decrease in settlement densities is Long Island, which has a very low value. There are several explanations for the unexpectedly low value. First, the island has the greatest
number of sites the lengths of which are not known ($n=11$); the arbitrary
30 meters used for missing values may not provide an accurate average
for sites on Long Island. Of greater significance is the discovery of only
two small sites along the southern 40 percent of the coast. This area has
been disturbed by the Diamond Crystal salt works, a large barrier cay has
created a shallow tidal flat that does not support marine organisms, and
the survey was not as thorough here as it was in other areas (Keegan and
Mitchell 1984b). Either our rapid survey failed to identify existing sites,
or the southern lee shore was less well suited for settlement than the
northern two-thirds of the island. When the southern sites are eliminated
from the calculation, the settlement density increases to a level com-
mensurate with the island's position in the sequence (i.e., 26.44 to 29.73).

Settlement densities corroborate the inferences reached through the
interpretation of catchment indexes. Islands in the southern subarea
have lower than expected densities. Densities for the central subarea
exhibit a steady decline that can be explained by timing differences. The
differences in settlement density in the central subarea are sufficiently
small to suggest that any timing differences were not significant. In sum,
the pattern closely matches that expected for a steady-state distribution.
Finally, the northern subarea, including Eleuthera, can be explained as fit-
ting the weighted distribution, with low densities attributed to shorter
periods of occupation.

Summary

On a regional scale, settlement patterns conform to the weighted distribution, with densities weighted toward the south of the central subarea (Acklins Island) and decreasing to the north and east. Within this
regional pattern, settlement distributions roughly conform to subarea
boundaries. The southern subarea (Great Inagua, Mayaguana) has settlement densities below those expected from either a weighted or a steady-
state distribution. These lower values have been explained as the product

of a poorer environmental quality. The central islands (Crooked Island, Long Island, Great and Little Exuma, and Cat Island) have settlement distributions that roughly conform to a steady-state distribution. Localized differences in environmental quality can account for any minor variations. Finally, the northern islands were shown to have lower settlement densities as a result of their position in the expansion sequence.

5

Honor Thy Mother's Brother:
Lucayan Social and
Political Organization

It is generally agreed that the Taino traced descent through the female line to a common ancestress (Keegan and Maclachlan 1989). It has also been reported that at marriage, a woman left her home to live in the home of her husband. To a large degree, those two sentences describe all that has ever been written about Taino social organization. Cross-cultural studies by sociocultural anthropologists reveal that even such limited information about a society's organizational features may make it possible to infer social relations in some detail. In this chapter, a reconstruction of Taino kinship and politics is the objective. This objective is important because the ways in which people relate to each other are the basis for all other aspects of culture.

Social organization is often overlooked by archaeologists. In fact, archaeologists have gone so far as to declare that you cannot excavate a kinship system. I hope that this chapter will convince people otherwise. It is imperative that we understand how and why people organized themselves. Where people live during their lives, how objects, resources, and positions are inherited, how communities and higher-order polities form and collapse all have significant effects that produce observable patterns in the archaeological record. The preceding discussion of island colonization demonstrated that social factors exerted significant influences. In this chapter, differences in the ways that men and women participate in their society will be shown to have similar large effects.

Social Organization

A major goal of anthropological research is to describe and explain the similarities and differences among human societies. Although archaeologists typically deal only with the material remains of human behavior, these remains are the product of people who organized themselves into groups. In order to adequately study the past, archaeologists must develop methods for relating the material consequences of human behavior to ethnological theories of human organization. A variety of schemes for accomplishing that end have been proposed, but none is completely successful. Even though certain organizing principles are universal, their specific combination is ethnocentric. In sum, every society must be re-created on the weight of the evidence left behind in the archaeological record. Yet, in this area we are investigating the less tangible aspects of culture—social structure and political economy, collectively termed social organization.

The division between social structure and political economy, especially in small-scale societies, is arbitrary. The basis for all social groupings is kinship, the interpersonal relations that arise from marriage and descent. In small-scale societies both within- and between-group relations tend to be dominated by kinship relations. However, as societies increase in size and scale their internal and external operations become increasingly differentiated (Johnson and Earle 1987).

The structure of all social groups reflects adaptations to social and physical environments. In this regard, patterns of *residence* and *descent* are especially important because they determine where an individual will live as well as the individual's rights and obligations with respect to other individuals and, when such exist, to the group's corporate resources.

A *rule of descent* affiliates an individual at birth with a particular group of relatives through maternal (matrilineal), paternal (patrilineal), both maternal and paternal (double), or nongenealogical (bilateral) groups of kin. Descent is especially important with regard to the inheritance of the rights and property that belong to kinspeople or to the kin group as a whole. For the Taino, access to land held communally by a group of kin and succession to the office of chief were determined primarily by descent traced through the maternal line.

Rules of residence describe the preferred living arrangements of couples following marriage. The possibilities include (but are not limited to) the married couple lives with the wife's parents (matrilocal); the couple lives with the husband's parents (patrilocal); the couple lives with the husband's maternal uncle (avunculocal); the couple lives independent of the parents (neolocal); and the couple chooses to live with either spouse's parents (bilocal). A society's residence preference, determined by what most people do rather than by what they say, in general reflects economic and social conditions.

Relations of residence and descent are referred to as *rules* because these categories of behavior tend to conform to predictable patterns (Goodenough 1955). It is not correct, however, to assume that rules of descent and residence are never broken. Steadfast adherence to rules may promote stability and order, qualities preferred by the group, but individuals possess tremendous creativity and actively work to manipulate rules to their advantage. Such flexibility and creativity provides the basis for successful responses to changing social and physical environments and provides nightmares for anthropologists who find exceptions to almost every rule.

Identifying general, typical, average, and probable patterns of residence and descent are nonetheless worthwhile activities. In some cases, the probabilities for a particular pattern are so low that the pattern can be disregarded. Such is the case, discussed below, in which the Spanish chroniclers described the Taino as practicing matrilineal descent and patrilocal residence. In other cases the exceptions are more important than the rules; for instance, when social arrangements are in flux because of changing environmental conditions. A final consideration is George Peter Murdock's (1949:202) conclusion that "alteration in the prevailing rule of residence is the point of departure for nearly all significant changes in social organization." It follows that archaeological evidence for changes in residence patterns (for example, house size, house shape, community arrangements) may reflect important instances of social change more accurately than do changes in pottery decoration. Yet, pottery decoration is today the most commonly used attribute for identifying social groupings (Rice 1987).

A final category is *kinship terminology*, the terms that people use to address each other. Because archaeologists lack informants who could be asked about terms of address it would seem impossible to determine kinship terms from archaeological evidence. It is, however, possible to reconstruct the probable kinship terminology based on other characteristics of the social system.

Anthropologists have defined six main types of kinship classifications:

Crow, Sudanese, Hawaiian, Eskimo, Omaha, and Iroquois. Each of these is associated with specific sociological characteristics and developmental histories (Murdock 1949; Fox 1967; Keesing 1975). Although these terms must be inferred from other nonarchaeological categories of evidence, they are of potentially great significance. For instance, if the Tainos were an avunculocal society, then it is likely they used a Crow-type kinship terminology (Byrne 1990). The significance of this inference is that Island Carib societies probably used Iroquois-type kinship terms. Based on ethnological information regarding the evolution of kinship systems, the Island Caribs and Tainos must have developed separate social identities long before the Antilles were colonized. This conclusion is supported by linguistic evidence as well (Allaire 1990).

The Political Economy of Matrilineal Society

Three factors have been commonly cited as influencing the emergence of unilocal residence patterns in which consanguineously related persons of one sex are systematically aggregated in extended families: the sexual division of subsistence labor, the prevalence and form of warfare in prestate-level societies, and aspects of gender relations, especially marital relations, arising from work and warfare.

The first of these to receive serious attention was the division of labor in a hypothesis suggesting that consanguineously related members of the harder working sex would be localized in the interest of efficiency and economic solidarity (Linton 1936; Murdock 1949; Driver and Massey 1957). If women do most of the work, then the usual pattern should be matrilocal residence in which husbands move to live with wives who remain with their mothers and sisters. If men do most of the work, then this pattern should be reversed in patrilocal residence. Subsequent crosscultural studies have revealed only weak and inconsistent associations between residence and the division of labor (Ember and Ember 1971; Divale 1974; Petersen 1982). While it is true, for example, that the division of labor is often matridominant in horticultural societies and that matrilocal societies are usually horticultural (Aberle 1961; Keesing 1975), the fact is that horticultural societies are far more often patrilocal.

The Embers (1971) found that in prestate-level societies in which warfare was prevalent the form of warfare exerts a strong influence on residence arising from men's having typically been the warring sex. If warfare features internal conflict among members of the same society, residence is usually patrilocal irrespective of the division of labor. When residence is not patrilocal under conditions of internal warfare, it is usually avunculocal. The Embers suggest that the more common patrilocal variant arises from the importance of alliances among fathers, sons, and brothers in the face of internal feuding and raiding. If the neighbors are hostile, the men of a descent group will not be dispersed at marriage.

In contrast, matrilocal residence occurs regularly only when warfare is exclusively external (i.e., fought with other societies) *and* when the division of labor is matridominant. As the Embers point out, the division of labor may not be responsive solely to techno-environmental factors internal to productive activities but may be responsive to other costs and benefits as well. If external warfare requires men to be absent from home for long periods of time, a society may be compelled to adopt a division of labor in which women do most of the subsistence work and may find that matrilocality provides a preferable alternative to households composed of unrelated women.

Divale (1974) suggests that matrilocality confers a political advantage on societies engaged in external warfare by dividing fraternal coalitions that might otherwise become factions in internal conflict. While agreeing that this advantage may be conferred, Marvin Harris (1979) argues that breaking up bands of brothers could hardly be the motive behind the residential choices of the men who would be members of such bands. Rather, the picture that emerges from Harris's interpretation of the cross-cultural literature is one in which matrilocality is adopted as an emergency measure that becomes institutionalized as the emergency persists. Harris does note, however, that an emergency need not exist for this form of residence to develop. If a man is able to compel the spouse(s) of his sister(s) to live in his community through whatever means, the same arrangement emerges.

For instance, begin with a village-based society in which married couples routinely live and work together, and residence is either patrilocal or a mixed pattern of choices reflecting the differing opportunities of individuals. This pattern is disturbed by a period of intense external warfare. Family life becomes increasingly matrifocal as women must rely more on themselves and on one another. Marital bonds are weakened by men's absence, and men return home to find wives replaced by sisters who, like

the men's wives, have returned to the more secure surroundings offered
by their natal households. Men come to rely more on their sisters and
less on their wives to take care of their interests at home. Eventually, the
situation is resolved in an arrangement whereby women never leave home
in the first place, and men divide their time between their natal and conjugal households.

This scenario provides the background from which Melvin Ember
(1974) sees avunculocality evolving. Avunculocality is a curious phenom-
enon in that it usually requires both sexes to change domicile. A man
moves in with a real or classificatory maternal uncle, where he is joined
by his wife unless he has married the uncle's daughter. Explaining why a
people would so complicate their domestic lives becomes all the more interesting in view of the custom's wide dispersal across societies of Africa,
Oceania, and the New World. Thus, the practice cannot be attributed to
the pecularities of a particular historical tradition but arose independently
on a number of occasions.

Ember (1974) portrays avunculocal residence as yet another emergency
measure that becomes institutionalized, emerging this time in response
to a recurrence of internal warfare in a society that had previously adapted
to external warfare through matrilocal residence. He notes that all avunculocal societies have internal warfare. They also have matrilineal descent groups, although there are others with both matrilineal and patrilineal descent groups (double descent) as well. Further, whereas polygyny
is relatively uncommon among matrilocals for a number of practical and
political reasons (Murdock 1949), its practice is widespread among avunculocal peoples. Indeed among societies with double descent, polygyny is
far more prevalent among the avunculocals than among the patrilocals.

Ember (1974) explains the co-occurrence of these phenomena as follows. Warfare seems to provide an impetus for the emergence of unilocal
residence and strong unilineal descent groups, whether patrilineal or matrilineal. If internal warfare resumes in a society with well-developed matrilineal descent groups, the incentives to form strong localized alliances
of consanguineously related males returns. The emergency arises from
established social practices providing little or no opportunity to base local groups on common paternity or to knit together larger alliances on
the basis of common patrilineal descent. Matrilineal descent provides the
one well-established nexus around which such coalitions can form, and
avunculocal residence effectively recomposes localized groups of matrilin-

eally related men who would have been dispersed under matrilocal residence (Fox 1967).

Widespread polygyny under avunculocal residence is significant in several ways. First, polygyny is more common, other things being equal, where high warfare mortality among males creates an imbalanced sex ratio in spouse pools (Ember 1974). Thus, Ember believes, the association of polygyny with avunculocality may indicate high warfare mortality among males and a high rate of widow remarriage. If so, this means that a woman's sons are less likely to share a common father, leaving common maternity as the sure basis of fraternal solidarity and strengthening the persistence of matrilineal descent groups. Second, polygyny provides the avunculocally residing man with all of the benefits enjoyed by patrilocally residing men but denied by matrilocality (Murdock 1949).

Through avunculocality a man can bring together multiple wives in a single domicile without their being sisters as in matrilocal residence and can thereby create marital alliances with a number of groups in the same way that patrilocally residing men can. Moreover, like his patrilocal counterpart, a powerful man can spend his entire adult life in a single domicile amassing and controlling wealth. Finally, it appears that avunculocal residence can offer powerful men opportunities they would not enjoy through patrilocality. Under patrilocal residence marital alliance amounts to keeping sons and exchanging daughters. Under avunculocal residence a man can potentially influence the marital destiny and residence of nieces and nephews as well as of sons and daughters.

A polygynous chief who succeeds a maternal uncle sends sons he has reared to the kin of their various mothers where they may succeed to positions of influence. In return he stands to receive the sons of sisters and half-sisters as coresiding nephews under his own influence, whom he controls through the manipulation of succession and access to resources. Likewise, he can influence the marital destinies of his daughters, because they reside with him, as well as those of his sister's daughters because of his prominence in their matrilineal group. Obviously, no one would accomplish this degree of influence without holding a good deal of political and economic power in the first place, but it is this extraordinary potential of avunculocality for the concentration of power within a system of kinship and marriage that leads me to propose that it may have become institutionalized among Classic Taino elites. In general, ethnohistorical accounts support this proposition.

In addition to its association with matrilineality and internal warfare, avunculocality is associated with the division of a society into warring chiefdoms. While the initial transition to avunculocality may well be a defensive measure in the face of internal conflicts in a matrilineal society, its institutionalization may result from efforts by chiefs and their subordinates to turn internal conflict to their own advantage by manipulating marriage, residence, and succession to concentrate power in the chiefdoms that become parties to internal conflict.

This is not to suggest that avunculocally organized chiefdoms achieve a higher level of political integration than do their matrilocal counterparts. To the contrary, matrilocally organized chiefdoms are fairly common and their ability to maintain internal peace to engage in external warfare is testimony to the size and integration of the polities they may achieve (Schneider and Gough 1961). Indeed, the emergence of the avunculocally organized chiefdom in response to internal warfare may represent a tightening of political boundaries and what amounts to their social fortification through the manipulation of ties of kinship and marriage by chiefs. In short, a key difference between the two kinds of matrilineal chiefdoms may turn on the personal power of chiefs and the way in which they maintain it.

Some evidence bearing on this postulated difference may be found in Textor's (1967) *Cross-Cultural Summary*. One finds that of 18 avunculocal societies 13 have inherited headsmanships, all of which are inherited matrilineally (Textor 1967: table 206). By contrast, of 31 matrilocal societies 17 also have matrilineally inherited headmanships, but 14 have other forms of succession or no headmen at all (Textor 1967: table 208). Interpreting these limited data cautiously, it seems that while matrilocality does not inhibit matrilineal succession to political office and the emergence of matrilineal descent groups may encourage it, the political processes that occur in these societies often allow individuals to pursue power through other avenues. Avunculocal residence, by contrast, seems to actively foster the mobilization of matrilineal ties for political purposes.

From a purely military perspective the greater reliance of avunculocal chiefdoms on matrilineal succession may seem contradictory. Outbreaks of warfare with neighbors are often intermittent with periods of alliance and trade, which makes them difficult to anticipate. A constant state of readiness is required, and political leaders must always be mindful of potential threats as well as of offensive opportunities. If chiefs must be successful military entrepreneurs to maintain the confidence of followers, it would seem that success should be achieved through demonstrated ability rather than ascribed by kinship.

However, the great advantage conferred by matrilineal succession in the avunculocal chiefdom is that it provides for orderly transfers of power while allowing considerable latitude in the choice of a successor. Under patrilineal succession, a chief is normally succeeded by one of his sons, whereas matrilineal succession may allow a chief to choose any of his sisters' sons, indeed virtually any man of his matrilineage. Melvin Ember points out that such latitude in the choice of a successor may actually be necessary, especially when there is high male mortality due to warfare. As discussed elsewhere, cases in which sons, wives, and sisters reportedly became Taino chiefs may reflect the high male mortality that followed the establishment of Spanish settlements.

Avunculocal residence assembles potential candidates in or near the chief's household and under his supervision. The succession may be contested, especially if a chief dies intestate, but the power of a chief to choose his successor from a variety of candidates he can call to live with him insures the allegiance of candidates and motivates them to achieve the chief's objectives to secure his favor.

In fact, military and political entrepreneurship may well have been the key elements in the emergence of the avunculocal chiefdom. The term *avunculocal chiefdom*, rather than *avunculocal society*, is used because a polity's being organized through avunculocal residence does not necessarily require the entire society to reside avunculocally. Recall that avunculocal residence seems to emerge in previously matrilocal, matrilineal societies that have experienced a recurrence of internal warfare. Because marriage distances are usually short in matrilocal societies, the men of a matrilineage can routinely assemble for political and ritual activities. As internal conflict resumes, the incentive to assemble the men of a matrilineal group more often and for longer periods increases. However, it is not feasible to localize all of the men all of the time, certainly not in a single household or village. Rather the objective of clan chiefs or of men who are simply successful war leaders is to assemble a retinue of capable and loyal followers from among their matrikin. Other individuals may continue to live matrilocally, and as avunculocality accustoms the population to the movement of women at marriage, still other couples may choose to live patrilocally. Thus, ethnographers have found a mixture of

residential choices among other avunculocal groups such as the Gitksan
(Adams 1973), the Trobriand (Weiner 1976), and the Trukese (Goodenough
1955). These choices reflect the different options available to married
couples, with avunculocal residence predominant in chiefly families. Since
these ethnographic observations describe periods after the cessation of
warfare, avunculocal residence may have been more common in earlier
times. However, it is not essential for avunculocal residence to be systematic for the avunculocal chiefdom to emerge.

What must happen for an avunculocal chiefdom to emerge is the
achievement of paramount status by a single matrilineal group. It is no
accident of history that avunculocal chiefdoms developed in highly circumscribed environments, islands or areas of highly concentrated resources such as those inhabited by peoples of the northwest coast of
North America. Circumscribed environments may foster internal conflict
that ceases only when one group achieves hegemony over the others
through greater numerical strength, better leadership, or command of a
strong defensive position centered on a prime site of habitation or astride
trade routes. Thus, if there are a series of such circumscribed environments in a region, a series of such polities may emerge. These polities
may continue to war and trade with one another because no one of them
can sustain the extension of its power beyond its circumscribed boundaries by conquering and incorporating others.

Thus far only the social dynamics conducive to a shift from matrilocal
to avunculocal residence, a process proposed for the Classic Taino, have
been discussed. The remaining question is that of why some societies
remain matrilocal.

Matrilocal residence seems to require a combination of internal peace
and absent husbands, compelling a matridominant division of home-based
subsistence labor. Whether external warfare must be one reason for men's
absence is not clear, because the Embers' analysis dealt only with warlike
societies (Ember and Ember 1971). A matridominant division of local labor could just as well be compelled by long-distance hunting, fishing, and
trading, which would tend to externalize warfare, but the extent to which
external military threat is necessary to induce internal peace is not clear
(Ember and Ember 1971). One point is clear, however: matrilocal residence is neither a sufficient condition for internal peace (as we saw in the
discussion of avunculocal residence) nor a necessary one. As the Embers
show, there are patrilocal societies with patridominant divisions of labor
practicing purely external warfare. Thus, the conditions of internal peace

are not to be found in the kinship system itself, but in the material conditions to which the kinship system is responsive. The existence of patrilocal societies with patridominant divisions of labor and exclusively external warfare suggests that male absence, rather than external threat, is the key condition of matrilocality.

Matrilocal society entails a potential prisoner's dilemma for men (see Gumerman 1986). Internal conflict threatens to divide men's loyalties between natal and conjugal groups, and if Ember is correct about avunculocality, men side with blood relations when this occurs. If a man is to be away from home for long periods he wants to be assured that his interests at home are protected. He can rely on his sisters, but he needs to be assured that other groups of men within the society will not prey on his resources in his absence. To be assured of this a man must be confident that other men's interests are better served by activities conducted away from home than by internal predation. This can happen in several ways. Severe external military threat assures that everyone will be a loser if internal war occurs. Alternatively, it could be that local resources simply are not worth fighting over in view of the higher returns from long-distance trading, raiding, hunting, and fishing. In either of these circumstances, or in some combination of them, interpersonal aggression may occur, but leaders will act to prevent it from escalating into violence because internal warfare is in no one's interest. To a large degree, political institutions arise from the structures that initially operated to organize the productive and reproductive activities of a group.

The Spanish Description of Taino Social Organization

The Spanish chroniclers who recorded Antillean cultures made the majority of their observations among the Classic Taino of Hispaniola. These reports have been generalized to other Taino groups on the basis of the Spanish assertion that all of the Taino had very similar cultural practices. The major exceptions to these general rules were the more warlike posture attributed to some groups and the more elaborate political structure of the Classic Tainos. For present purposes it is assumed that a simpler political organization was the primary difference between the Lucayans of the Bahamas and the Classic Tainos of the Greater Antilles.

An additional caveat is also warranted at this point. There are problems with many of the Spanish descriptions of the Tainos stemming from their unfamiliarity with matrilineal organizations and their choice of terms when describing certain actions. In addition, archaeologists have developed inferences based on Spanish descriptions, but they have sometimes failed to read the documents with a critical eye or alternatively have selected only those descriptions that best fit a particular theory while ignoring contradictory reports. The result is sometimes contradictory conclusions. For instance, it is sometimes reported that only one language was spoken throughout the northern Caribbean, a conclusion that comes from a statement by Las Casas, "En todas estas islas hablaban una sola lengua." Yet, as Granberry (1987) has so clearly documented, Las Casas was referring to a *lingua franca*, a language shared for political and commercial purposes, and several other languages and dialects were also spoken.

The Tainos are reported to have had a matrilineal descent system (Fewkes 1907). Supporting this report is the Taino myth of an immortal being who had a mother with five names and a maternal uncle (Rouse 1948). In practice, matrilineal descent was expressed in the inheritance of rank through the female line, with females sometimes inheriting chiefly positions (Sued-Badillo 1979; Wilson 1990a). Zemis, representations of the lineage's ancestors (Rouse 1948, 1982; Fewkes 1907; Stevens-Arroyo 1988), were also passed through the female line, and women are reported to have been both the producers and the distributors of certain high-status goods (e.g., wooden stools and household objects, "a thousand things of cotton") (Las Casas 1951; Wilson 1990a; cf. Petersen 1982). Since private property is not reported as an important item of inheritance, even though it did exist among the upper ranks, it is inferred that access to corporate resources was the primary good obtained through matrilineal inheritance.

The Spanish also reported that the eldest son would, on occasion, inherit the rank of lineage chief from his father (Rouse 1948; Alegría 1979). Such inheritance could result from patrilineal descent, but this option appears to be an exception to general practices that may have been brought about by the Spanish disruption of the indigenous social system (Sauer 1966; Cook and Borah 1971b; Sued-Badillo 1979; Wilson 1990a).

The Spanish reported that the Taino residence pattern was patrilocal (Rouse 1948). However, this pattern of residence is not consistent with the residence possibilities of matrilineal systems (Aberle 1961; Fox 1967). This erroneous report probably reflects a confusion of where the *wife* resided with where the *husband and wife* resided in relation to the husband's lineage (see Goodenough 1955). In other words, although the wife resided patrilocally by moving to her husband's village, the husband resided avunculocally (with his mother's brother) in the village of his lineage.

Social Organization and the Evolution of Lucayan Settlement Patterns

The evolution of Lucayan settlement patterns described in chapter 4 can be viewed as expressing adjustments in residence over time in three main phases: an initial phase in which settlements were randomly distributed, a second phase during which settlements converged to form regularly spaced settlement pairs, and a final phase characterized by the clustering of settlement units and the development of plaza communities.

Initial Colonization of the Bahamas

Colonizing populations share a variety of adaptive strategies derived from the exigencies of migration into unoccupied territories. These strategies include a generalized use of the environment, a rapidly growing population, and spatial mobility; all of which conspire to promote the maintenance of a flexible social organization (Cherry 1981, 1985; Kirch 1984; Terrell 1986; Keegan and Diamond 1987). During the initial phase of colonization land and other resources tend to be so abundant as to obviate the need to control them through strong descent groups. As Sahlins (1961) has suggested: "Expansion in an open environment may well be accompanied by segmentation, the normal process of tribal growth and spread. But in the absence of competition small segments tend to become discrete and autonomous linked together primarily through mechanical solidarity."

Tracing descent through the female line provides a means for loosely integrating relatively large segments of a population. In horticultural economies where land tends to be abundant in relation to seasonal labor demands, matrilineal descent provides a method for establishing rights of access to land through lineage membership and also serves to foster cooperation among the members of a group. Further, the risks incurred during island colonization would strengthen the bonds between colonists and the parent community on adjacent islands (see Rouse 1982), and if males are frequently absent on overwater voyages there exists a stimulus for matrilocal residence.

That the initial colonists of the West Indies were matrilineal and matrilocal can be inferred from several sources. First, mainland Arawakan peoples who in recent times lived closest to the river mouths from which the ancestors of the Tainos departed for the islands were typically matrilineal and matrilocal (Steward and Faron 1959). Second, matrilineal descent is usually accompanied by a preference for matrilocal residence (Aberle 1961), and this residence preference is the necessary precursor to avunculocal residence (Murdock 1949; Fox 1967). Finally, as we have seen, ethnohistoric reports identify matrilineal descent reckoning and avunculocal residence as the predominant patterns among the Classic Taino at contact.

In the earlier discussion of the transmission of matrilineal institutions to the Bahamas the presence of these institutions in Hispaniola at contact was cited as circumstantial evidence. In point of fact, however, the distinctions between the Classic and the Lucayan Tainos are to a large degree arbitrary. There may have been linguistic and other cultural differences within and between Taino groups, and the Classic Tainos certainly had much larger communities, but the Bahamas may be viewed as a hinterland of a larger political region centered on the Greater Antilles. In sum, there is a sound basis for concluding that the initial colonists of the Bahamas were predominantly matrilineal. There is also good reason to infer that the initial pattern of residence was predominantly matrilocal, so the following discussion will focus on changes in residence patterns that reflect adjustments to changes in sociopolitical arrangements expressed as changes in settlement patterns.

The Lucayan colonization practice of moving to the nearest available island rather than to the biggest may be viewed as a satisficing strategy, a simple matter of convenience. Yet, as the ethnohistoric accounts make clear, these people were accomplished seafarers with large vessels who traveled long distances to trade (Daggett 1980; Dunn and Kelley 1989). It thus seems unlikely that they would settle nearby islands simply to save time if farther islands offered better resources. The nearby islands were certainly good enough until the population approached a comfortable carrying capacity, but it also seems likely that nearby islands were decisively preferred because the system of kinship and marriage worked better if these islands were settled first. Seemingly, measures were always taken to settle a new island with people who could marry one another, but in addition settlers may have preferred to stay in easy communication with the parent community where additional spouses were available. In this way, entire domestic groups could routinely engage in interisland visitation without incurring unnecessary hazards. In short, we are suggesting that the islands would not have been settled as they were unless people organized in unilineal descent groups were doing the settling. The only unilineal descent groups we know about in the region from historical accounts were matrilineal.

Population expansion would have occurred through the creation of sublineages in response to population growth. New communities would then be established by the "drift" method of segmentation in which one of the sublineages moved away to found a new community (Fox 1967). In its simplest form the drift method involves a moiety division of the lineage with two sibs remaining in the parent community and matrilineal relatives of both moving to the new community (Murdock 1949:215; Fox 1967). Under conditions of resource abundance, the impetus to move would have been the pull of greater economic potential in previously unoccupied territories versus the push of intracommunity competition (Keegan and Butler 1987). This economic stimulus would have permitted the continuation of amicable relations between the parent and daughter communities. In addition, the differential pattern of growth exhibited by unilineal descent systems, with some lineages growing and others going extinct (Fox 1967), combined with the risks of colonization would have also favored the continuation of intercommunity communication and cooperation.

It is in this method of segmentation that we find our notion of social distance. On the one hand, the risks of colonization, unilineal corporate-group longevity, and matrilineal kinship relations that crosscut communities favor communication and cooperation (centripetal forces); on the other, the attraction of economic advantage favors segmentation (centrifugal forces). The spatial displacement of males from communities in which they maintain a vested interest would thus act to constrain the spatial separation of parent and daughter communities. However, because these interests were probably quite small at this time (i.e., no corporate property to control), the distance between communities could be fairly large. In sum, the initial period of population expansion would have been characterized by the localization of female kin groups and the spatial displacement of some males.

Although matrilocal residence is suggested as the prevalent pattern, social and economic factors would favor flexibility and individual choice in residence decisions during the initial phase of colonization. We would therefore expect individuals to reside in the community that best satisfied their productive and reproductive needs. If new communities were created through the drift method of segmentation in which a moiety division of husband givers and husband takers was duplicated in every community, then individuals could maintain the same general pattern of residence regardless of the community in which they resided. The only difference between communities would be the specific individuals who comprised the two sibs in each one.

The Emergence of Settlement Pairs

Even when descent is traced through the female line, it is usually males who assume the positions of authority within the lineage, especially with regard to external relations (Schneider 1961). Although matrilineal descent reckoning may at first favor the localization of related females because of male absence reinforced by the nature of the productive activities, if males are required to reside matrilocally there exists an inherent instability in the society. This instability results from a male's need to participate in his lineage while resident with his wife's lineage.

One means by which to balance such competing demands is to establish villages in close proximity, thus reducing the distances that males must travel to participate in their lineage affairs and resulting in the short marriage distances typical of matrilocal societies. So long as male participation in the lineage is flexible, and male distance from their lineage group is outweighed by the advantage of localizing related females, the society should not become critically unstable. However, the advantage of maintaining a corporate group of related females may eventually be outweighed by other sociopolitical factors that require heightened participation by males. Under such conditions the localization of matrilineally related men and their spouses may develop (Fox 1967; Ember 1974).

The shift from widely spread communities to settlement pairs can be explained as resulting from population growth to a level at which lineage membership was important for defining access to productive resources. Under such conditions, males should attempt to minimize their distance from their matrilineage's corporate usufruct. One possible solution is the continuation of a matrilocal residence pattern accompanied by the spatial convergence of sublineage segments. Each community contains a minimum of two sibs, with both contributing matrilineal relatives to the new community; if the rule of exogamy is retained, the original sibs are converted automatically into matrimoieties (Murdock 1949:215). A slight spatial separation between the communities provides the basis for controlling a larger territory, while allowing men in both communities to observe the rule of exogamy and reside matrilocally without leaving their village or natal territory. Settlement pairs thus reflect social integration as an economic strategy. A similar settlement system known as village clusters characterizes the Trobriand Islanders, a matrilineal and avunculocal society (Powell 1960; Weiner 1976; Rubel and Rosman 1983).

Because communities of a pair so often differ in size it seems impossible that islands were endogamous while communities were exogamous. Yet the occurrence of community pairs in this phase suggests some clear reason for maintaining the division between them. Given what we have seen thus far of the ethnohistory of the Tainos, the most probable explanation would be that the moiety division of communities reflected a moiety division of society as a whole premised on bilateral cross-cousin marriage. Such moiety divisions are commonplace among Amazonian peoples. If such communities represent single, localized matrilineages or two or more lineages of the same moiety, then they may have been exogamous, exchanging spouses with the paired community as well as with opposite moiety communities on adjacent islands.

Settlement pairs emerged in conjunction with a growing population and the end of opportunities to expand onto nearby islands. It is also apparent that the communities involved are not simply equal pairs. Only six of the settlement pairs involve communities of nearly equal size. The emergence of settlement pairs thus appears to reflect the emergence of a dominant lineage or lineages. This settlement system may therefore be interpreted as evidence during this phase of increased sociopolitical integration that may be based on matrilocal residence patterns or on an initial expression of avunculocal residence among the emerging upper ranks.

Settlement Clusters and Plaza Communities

The final settlement pattern of site clusters and joined pairs reflects the increasing political integration of the growing Lucayan population.

Taino individuals can be distinguished as commoners (those lacking positions of authority in their lineage) and chiefs (who the Spanish called *caciques*, and who held positions of authority). Both chiefs and commoners were likely to change their place of residence several times during their lifetime. Children began by living with their parents. During adolescence, boys would usually move to their maternal uncle's house in the village of their lineage (avunculocal residence). At marriage, Taino commoners are reported to have provided bride service as compensation to the lineage that provided their spouse (Fewkes 1907), at which time the couple resided matrilocally with the wife's family. Taino chiefs apparently could avoid such bride service by paying movable property to the wife-giving lineage. Finally, at the completion of bride service the couple would move back to the husband's matrilineage where they would reside avunculocally.

These marital practices are especially interesting because bride service, in effect temporary matrilocal residence during which a man provides services to his in-laws in payment for their daughter, amounts to a transitional compromise between matrilocality and avunculocality. Chiefs who bought out their bride service had for all practical purposes instituted bride price, which was construed as a substitute for bride service simply because commoner men served it.

The attribution of bride service instead of outright matrilocality to the Classic Tainos suggests that a growing proportion of the population felt the impetus to recompose matrilineally related groups of men. The Spanish accounts are not clear regarding qualifications for cacique rank or the number and kinds of distinctions among those of noble rank. On one point they were clear: there were many caciques. In one case a paramount chief is cited as having assembled 300 caciques (Wilson 1990a). If this actually occurred, the size of the total population of the chiefdom suggests that a man who was simply head of a small village or of a large family could be regarded as a cacique. Thus, the picture that emerges from the Spanish accounts, clouded though they were by the Spaniards' previous ignorance of matrilineal institutions, is one of a society with considerable variability in residential practices. Sooner or later, the institution of bride service allowed all men to rejoin their matrikin, with the length of service dependent on the status or rank of the individual and that of the descent group to which he was affiliated.

At the top of the society, avunculocality would have occurred as soon as selected nephews reached adulthood, and high-ranking polygynous men brought wives to live with them immediately after marriage. At the bottom of the society a connubial cycle prevailed. Sons reared in one family might join a second upon marriage and move to a third upon completion of their suitor service. Meanwhile the original family would be collecting temporarily residing sons-in-law and older, permanently settled nephews, with the question of who went where and when determined by some mixture of political advantage, practical expedience, and personal preference. The mixture of residential arrangements at the bottom of the society could easily confuse a modern ethnographer (see Goodenough 1955), let alone a sixteenth-century Spaniard.

Archaeological evidence for these developments is observed in the cluster of sites on Acklins Island in a settlement pattern similar to that in the Trobriand Islands where socially discrete hamlets of extended families composed of matrilineally related men, their spouses, young children, and adolescent nephews occupy large dwellings that together form a village (cf. Rouse 1948 and Weiner 1976). One lineage at each village was probably dominant in the sense that that lineage or clan head was the chief of the village and in some cases the chief of a district or of a region. With the emergence of chiefs, male status was enhanced and the localization of males in their lineage's village would have promoted the shift to avunculocal residence (Murdock 1949; Fox 1967).

Furthermore, at site MC-6 on Middle Caicos, one plaza is clearly dominant, and its central court has stones aligned to chart astronomical events (Sullivan 1981; see Castellanos 1981; Alegría 1983). The distribution of exotic materials imported from the Greater Antilles provides evidence for a moiety division of this dominant plaza group that conforms to the identification of matrimoieties as the minimum structural unit of matrilineal and matrilocal/avunculocal societies. Site MC-6 is, however, unusual in comparison to other Lucayan sites, and it appears to have been a Classic Taino outpost established to maintain access to marine resources and a seasonal source of salt (Sullivan 1981). In this regard MC-6 may be more characteristic of Classic Taino than of Lucayan spatial organization (Alegría 1983). The two sites on Middle Caicos at which plaza communities have been identified (MC-6, MC-12) are therefore interpreted as reflecting external influences, so the following consideration of the emergence of settlement clusters in the Bahamas will be restricted to developments on the islands to the north.

The transition from settlement pairs to settlement clusters appears to reflect some combination of long-distance trading and interisland raiding in conjunction with continued population growth. Columbus reported that exchange was regularly conducted between the central Bahamas and Cuba, and he observed dugout canoes that could carry 40 to 45 men (Dunn and Kelley 1989). Given the size of most archaeological sites in the central Bahamas, canoes of this size must have carried men who resided in several communities. In sum, long-distance exchange involved a supracommunity organization of males. Because matrilineal descent was the dominant principle for the organization of males in cooperative ventures, long-distance exchange provided a stimulus for the localization of matrilineally related males. As has been argued, the localization of matrilineally related males finds its most complete expression in avunculocal residence.

That scale of long-distance exchange would have required the participation of a chief. On the one hand, the coordination of efforts by males who usually reside in different communities required an individual whose power and influence extended beyond the community in which he resided. On the other, the construction of large oceangoing canoes or the procurement of such canoes through exchange required an individual who could marshall resources that exceeded those available to the typical household. In sum, the presence of chiefs is inferred from activities that exceed the scale of single households and autonomous communities.

Recent excavations at the Delectable Bay settlement complex on Acklins Island provide evidence for long-distance exchange that exceeded by several magnitudes the scale of exchange in the remainder of the Bahamas (Keegan 1988). In the Delectable Bay site, AC-14, 27.3 percent by weight of the pottery assemblage was imported from the Greater Antilles. In comparison, Sears and Sullivan (1978) have reported that imported pottery comprises less than 1 percent of the ceramic assemblages at Lucayan sites in the Bahama Islands, and about 10 percent of the assemblages at sites in the Turks and Caicos Islands. Such heightened participation in long-distance exchange is consistent with Columbus's report (Dunn and Kelley 1989) that a "King" (paramount chief) who held hegemony over all of the central Bahamas resided on Acklins Island (Keegan 1984a; Keegan and Mitchell 1986).

To date, the possible role of interisland raiding in the evolution of Lucayan societies has not been explored. Interpretive difficulties arise from the fact that raiding is presently archaeologically invisible, and the only reports of raiding are colored by Columbus's views (Allaire 1987; Davis and Goodwin 1990). Columbus reported observing men on Guanahani (Columbus's "San Salvador") who had scars that were received when raiders from the northwest came to "capture" them (Dunn and Kelley 1989). Given the size of Lucayan settlements it is unlikely that conquest warfare or the taking of captives actually occurred. Here is a case where Columbus is attributing European motives (conquest, slavery) to the native population.

It is, however, quite clear that the Lucayans were prepared to defend themselves. Columbus was not met by a cross section of the population; he was met by young people ("mancebos") carrying spears. Since Columbus states that he saw only one quite young girl, some have concluded that Columbus was met only by men. Dunn and Kelley (1989:67n1) have pointed out that the Spanish masculine plural cannot be used to support the view that Columbus was met only by men. Even so, the context of Columbus's statement supports the interpretation that these young people were there to defend their village.

Rather than speculate on the reasons for long-distance exchange and interisland raiding, interpretations are limited to their sociological impacts. Both activities would have promoted the localization of matrilineally related men. And, as the scale of both increased, a consolidation of power in dominant lineages would have emerged through the coordination and political integration of the men who belonged to the dominant lineages. One expression of such consolidation was the growth of villages through the incorporation of additional settlement units. The fullest expression of such village growth is the settlement cluster at Delectable Bay, Acklins Island.

Conclusions

In contrast to Judeo-Christian ethics, which command "Honor thy mother and father," the major canon of the Taino family was "Honor thy mother's brother." The complexities of such allegiance are practically incomprehensible to members of a society such as ours in which families communicate more often by telephone than in person. Yet in relatively small-scale societies in which individuals reside in villages in which almost everyone is related through marriage or descent, avunculocal residence provides an effective solution to significant organizational problems.

Knowledge of the northern Caribbean chiefdoms has come largely from contact-period documents (Wilson 1990a). These documents report that the Tainos of Hispaniola were organized into five paramount *cacicazgos*. A cacicazgo is a regional polity that is ruled by a cacique (chief) and is composed of a number of communities, each of which is ruled by a village headman. Chiefs used their military and political entrepreneurship to maintain the loyalty of an extended network of kin. Taino society was strongly stratified, ruled by caciques who were followed in descending order by *nitainos* (nobles or clanlords) and *naborias* (commoners) (Moscoso 1981).

In the present study, the development of the Taino cacicazgos has been presented as the organizational outcome of adjustments between demography, economy, and ecology and employs the logic of cultural or vulgar materialism. A second perspective has promoted a Marxist model of exploitation in which religious ideology was manipulated by elites to control the disposition of the surplus of social production (Moscoso 1983, 1987). Both perspectives are in need of additional archaeological investigation along the lines of diachronic studies undertaken elsewhere (e.g., Kirch 1984; Earle 1987). However, the materialist view provides a parsimonious explanation for the observed phenomena and is able to subsume the expectations generated by the Marxist.

6

Diet for a Small Island:
Lucayan Subsistence Economy

The ways in which people make their living comprise the most elemental aspect of human society. One way in which archaeologists have sought information about lifeways is by studying the plant and animal remains in archaeological sites (Wing and Brown 1979). For many years these studies emphasized the identification and description of faunal and floral remains to the exclusion of formal economic study. However, in recent years archaeologists have gone beyond the static identification of food remains to develop models for explaining and predicting the timing and direction of changes in prehistoric subsistence economies (Earle and Christenson 1980; Keene 1982; Keegan and Butler 1987). Such reconstructions of prehistoric diets require a multidimensional approach.

Theories of Subsistence Behavior

Despite differences in their subjects, some anthropologists, economists, and ecologists have adopted similar, one might say convergent, theories of food-getting behavior. These approaches have been reported under a variety of different names—price theory in microeconomics (Hirshleifer 1980), optimal foraging theory in ecology (Krebs 1978), and formalist economics in anthropology (Johnson 1982). Whether one is interested in "bumblebee economics" or "careful consumers," the underlying logic is the same: behavior is patterned by the allocation of scarce means to competing ends (Heinrich 1979). The means are always limited (e.g., time, space, energy, income) but the alternative ways of spending the means are potentially infinite.

The use of such theories is based on the assumption that animals, and especially humans, tend to behave rationally and that rationality is reflected in their allocation of means (Krebs 1978; Krebs and Davies 1981). In contrast to capitalist economies, in which scarce means are allocated toward the goal of maximizing profits, subsistence economies are viewed as attempting to minimize the costs of production. In other words, they seek the most resources for the least effort. This cost-minimization goal has found its fullest expression in studies of time allocation. Time is devoted to any one activity to allow the maximum amount of time for other activities (Johnson 1975; Johnson and Behrens 1982; E. Smith 1983).

There are, of course, limits to the theory. It is sometimes difficult to defend the premise that people are behaving rationally, and time is not always the factor in most limited supply. Furthermore, the theories are based on a logic of behavior under conditions of scarcity and stress, conditions that certainly do not apply in many situations. Finally, the theories require complicated mathematical calculations and currency measurements that are beyond the capabilities of their subjects. Animals do not measure the nutritional content of prey types and then run computer algorithms to determine which prey type to pursue. Nonetheless, natural selection will favor those animals that make the most efficient use of their environment.

Given these limitations, it may seem that the theories are of no possible utility (e.g., Martin 1983, 1985; cf. Smith and Winterhalder 1985). Yet, such theories are important because they provide specific measurements and predictions concerning behavior under specified conditions. By comparing actual or observed behavior with that predicted by abstract theory we gain insight into the factors that influenced behavior. Furthermore, theories help to isolate the significant variables, especially variables that are common to seemingly unrelated activities. For instance, the relationship between food getting, recreation, and ceremonies may appear impossible to specify, yet all can be expressed in terms of time allocation. Such well-structured approaches direct scientific research in ways that improve our understanding and evaluation of complex human behaviors (Johnson 1980; Orians 1980).

Price Theory

Microeconomic price theory provides a set of hierarchically integrated models that are used to address questions of resource allocation at group (aggregate) and individual (disaggregate) levels of analysis (Hirshleifer 1980; Mansfield 1982). Most anthropological studies have focused on decision making by individuals. At the group level, questions of total currency demand and changes in the means of production can be addressed with a technique known as equilibrium analysis.

Equilibrium analysis describes the aggregate relationship between the two sectors of the economy called supply and demand in a mutual and voluntary market relation (fig. 6.1). While money is used as the index of prices (called a currency) in market economies, price is simply a ratio of

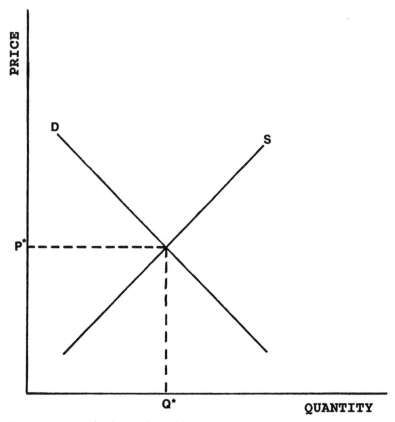

FIGURE 6.1. Supply/demand equilibrium.

quantities that can be expressed in units that are relevant to cultures that do not use money (e.g., calories per hour of effort, grams of protein per hour of effort) (Keegan and Butler 1987). By defining price (i.e., currency) in culturally relevant units, the market equation is transformed into a method for evaluating nonmarket production and consumption decisions.

The demand curve, which corresponds to the perspective of a consumer, is downward sloping because the amount of a good desired is inversely related to price—as price increases, less is demanded (Earle 1980, 1985; Hirshleifer 1980). The aggregate supply curve, which corresponds to the perspective of a producer, defines the inverse relationship—the higher the price, the more the supplier wants to produce. The relationship between aggregate supply and aggregate demand approaches a locally stable equilibrium at the intersection of the curves. Because individuals in subsistence economies embody the perspectives of *both* the consumer and the producer, subsistence systems always correspond to locally stable equilibriums (Keegan 1986b; cf. Chayanov 1966).

Equilibrium analysis provides a technique for evaluating the specific determinants of subsistence change. At this aggregate level of analysis the intensification of production is reflected in a shift of either the supply curve or the demand curve in a way that increases total output. A shift in the demand curve to a higher level of output is accompanied by an increase in the equilibrium price (fig. 6.2). This increase in price occurs because the new equilibrium point is at a higher position on the supply curve. A shift in the supply curve to a higher level of total output is accompanied by a decrease in the equilibrium price, with this decrease reflecting a more cost-efficient mode of production (fig. 6.3). To this point, changes in the supply-demand equilibrium have been expressed in terms of increasing output because subsistence change is most often studied as progressive—the Western view of economies being focused on growth. However, the technique is also amenable to situations of decreasing total output.

Economists define aggregate demand as the sum of tastes, wants, or preferences. They view the reasons for particular preferences to be outside their sphere of competence and focus their attention on examining the net effects of given preferences (Hirshleifer 1980). This approach to the study of demand is called utility analysis, with utility defined as a hypothetical magnitude that serves as an index for preferences (Lancaster 1971).

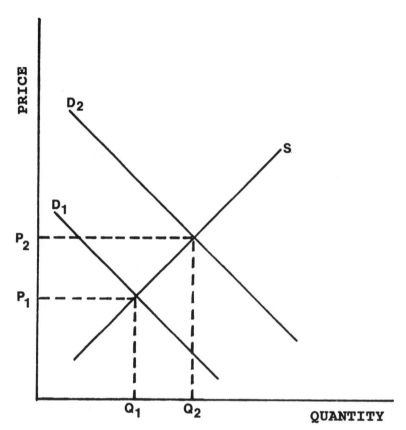

FIGURE 6.2. Changes in the supply/demand (S/D) equilibrium resulting from an increase in demand (D_1 to D_2).

Ecologists and anthropologists who have adopted ecological models tend to equate demand with nutritional needs (Johnson and Behrens 1982; Johnson 1982). This need-based definition of wants results from the relative ease with which nutritional requirements can be measured for quantitative analysis. Furthermore, it is obvious that people must satisfy their nutritional requirements to ensure long-term survival and reproduction. However, this need-based definition produces an inelastic demand curve that is unlikely to characterize actual demand (fig. 6.4). What is needed is a more flexible definition of demand.

For human subsistence economies, the household can be viewed as the primary economic decision-making unit, and demand is expressed as the sum of the wants of household members. An aggregate of households

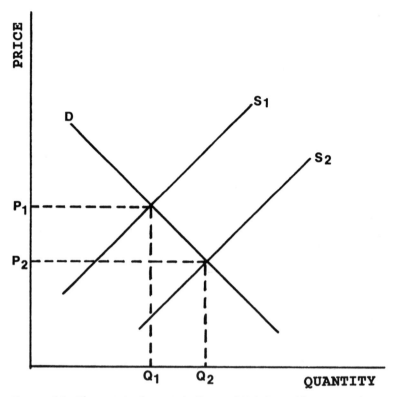

FIGURE 6.3. Changes in the supply/demand (S/D) equilibrium resulting from an increase in supply (S_1 to S_2).

sharing cultural values, living in similar physical and social environments, and faced with similar production opportunities will share similar perspectives on what constitutes a standard of living or quality of life. This similarity in wants is used to define aggregate demand as a function of the number of households. When separate households are comprised of equivalent members with regard to age and sex, aggregate demand can be further reduced to a function of population numbers (Keegan, Johnson, and Earle 1985). At a general level, an increase in demand should be apparent as an increase in the number of households and as an increase in population numbers. (The demand side of this linkage between economy and demography is developed further in the next chapter.)

The factors of supply include the variables that determine the rates at which currency is captured. The effects of supply-side variables can be

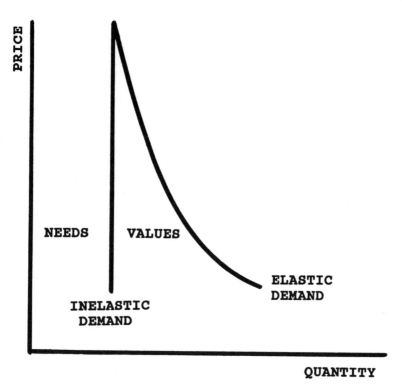

FIGURE 6.4. Relationship between physiological needs and cultural values with regard to the elasticity of demand.

measured with regard to resource density, search costs, transportation costs, and handling costs. Resource density influences the rate at which a resource is encountered, which will affect the time devoted to searching for total currency wants. A decline in resource availability will lead to the expansion of diet breadth (i.e., more food types are added to the diet), while an increase in resource density will promote the contraction of diet breadth (Winterhalder 1981). It should be noted that these effects are limited to resources in the optimal set. The availability of resources that are not in the optimal set will have no influence on subsistence decisions. (Supply-side variables are the focus of optimization analysis, described later in this chapter.)

Basic changes in the economy can be broken down at the aggregate level into changes in the demand side and changes in the supply side (fig. 6.5). One response to an increase in total demand (resulting, for in-

CHANGE IN EQUILIBRIUM		CHANGE IN PRICE	CHANGE IN QUANTITY
Restrict Demand		0	-
Increase Demand:	Expand Area of Production	0	0
Increase Demand:	Intensify Production	+	+
Increase Supply		-	+

FIGURE 6.5. Changes in price and quantity resulting from changes in supply and demand. Symbols refer to no change (0), an increase (+), or a decrease (-) in the equilibrium value.

stance, from a growth in population) is expansion to a previously unoccupied or underused area either by the entire group or by some portion of the group. There is no change in either price or quantity as a result of this move. A second response to such an increase is to work harder using available techniques or to include known but previously underused resources. The result is an increase in both total output and total price.

Changes in the supply side involve an increase in the cost efficiency of production; the result is an increase in output at a lower price. For instance, as people become more familiar with a resource or a new technology they should become more efficient in its use. Second, in response to a decline in supply resulting from increasing costs or declining returns, the members of a group could decide to accept lower total outputs. Because levels of want usually exceed the level of physiological need, such belt tightening could continue until people can no longer survive on the available output.

The next step in the analysis is to specify the supply-side inputs using optimization analysis, which affords an opportunity to examine behavior in specific cases. In the Lucayan economy we expect an initial condition in which price and quantity do not change because the increase in demand due to population growth is relieved through expansion. After all of the Bahamas were occupied intensification should be observed as changes in the factors of supply.

Optimal Foraging Theory Analysis

Models developed in evolutionary ecology under the umbrella of optimal foraging theory provide a simplified format for evaluating supply-side behavior in subsistence economies. Since optimal foraging theory has been discussed in detail elsewhere, it will only briefly be reviewed here (see Winterhalder and Smith 1981; E. Smith 1983; Keegan 1986b).

It should be noted that the use of optimal foraging models in anthropology has been wrongly criticized out of the misplaced belief that these are animal or noncultural models (Martin 1983, 1985; Smith and Winterhalder 1985). In fact, optimal foraging theory is simply an extension of price theory that was developed to investigate nonmarket economies. The foundation of optimal foraging theory, the marginal-value theorem, is also the basis of utility theory in microeconomics (cf. Charnov and Orians 1973; Hirshleifer 1980).

Optimal foraging models require the specification of a goal, a currency, a set of constraints, and a set of options. Formal economic studies of nonmarket economies have come to emphasize cost minimization as the most common *goal* (Earle 1980; Johnson and Behrens 1982; Keegan 1986b). Stated more explicitly, subsistence decisions are evaluated with respect to the objective: satisfy currency wants at the minimum cost of currency production.

In studies of foraging behavior, a nutritional *currency* is usually employed. However, a currency can be any unit common to the behavior that is being optimized. Calories have been used as the primary currency for examining forager decision making because the food quest is viewed as the activity that most affects the time available to pursue other activities (Reidhead 1980; Winterhalder 1981; Keene 1982). Studies of extant tropical forest societies whose production strategies are similar to those proposed for the prehistoric Caribbean have emphasized the importance of protein as a limiting currency (Ross 1978; Roosevelt 1980; Keegan 1986b). In the present study, both calories and protein have been evaluated.

Constraints are factors that limit an individual's ability to capture the

currency. Constraints include technology, resource distributions, and resource abundance. In a time-allocation framework, time serves as the sum
of constraints. In other words, time is the common denominator of effort;
it is common to all activities. Finally, *options* are the various food items
that could be eaten to obtain the currency. Options are ranked relative to
each other with regard to their currency returns per handling time. Handling time is the amount of time required to capture, process, and consume that food item.

It is also necessary to distinguish how several different kinds of costs
are calculated. *Search* costs are those devoted to locating resources in a
fine-grained environment and are thus a measure of resource abundance.
These costs are calculated as the amount of time spent looking for game.
A forager searching in a fine-grained environment will encounter prey in
proportion to their actual numbers because the prey are evenly distributed. In horticultural economies the time devoted to land preparation is a
type of search cost because this investment influences the availability of
resources in the garden patch (Keegan 1986b). Search costs may be significantly affected by the organization of productive task groups, for instance, when individuals cooperate in land clearance or when foragers
share the resources they procure. Search costs affect the *average* rate of
currency return from all procurement strategies. Thus, an increase in
search costs will lead to an increase in the number of food items in the
diet (expansion of diet breadth), while a decrease will produce a contraction of diet breadth.

Transportation costs include the time spent traveling between patches
in a coarse-grained environment. A coarse-grained environment is one in
which prey types are not evenly distributed but are clustered in different
patches. An increase in travel time between patches should lead to a res-
triction of foraging to the higher-ranked prey types, while a reduction of
travel time will promote an expansion of diet breadth (Hames and Vickers
1982). As travel time approaches zero, search costs will define the optimal set.

Lastly, *handling* costs are those devoted to the capture, processing, and
consumption of one unit of a resource. These costs are used to measure
the marginal rate of currency capture (e.g., calories per handling hour),
which provides a ranking or utility index for resources. These rankings
list the order in which prey should be added to the optimal set. Handling
costs are affected by the size of the group involved in resource capture
and the technology of resource capture and processing. An increase in

handling costs will result in a contraction of diet breadth, of resource specialization, or of both, while a decrease would result in diet-breadth expansion.

Optimal foraging models as developed in ecology provide specific predictions concerning when shifts in time allocation between discrete resource patches and in diet breadth will occur. The models direct attention to changes at the margin, and it is in the identification and explanation of marginal shifts that larger-scale changes in subsistence production have their roots.

Consumption Profiles

Given sufficient data, optimal foraging models could be used to predict the proportional contribution of every individual food type to the optimal diet. In practice, this level of specificity has only been attempted in linear-programming analyses (e.g., Reidhead 1980; Keene 1982; Johnson and Behrens 1982). However, since linear-programming analysis examines changes in *average* (versus *marginal*) return rates, the results of linear-programming analyses typically do not match long-term, diachronic patterns of subsistence change (Reidhead 1980).

The difference between these return rates is that average returns are averaged over a long period of time and therefore are not sensitive to short-term fluctuations (e.g., seasonality, depletion). On the other hand, marginal return rates are measures of the instantaneous return, and they are thus more sensitive to immediate constraints, but they are accurate for only an instant in time. The trade-off is between generality and precision. In some instances the trade is not too great, for example when short-term variation in the availability of a resource is small. In these cases the marginal and average return rates converge.

Even where such specificity is possible, it will be of limited use if we are unable to determine the degree to which the optimal diet accurately characterizes prehistoric subsistence behavior. Unfortunately, direct archaeological tests of theoretical predictions are often limited by preservational biases and the limits of inferential techniques. It is, for example, possible to identify the root crops in Classic Taino gardens from ethnohistorical sources, but these cultigens are not easily distinguished in archaeological deposits, and their measurement is limited to that of presence or absence rather than of proportional contribution.

To some degree the problem of preservational biases can be circumvented through osteochemical analyses. Stable isotope and trace-element methods provide the means for evaluating prehistoric consumption practices in particular instances. These techniques are not sufficient, however, to distinguish between every individual food type in the diet, and we must therefore limit our interpretations to distinctions between food groups. In this regard, osteochemical techniques do not provide a direct reconstruction of diet in the sense that a diet is the sum of contributions from individual food types. Rather, osteochemical techniques identify consumption profiles that reflect the relative contributions of different food groups.

Stable-isotope analysis provides an effective technique for tracing the flow of certain dietary components through food webs. The method is based on two observations. First, physical and chemical processes produce measurable differences in the stable carbon and nitrogen isotope ratios of different classes of plants (Bender 1968; Delwiche and Steyn 1970; B. Smith and Epstein 1971; Delwiche et al. 1979). Second, these differences in plant isotopic compositions are maintained or increased as carbon and nitrogen pass up food chains into the tissues of primary and higher-order consumers (fig. 6.6) (Miyake and Wada 1967; DeNiro and Epstein 1978, 1981; van der Merwe 1982).

The demonstration that the protein or collagen component of bone reflects the isotopic composition of a vertebrate's diet has led to the use of isotope ratios of archaeological bone collagen to analyze prehistoric diet (e.g., Vogel and van der Merwe 1977; Burleigh and Brothwell 1978; Bender, Baerris, and Steventon 1981; DeNiro and Epstein 1981; Sillen, Sealey, and van der Merwe 1989). Recent studies have demonstrated that the carbon (Tauber 1981; Chisholm, Nelson, and Schwartz 1982; Sealey and van der Merwe 1985) and nitrogen (Schoeninger, DeNiro, and Tauber 1983) isotopic compositions of marine and terrestrial food sources are often sufficiently different to allow their relative contributions to prehistoric human diets to be estimated from the corresponding isotope ratio in bone collagen.

Lucayan Diet

The Lucayans practiced a mixed economy of root-crop horticulture and hunting-fishing-collecting (Sears and Sullivan 1978). The components

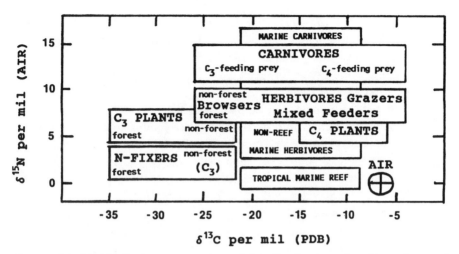

FIGURE 6.6. An idealized representation of the distribution of stable carbon and nitrogen isotopes in terrestrial and marine environments. Courtesy of Stanley Ambrose.

of their diet have been identified from historic reports and from the analysis of excavated faunal and botanical samples. Included in their diet was cultivated roots and tubers, maize, terrestrial animals, marine fishes, and marine mollusks (Fewkes 1907; Rouse 1948; Wing 1969; Sullivan 1981; Wing and Reitz 1982; Wing and Scudder 1983; Keegan 1986a). Maize was apparently a late introduction and may have been the focus of intensification in the Greater Antilles at the time of Spanish contact (Keegan 1987; cf. Lathrap 1987).

The first task in reconstructing prehistoric diets involves compiling a list of the plants and animals that were consumed. Since the majority of historic reports described Taino subsistence in the Greater Antilles, the working hypothesis is that the Lucayan menu corresponded in general, if not in detail, with that described for the Antillean Tainos. This hypothesis, along with the accuracy of the ethnohistoric reports, has been and will continue to be tested by collecting archaeological documentation.

The Spanish chroniclers reported that manioc (*Manihot esculenta*), sweet potato (*Ipomoea batatas*), yautía or cocoyam (*Xanthosoma* sp.), arrowroot (*Maranta* sp.), llerén (*Calathea allovia*), yampee (*Dioscorea* sp.), peanut (*Arachis hypogaea*), maize (*Zea mays*), beans (*Phaseolaris* spp.), cucurbits (*Cucurbita* spp.), and a variety of fruit trees were cultivated by the

Tainos (Fewkes 1907; Rouse 1948; Sauer 1966; Guarch 1974). Manioc was
the staple crop and was intensively cultivated on mounds at contact
(Sturtevant 1969). Maize is reported as having been grown for roasting
ears and to some extent for bread grain, but it was not a major foodstuff
(Sauer 1966; Keegan 1987).

As is typical of most islands, the Bahamas have a depauperate terrestrial fauna. Indigenous terrestrial animals are limited to a small rodent,
the hutia (*Geocapromys* sp.), rock iguana (*Cyclura carinata*), a variety of
small reptiles (e.g., *Anolis* sp.), land crabs (*Cardisoma* sp., *Gecarchinus*
sp.), and a variety of birds (Wing 1969; Sullivan 1981; Wing and Reitz
1982; Wing and Scudder 1983). The Tainos kept domesticated Muscovy
ducks (*Cairina moschata*) and dogs (*Canis familiaris*), although only the
latter are reported ethnohistorically and have been identified in Bahamian archaeological deposits (Sauer 1966; Sullivan 1981; Wing and Scudder
1983).

The analysis of Lesser and Greater Antillean archaeological deposits
has indicated that there was an early emphasis on terrestrial prey (especially land crabs), which was followed by a rapid and almost complete
shift to marine sources of animal protein (Carbone 1980b; Goodwin 1980;
Wing and Scudder 1980; A. Jones 1985; Keegan 1989d). Because the majority of known Lucayan sites are coastal and apparently date to the terminal period (post–A.D. 1200), there is presently no empirical evidence for
a similar shift in Bahamian diet. The four Lucayan sites with analyzed
fauna have maximum terrestrial biomass per maximum total vertebrate
biomass estimates of less than 12 percent. In other words, less than 12
percent of the meat in their diet came from land animals. Iguana and land
crabs were the most common land animals, with combined totals that
comprise about 9 percent of the maximum total vertebrate biomass (fig.
6.7) (Wing 1969; Wing and Scudder 1983). In sum, about 75 percent of the
terrestrial biomass came from Iguanidae and land crabs; this leaves only
25 percent of terrestrial biomass, which comprises less than 3 percent of
the total animal biomass, to be accounted for by all other land animals.
The very minor position of these other animals in the diet indicates that
they would not have a significant impact on the isotopic composition of
human bone collagen.

The main component of prehistoric Antillean vertebrate faunal assemblages is marine fishes (Wing and Reitz 1982). In the Bahamas, marine
fishes account for more than 80 percent of the estimated maximum vertebrate biomass in the four sites with analyzed assemblages (Wing 1969;

FIGURE 6.7. Iguana. After Oviedo 1547.

Sullivan 1981; Wing and Scudder 1983; Keegan 1986a). With very few exceptions these fishes have diets characterized by the seagrass/coral reef food chain (i.e., ^{13}C enrichment and nitrogen fixation at the base of the food chain).

In addition to fishes, several large aquatic animals have also been identified in Antillean sites. These include marine turtles (Chelonidae), porpoise (Delphinidae), West Indian monk seal (*Monachus tropicalis*), and manatee (*Trichechus manatus*) (Wing and Reitz 1982). Of these animals only the manatee has not been identified in Bahamian sites, and although present, the others occur at such low frequencies that their contributions to diet must be regarded as inconsequential with regard to isotopic analysis (Sullivan 1981; Wing and Reitz 1982; Wing and Scudder 1983). The lack of evidence for marine turtle use is especially surprising, and it may reflect inadequate sampling of prehistoric faunal assemblages.

The final category of subsistence remains is marine mollusks. Molluscan shell is the most abundant refuse in prehistoric sites in terms of both volume and mass (Sullivan 1981). Despite this abundance, molluscan shell represents relatively small edible packages.

In summary, Lucayan diet can be described as consisting of inputs from five general sources: cultivated roots and tubers, maize, terrestrial animals, marine fishes, and marine mollusks. These foods were distributed in three habitats: the forest, the coastal strip, and the sea.

Terrestrial Habitat

The main component of the forest habitat was gardens. These were probably prepared in coastal accumulations of humic-enriched sandy soil and would have followed the pattern of other tropical gardens (e.g., Ruddle 1974; Johnson 1983). Gardens provided a stable patch whose output could be modified in response to changing needs. Root-crop horticulture provides high total and marginal rates of return. Average yields of manioc in Brazil are reported as 14.2 million calories per hectare (Roosevelt 1980: table 1). Using a conservative estimate of human caloric needs (2700 calories per day), 14 adults could have been supported on one hectare of land. The availability of calories in other foods with higher net return rates would have precluded complete reliance on manioc production.

Manioc does not require fertile soils for efficient tuber production, so a single plot can be cultivated for many years. Yields from long-term manioc gardens can be increased by intercropping other cultigens (e.g., sweet potatoes, cocoyams). These crops do not interfere with the growth of manioc plants, they increase yields per hectare for the additional investment of planting and harvesting, they aid in preventing weed growth, and they fill areas that would otherwise go unused (Ruddle 1974; Keegan 1986b). It is likely that the initial colonists planted small gardens with a diversity of crops.

Garden size would have been set by caloric returns from manioc. As population increased, garden size would have increased, and other cultigens would have been added. Long-term use of a single plot of land is not practiced in the tropical forest today because protein requirements also are met through garden production and protein-producing cultigens usually cannot be grown on a single plot more than one or two years (Carneiro 1960, 1961; Johnson 1983; Keegan 1986b).

The principal shortcoming of manioc is its low protein content (Roosevelt 1980). Because human nutritional requirements cannot be satisfied by manioc alone, other sources of protein had to be sought. In addition to the animal protein sources discussed below, a number of cultigens could have been added to the garden as protein supplements (e.g., maize, beans, groundnuts). These cultigens are more expensive in terms of harvesting and processing, they contribute to a more rapid exhaustion of garden soils, and they are only available during specific seasons.

Maize is the most cost efficient of the high protein cultigens. From Johnson's (1983) studies it was estimated that maize has a marginal return rate of 20 grams of protein per hour of labor (Keegan 1986b). This return rate is higher than that for many other Lucayan foods, which would have promoted its acceptance when it became available after about A.D. 1200 (Keegan 1987). The disadvantages of maize production are the plant's need for fertile soils, its availability during only one season of the year, and the high cost of storing and processing maize when it is grown for use throughout the year. Thus, maize is only a partial solution to the problem of protein production.

Marginal return rates for animal species that inhabit the forest favor their use over horticulture. These animals could not, however, satisfy total needs. Their combined densities are equivalent to 1,861,950 calories per hectare, which could support only two individuals for a year if every animal was captured, an extremely unlikely occurrence. In economic terms, intensive use would rapidly reduce the frequency of encounters (i.e., animals would not be seen very often) with the result being a decline in the average return rate to a level below the marginal rate for other food sources (including horticulture). When this decline reached that level, those other foods would be added to the diet (Winterhalder and Smith 1981; E. Smith 1983). For the Lucayans, this other source of protein was the sea.

The inference from the economic model is that terrestrial animals were pursued whenever they were encountered. It is probable that game was taken in or near gardens (Linares 1976) and during visits to the coast. The forest is a difficult patch to traverse, and hunting trips in the forest were probably infrequent, especially after the decline of initially high prey densities. Since all of these small game were regular visitors to the coastal strip, the most efficient strategy would be to forage in this area. Travel along the coast is less difficult, and other food sources would also have been encountered (e.g., wild plants, littoral mollusks).

The one exception to the forest hunting proscription is land crabs, which congregate in low areas that provide for moist burrows. These locations could be identified, and hunting could be accomplished with guaranteed results. But even land crabs can be taken on the coastal strip, especially when they congregate for mating (Gifford 1962; deFrance 1988).

Coastal Habitat

The coastal strip is comprised of the beach patch and the rocky intertidal patch, and it also provides access to marine habitats. The beach patch was the site of seasonal monk seal aggregations, turtle nesting grounds, and the accidental beaching of cetaceans. In addition, terrestrial animals frequent this patch. Because settlements were located on the coast, the Lucayans were in a position to monitor activities on the beach.

The highest average return rate was available in the beach patch, although the highest return species were not available in all locations (e.g., green turtles, monk seals, and cetaceans). Turtles would have been available from April to July, and monk seals for about six weeks centered on December. Both should have been the focus of procurement efforts during their seasonal abundances.

The rocky intertidal patch supports dense aggregations of West Indian top shells, nerites, and chitons. Top shells have a relatively high net return rate. However, the use of top shells is limited by two factors. Rocky intertidal zones are small, averaging less than 3 meters wide, and they are irregularly distributed. These snails also are easily exploited and would have rapidly disappeared following the start of human predation. The other common littoral mollusks have lower return rates. These low values suggest that they were exploited during periods of food shortage. In any case, chitons and nerites should have been among the last items added to the diet. The return rates for marine mollusks were estimated in experimental studies described in detail elsewhere (Keegan 1985).

Marine Habitat

The marine environment is comprised of a tidal flat patch and a reef patch. The tidal flat patch can be further divided by procurement strategies into infaunal mollusk collecting (i.e., in the mud/sand substrate), epifaunal mollusk collecting (i.e., on the substrate), and fishing.

The Codakia clam, *Codakia orbicularis*, is the most commonly used infaunal mollusk species. The clams occur at high densities beneath shallow grass flats and would have provided a stable resource supply (see

Botkin 1980). In terms of weight, Codakia provided a more significant source of food than did intertidal mollusks (Sullivan 1981; Rose 1982). However, Codakia has low net return rates of both calories and protein, which raises the question of why these clams were eaten. One possibility is that these rates have been underestimated. For instance, a study of bivalve collecting in Australia indicated a caloric return rate that is twice that estimated for *Codakia orbicularis* (Meehan 1977). Historic evidence presented below suggests that even if the return rates were underestimated, the ranking relative to other food items is accurate. Codakia should therefore have been one of the last items added to the diet.

The epifaunal gastropod, *Strombus gigas*, is the highest ranked marine resource. It is available at relatively high densities on shallow grass flats and was a significant component of the diet. The high return rates indicate that *Strombus gigas* was in the initial optimal diet. Foraging trips over the shallow grass flats would have also led to encounters with marine fishes (e.g., bonefish).

The net return rate for fishes has been calculated as an average for all fishing strategies. Higher returns could have been obtained by pursuing particular strategies, such as the capture of fishes encountered during *Strombus gigas* collecting trips, but present evidence is not sufficient to discriminate the return rates for alternative strategies (Johannes 1981; Keegan 1982c, 1986a; Kirch 1982). The average values for all fishing strategies place fishing just below rock iguana in the ranking of protein returns (Keegan 1985).

Changes in Patch Selection and Diet Breadth

A number of questions arise in relation to the food quest. In which patch should food be sought first? How much time should be devoted to the food quest in each patch? When should new foods be added to the diet? More complete information on time allocation and predation rates is needed before a quantitative solution for patch-selection decisions can be calculated.

In the Lucayan case, a qualitative solution can be proposed because the net return rates for the second through eighth ranked resources are sufficiently similar to analyze dietary change in a diet-breadth framework (table 6.1). This approach is based on the identification of horticultural production as part of the original subsistence endowment, and on the dis-

TABLE 6.1 Return Rates and Rankings of Lucayan Food Types and Food Groups

Food source	Avg. weight/ individual (kg)	Kcal/ kg	Grams protein per kg	Handling time (hr/kg)	Pop. density (kg/ha)	E/h	gP/h	Rank E/h	Rank gP/h
Chelonia mydas (green turtle)	19	1,300	2.2	.026	2,609	50,000	84	1	1
Geocapromys sp. (hutia)	1.4	1,500	1.5	.12	21	12,500	13	2	5
Cardisoma sp. (land crab)	.2	1,500	1.5	.12	21	12,500	13	2	5
Strombus gigas (green conch)	.17	800	1.3	.09	850	8,889	14	4	4
Cyclura carinata (rock iguana)	.7	2,000	2.4	.24	15	8,333	10	5	6
Horticulture									
root crops (esp. *Manihot* sp.)	n/a	n/a	n/a	n/a	n/a	5,000	n/a	6	—
seed crops (esp. *Zea mays*)	n/a	n/a	n/a	n/a	n/a	n/a	20	—	2
Marine fishes (average)	.25	1,000	1.9	.22	n/a	4,545	9	7	7
Cittarium pica (top shell)	.035	800	1.3	.25	1,750	3,200	5	8	8
Chiton sp.	.005	800	1.3	.5	500	1,600	3	9	9
Codakia orbicularis (codakia clam)	.01	800	1.3	1.39	4,000	576	1	10	10
Nerita sp. (nerites)	.002	800	1.3	1.4	400	471	<1	11	11

E/h = calories per handling hour.
gP/h = grams of protein per handling hour.

tribution of higher ranked resources in forest, coastal, and marine patches. Furthermore, the location of permanent settlements on the coast would eliminate significant differences in the time invested in traveling between patches.

The logic behind the use of the diet-breadth model rather than the patch-selection model is as follows. Although the patch-selection model compares average returns from different patches (including transportation time) and the diet breadth model compares marginal returns to overall foraging efficiency, the marginal return rates calculated for Lucayan food sources include some time investments that are better considered as search time (search time is a component of average return calculations). This conflation of average and marginal returns is a result of the character of information available to calculate those rates. A second factor is that foraging from a central place should require similar investments in the time required to travel between patches. The high-ranked items in the Lucayan diet all have population densities that would have been rapidly depleted after the start of human predation. This reduction of animal densities would produce a reduction in the average return rates. Since the marginal rate for high-ranked items are similar, as is the time invested in traveling between patches, the marginal return rates should approximate the long-term decision-making problem. In other words, foraging decisions can be modeled as reflecting a selection between habitats based solely on short-term differences in resource distributions in each of the patches. This type of patch selection is so fine-grained (homogeneous) that it closely resembles and even operates like the environment characterized by the diet-breadth model.

The diet-breadth model predicts that diet breadth will be expanded (i.e., items added to the diet) when the marginal return rate for a resource is equal to the average return rate for all higher-ranked resources. Because manioc cultivation was practiced when the Bahama archipelago was colonized, the higher-ranked resources would also have been in the original optimal set (i.e., hutia, land crabs, queen conch, and rock iguana). This analysis suggests that despite their current absence in archaeological samples, green turtles and monk seals would have been captured during their seasonal availabilities. The food items mentioned above should have provided a diet sufficient to preclude the need to eat any other foods. One qualification to this conclusion is that high-ranked fishes were probably pursued when encountered during foraging on the tidal flats (e.g., bonefish).

Terrestrial animals in the Bahamas are susceptible to overexploitation. Their availability would have rapidly declined after a short period of intense predation and as human population growth increased the demand for these foods. The first response would be migration to unexploited areas. The rapid decline in high-ranked terrestrial animals would have encouraged the rapid expansion of people to unoccupied islands. When new areas were no longer available, then the intensification of foraging in the marine habitat should have occurred.

The redistribution of population was no longer a cost-efficient option when the presence of other settlements prevented people from moving into pristine areas. When such social circumscription occurred, the currency demands had to be satisfied in the vicinity of the village over a longer period of time. In response to the combined effects of increased demand due to population growth and declining returns due to long-term exploitation, the intensification of production would focus on only two options: increased use of marine habitats and changes in garden breadth. The total contribution of land animals would have continued to decline as human population numbers increased. In marine habitats *Strombus gigas* would have been the initial focus, followed by fishes, and ending with the highest-ranked littoral mollusc, *Cittarium pica*. But West Indian top shells, *Cittarium pica*, would have also been rapidly exhausted in areas of human settlement.

During the final phase, the lowest-ranked foods would have been added in turn (i.e., nerites, chitons, and Codakia). *Strombus gigas* would have been sought at more distant locations, and a variety of more intensive fishing strategies would have been introduced. It is likely that fish traps were introduced early in this phase as the availability of visible, diurnal species such as bonefish declined and as fishes had to be sought at more distant locations such as the barrier coral reef. Horticultural production would have been intensified through the addition of beans, groundnuts, and maize, all of which are high protein- and oil-producing cultigens. Fields may have been fallowed for shorter lengths of time, although the sandy soils may have supported production for longer periods than was possible on other tropical soils (as in the Yucatan Peninsula, Mexico; Roosevelt 1980). Nitrogen-fixing legumes would have helped to maintain soil fertility.

The preceding evidence can be divided into three discrete diets. An initial diet composed of root crops, land animals, and a few high-ranked marine species was followed by a second diet that included the consumption of more marine foods, a continuing contribution from root crops, and a precipitous decline in the contribution from land animals. In the third diet, land animals were reduced to a minor level of use, marine production was further intensified, and horticulture was expanded to include higher-cost cultigens, such as maize and beans, which provided higher total protein returns from the garden. It is this final pattern that is evident in the Lucayan faunal samples that have been analyzed to date (Sullivan 1981; Wing and Reitz 1982; Wing and Scudder 1983).

A significant question that is difficult for archaeologists to answer concerns the relative contributions of plants and animals to the diet. The hard structures of animals favor their preservation in archaeological deposits, and even when plant remains are preserved it cannot be determined what quantity of the plant was being consumed. Given the high caloric productivity of manioc (Roosevelt 1980) and the higher ranking of the marginal caloric return rate from horticultural production in comparison to marine fishes, it is reasonable to expect that cultigens comprised at least 50 percent of the Lucayan diet (Keegan 1986b, 1989d). Ethnographic reports of similar tropical horticulturalists indicate that cultivated plants comprise 50 to 95 percent of the diet (Keegan and DeNiro 1988).

Stable-Isotope Analysis of Consumption

The three diets just described were proposed on the basis of data gathered from ethnographic analogy, ethnohistoric reports, ethnobiological analyses, and formal economic models. To determine how well these diets reflect the actual subsistence practices of the Lucayans a different analytical technique must be used, for to do otherwise would be to engage in circular reasoning. Stable-isotope analysis provides such a technique (Ambrose 1987; Keegan 1989c).

Isotopes occur in nature as forms of an element with different atomic weights. Their weight differences are the result of different numbers of neutrons in their nucleus. Stable isotopes maintain their atomic weights through time, while unstable isotopes decay into another form. Carbon, for example, has three forms. Carbon 12 (12 neutrons) and carbon 13 (13 neutrons) are stable, while carbon 14 (14 neutrons) is unstable and decomposes at a known half-life. The decomposition of carbon 14 is what makes it useful for dating organic remains from the past.

Carbon and nitrogen are two of the main building blocks in organic tissues. They are obtained from the atmosphere by plants along a number of different biochemical pathways. Different classes of plants assimilate carbon and nitrogen isotopes in different ratios (Farnsworth et al. 1985: 102). Studies have shown that the different isotopic signatures of plants are maintained as one moves up the food chain.

The link that makes the analysis of prehistoric diets possible comes from the preservation of stable-isotope ratios in bone. It has been shown that the stable-isotopic composition of bone protein (collagen) reflects the isotopic composition of the animal's diet (DeNiro and Epstein 1978, 1981). Isotopic compositions are expressed in δ notation (see Chapter Appendix), which is the ratio of stable isotopes in a sample to those in a standard expressed in parts per thousand (per mil).

Isotopic Analysis of Diet

The isotopic analysis of bone collagen requires measurable differences in the isotopic compositions of food sources at the base of food webs. These differences are passed on to consumers, whose isotopic composition reflects the proportionate contribution of the different foods that were consumed. The human body uses a variety of biochemical reactions to convert foods into "flesh and blood." During these reactions the body may be selective in the isotope of an element that is used to construct a particular tissue. For instance, because carbon-13 is heavier than carbon-12 it moves more slowly in chemical reactions and therefore is used less easily. Isotope discrimination during the metabolic transformations of food into tissues is called fractionation. Fractionation produces measureable and constant differences between the foods that were consumed and the consumer's various tissues (e.g., fat, muscle, hide, bone, bone protein). These differences have been measured to define fractionation factors (DeNiro and Epstein 1978, 1981; van der Merwe 1982). Fractionation factors can then be used to translate the isotope ratios of preserved fossil materials (e.g., bone collagen, crab exoskeleton chitin) to the isotope ratios of the parts of an animal that were eaten. Thus, the isotopic composition of all food items can be expressed in comparable units.

The initial step in evaluating the Lucayan diets involved measuring or estimating the isotopic compositions of dietary items (table 6.2). This was accomplished in three ways. First, edible parts of fishes, mollusks, and cultigens were measured directly. Second, values for the flesh of crabs were converted from measured exoskeleton chitin values (Schimmelmann 1985). Third, the isotopic compositions of flesh for terrestrial animals and for archaeological fishes were converted from bone collagen isotope ratios. The isotopic relationship of flesh to bone collagen was based on earlier reports for terrestrial animals and on measurements of both tissues in 17 modern fishes (DeNiro and Epstein 1978, 1981; van der Merwe 1982; Keegan and DeNiro 1988).

The second step in dietary reconstruction involved isotopic analysis of bone collagen from 17 Lucayan skeletons (table 6.3). These skeletons are from burials in caves and were not associated with materials that could be used to date them (Keegan 1982b; Keegan and DeNiro 1988). The isotopic composition of these individuals' diets were estimated as follows. Fractionation factors between human bone collagen and diet have not been measured directly, but indirect estimates in previous studies suggest a +5±1.0 per mil increase in $\delta^{13}C$ values and about a +2.5 per mil increase in $\delta^{15}N$ values for bone collagen relative to diet (Burleigh and Brothwell 1978; DeNiro and Epstein 1978, 1981; van der Merwe 1982; Sillen, Sealey, and van der Merwe 1989). These values were subtracted from the bone collagen values listed in table 6.3 to obtain the diet values plotted in fig-

T A B L E 6.2 $\delta^{13}C$ and $\delta^{15}N$ Values (in per Mil) of Plants and Animals that Contributed Directly or Indirectly to the Lucayan Diet

	$\delta^{13}C$	$\delta^{15}N$
Plankton	−22 to −16[a]	+0 to +6[b]
Autotrophic sulfur bacteria	−38 to −20[a]	n/a
Seagrasses		
Thalassia testudinum (turtle grass)	−6.2	+0.9
Syringodium filiforme (manatee grass)	−12.8	+2.0
Macroalgae	−28 to −9[a]	
Laurencia sp. (brown alga)	−15.7	+6.2
Laurencia sp.	−15.7	+6.1
Batophera sp. (green alga)	−5.8	+1.7
Halimeda sp. (calcareous green alga)	−12.0	+2.2
Unidentified encrusting red alga	−14.3	+2.3

(*continued*)

Table 6.2—*continued*

	$\delta^{13}C$	$\delta^{15}N$
Invertebrates		
Unidentified encrusting black sponge	−5.4	+3.9
Adocia carbonaria (sponge)	−15.0	+0.1
Chondrilla nucula (sponge)	−13.3	+5.2
Porites porites (finger coral)	−12.5	+3.7
Unidentified Serpulidae (worm)	−11.5	+4.8
Tripneustes esculentus (urchin)	−12.4	+3.8
T. esculentus	−4.5	+2.5
Diadema antillarium (black urchin)	−6.7	+2.3
Unidentified Holothuriidae (sea cucumber)	−9.3	+2.4
Unidentified Holothuriidae (sea cucumber)	−10.3	+5.0
Bittium varium (gastropod)	−13.0	+6.3
Atrina rigida (pelecypod)	−13.4	+6.3
Tellina listeri (pelecypod)	−9.8	+2.6
Nerita versicolor (littoral gastropod)	−5.7	+2.1
N. versicolor (gut contents)	−6.6	+1.0
N. versicolor	−7.8	+2.9
N. versicolor	−15.8	+3.3
Chiton squamosus (littoral gastropod)	−8.2	+3.3
C. squamosus (gut contents of above)	−8.0	+1.4
C. squamosus	−8.9	+4.1
C. squamosus	−8.9	+2.1
Strombus gigas (megagastropod)	−12.6	+2.1
S. gigas (gut contents of above)	−12.3	+1.3
Codakia orbicularis (pelecypod)	−22.3	+2.0
C. orbicularis	−23.8	+1.9
C. orbicularis	−22.9	+0.4
Decapods[c]		
Calinectes sapidus (blue crab)	−16.5	−4.0
Panulirus argus (spiny lobster)	−12.3	−5.7
Grapsus sp. (littoral crab)	−10.1	−6.0
Modern fish (from Grand Bahama)		
Haemulon flavolineatum (yellow grunt)	−10.5	+8.1
H. flavolineatum	−10.5	+7.7
H. flavolineatum	−10.9	+7.2
H. flavolineatum	−10.3	+8.2
H. flavolineatum	−10.5	+7.9
H. flavolineatum	−10.9	+7.2
H. album (margate)	−11.1	+6.9
H. parra (sailor's choice)	−10.8	+7.1
H. sciurus (blue-striped grunt)	−11.1	+7.0
Lutjanus mahogani (hog snapper)	−11.2	+6.2

(*continued*)

Table 6.2—*continued*

	$\delta^{13}C$	$\delta^{15}N$
L. griseus (gray snapper)	-9.9	+8.2
L. griseus	-15.7	+7.8
L. jocu (dog snapper)	-11.9	+7.8
L. synagris (lane snapper)	-10.1	+8.6
Epinephelus guttatus (Nassau grouper)	-13.0	+7.6
E. striatus (red hind)	-12.9	+7.3
Balistes vetula (queen triggerfish)	-11.6	+7.3
B. vetula	-11.8	+8.2
Holocentrus rufus (squirrelfish)	-11.1	+7.8
Ocyurus chrysurus (yellowtail)	-12.2	+7.1
Calamus bajonado (jolthead porgy)	-10.9	+6.0
Anisotremus virginicus (porkfish)	-13.2	+7.5
Caranx fuscus (blue runner jack)	-12.0	+7.5
Cephalopholis fulva (coney)	-12.9	+8.0
Priacanthus cruentatus (bigeye)	-15.1	+6.5
Hemiramphus sp. (halfbeak)	-16.2	+9.7
Hemiramphus sp.	-16.9	+9.6
Hemiramphus sp.	-15.4	+9.9
Hemiramphus sp.	-17.0	+9.3
Hemiramphus sp.	-16.5	+8.1
Hemiramphus sp.	-16.4	+9.9
Terrestrial animals[d]		
Geocapromys sp. (hutia)	-24.1	+4.1
Cyclura carinata (iguana)	-19.5	+6.0
Gecarchinus sp. (land crab)	-23.8	-2.3
Cultigens[e]		
Zea mays (maize)	-10.8	n/a
Z. mays	-10.1	+10.0
Dioscorea sp. (yam)	-25.1	+7.6
Dioscorea sp. (red yam)	-26.3	+3.7
Dioscorea sp. (white yam)	-27.0	+5.2
Dioscorea sp. (black yam)	-27.3	+2.8
Xanthosoma sp. (cocoyam)	-26.1	+4.3
Manihot esculenta (manioc, cassava)	-27.6	+2.4
Ipomaea batatas (sweet potato)	-25.7	+3.8
Colocasia esculenta (eddoe)	-24.4	+3.2

Source: Keegan and DeNiro 1988.

[a]From Fry et al. 1982.

[b]From Minagawa and Wada 1984.

[c]From Schimmelmann 1985.

[d]Measurements were made on bone collagen (hutia and iguana) and chiton (land crab).

[e]Not all cultigens were consumed prehistorically; values are presented to reflect the isotopic signatures of tropical cultigens.

TABLE 6.3 $\delta^{13}C$ and $\delta^{15}N$ Values (in per Mil) of Bone Collagen of
Lucayan Individuals from the Bahamas and a Saladoid
Individual from Puerto Rico

Acc. No.[a]	Location[b]	Sex/Age[c]	$\delta^{13}C$	$\delta^{15}N$
—	GB	U/A	−13.1	10.3
—	GB	U/A	−13.5	6.5
4683	AB	F/J	−15.7	8.6
4684	EL	M/A	−12.5	10.5
4685	EL	M/A	−12.3	10.0
4686	EL	M/A	−13.4	10.5
4682	RC	M/A	−10.7	10.8
4689	SS	M/A	−13.3	10.8
4690	SS	U/A	−15.9	9.8
4687	LI	F/A	−15.8	11.1
4692	CR	M/A	−13.2	10.6
4693	CR	F/A	−13.6	10.5
4694	CR	M/A	−14.1	11.9
4696	CR	F/A	−14.1	9.7
4698	CR	F/A	−13.9	10.2
—	PS	U/U	−10.8	8.9
—	PS	F/A	−9.6	8.3
—	Puerto Rico	U/U	−19.1	9.4

Source: Keegan and DeNiro 1988.

[a]Yale Peabody Museum accession numbers (see Keegan 1982b).

[b]Grand Bahama, GB; Great Abaco, AB; Rum Cay, RC; Long Island, LI; San Salvador, SS; Eleuthera, EL; Crooked Island, CR; and Providenciales, Turks and Caicos Islands, PS.

[c]Male, M; Female, F; Adult, A; Juvenile, J; Undetermined, U.

ure 6.8. These converted diet $\delta^{13}C$ and $\delta^{15}N$ values are used in the following analysis.

A fundamental question in isotopic studies concerns what is being measured. Although the investigator is attempting to measure *in vivo* values that characterize the animal's diet, the possibility exists that processes have altered the isotope ratios following the animal's death (Sillen, Sealey, and van der Merwe 1989). DeNiro (1985) has shown that prehistoric bone collagen samples that have atomic carbon-to-nitrogen (C/N) ratios in the range 2.9 to 3.6 (values that characterize collagen from fresh bone) retain their *in vivo* $\delta^{13}C$ and $\delta^{15}N$ values. The C/N ratios of the human collagen samples were calculated from the volumes of CO_2 and N_2 produced when the samples were combusted. The collagen samples prepared from prehistoric fish (table 6.2) and human bones (table 6.3) had

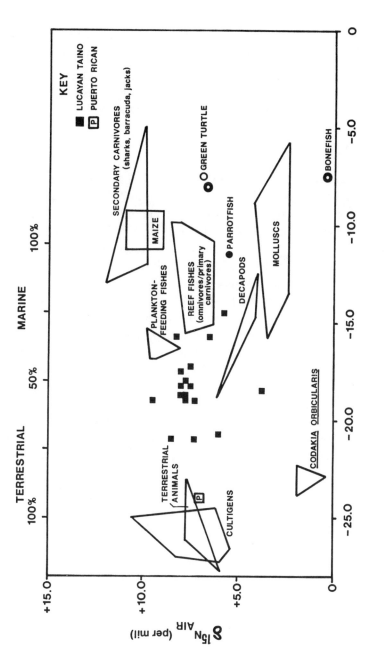

FIGURE 6.8. $\delta^{13}C$ and $\delta^{15}N$ values of the consumed portions of foods and of the diets of Lucayan individuals (data from Keegan and DeNiro 1988). Food values are represented by polygons for groups for which at least three specimens were sampled, in which case the polygons cover the extreme values, by a square for maize, in which case ±1 per mil to the mean $\delta^{13}C$ and $\delta^{15}N$ values reported in DeNiro and Hastorf (1985), and by points for cases in which only two specimens were analyzed.

C/N ratios between 3.0 and 3.5 and between 2.9 and 3.4, respectively. Thus, postmortem processes do not appear to have significantly altered the isotopic record of what these individuals ate.

Carbon Isotope Distributions

The Lucayan diet can be divided into marine and terrestrial components, a dichotomy also reflected in carbon isotope ratios. The marine organisms have $\delta^{13}C$ values that are 7 to 20 per mil less negative than those of the terrestrial foods. The distributions of ^{13}C values in marine and terrestrial foods reflect differences in the $\delta^{13}C$ values at the base of the food chains in the two environments, in that terrestrial plants utilizing the C_3 photosynthetic mode have more negative $\delta^{13}C$ values than seagrasses and corals (Bender 1971; Fry et al. 1982; Minagawa and Wada 1984).

Several exceptions to the general pattern are apparent (fig. 6.8). These exceptions can be attributed to three additional carbon pathways: the C_4 photosynthetic pathway used by maize (Bender 1971); the particulate organic carbon of marine phytoplankton, which produced the more negative values for plankton-feeding fishes (Fry and Sherr 1984); and the contribution of carbon from autotrophic sulphur bacteria to the infaunal pelecypod *Codakia orbicularis* (Fry and Sherr 1984; Berg et al. 1985). Zooplankton-feeding fishes merit attention as a potential dietary source of more negative $\delta^{13}C$ values, but they are eliminated from the present analysis because they comprise less than 0.6 percent of the estimated total vertebrate biomass in Lucayan archaeological faunal assemblages (Wing 1969; Wing and Scudder 1983). Although maize and *Codakia orbicularis* have $\delta^{13}C$ values that run counter to the significant difference between marine and terrestrial food groups, their effects on diet $\delta^{13}C$ would have, to some extent, canceled one another.

A preliminary reconstruction of the Lucayan diet can be obtained by calculating the diet $\delta^{13}C$ values that would result from eating different combinations of marine (mollusks, reef fishes) and terrestrial foods. The marine group has an average $\delta^{13}C$ of –11 per mil, while the terrestrial group has an average $\delta^{13}C$ value of –25 per mil. Using these averages, the diet $\delta^{13}C$ values calculated for the Lucayan individuals can be interpreted. For instance, a diet $\delta^{13}C$ value of –11 per mil would suggest complete reliance on marine foods, a diet $\delta^{13}C$ value of –25 per mil would suggest complete reliance on terrestrial foods, and a diet $\delta^{13}C$ value of –18 per mil would suggest equal contributions from both. These ideal consumption combinations are plotted along the upper margin of figure 6.8. Based on an estimated ±1 per mil uncertainty in the fractionation factor between diet and bone collagen, the diets of Lucayan individuals range from an estimated 71±7 percent reliance on terrestrial foods (-21.0 per mil) to an estimated maximum of 74±7 percent reliance on marine foods (-14.6 per mil) (fig. 6.8).

One individual from the Hacienda Grande site, an initial period Saladoid settlement on Puerto Rico (Period II, A.D. 100–600; see Rouse 1986), was included to aid in the interpretation of the Lucayan samples. The sample was included because it represents the earliest phase in the Island Arawak expansion that reached the Bahamas by A.D. 700. Furthermore, a similar set of food items was available to both Puerto Rican and Bahamian populations (Fewkes 1907; Rouse 1948; Keegan 1987). In addition, similar environmental characteristics of the islands in the northern Caribbean support the assumption that the isotopic compositions of food items were equivalent.

The Puerto Rican individual exhibits a 93±7 percent reliance on terrestrial foods (diet $\delta^{13}C$ value of -24.0 per mil). This value is consistent with archaeological reconstructions of the initial Saladoid diet as consisting of cultivated tubers and land crabs with a very minor contribution from the marine environment (Goodwin 1980; Jones 1985). Following the initial period of settlement, archaeological evidence documents a shift from inland to coastal settlement locations with a corresponding increase in the consumption of marine food items. This shift has been interpreted as reflecting the optimal path of diet-breadth expansion (Keegan 1989d). As discussed above, a similar but less pronounced shift has been proposed for the Lucayans.

If the above interpretation is correct, the range in $\delta^{13}C$ values estimated for the diets of Lucayan individuals can be interpreted as reflecting a shift in consumption practices through time. The three most negative $\delta^{13}C$ values (all around -20 per mil) might characterize the first of the proposed diets, in which land animals were abundant and only the highest-ranked marine organisms were consumed. The second dietary pattern would account for the majority of Lucayan individuals ($n=11$), whose diet $\delta^{13}C$ values of -18.1±1 per mil can be accounted for by about equal contributions from marine and terrestrial sources. The remaining three individuals exhibit ideal consumption patterns in the 66 to 74±7 percent marine range (diet $\delta^{13}C$ values of $-15.2\pm.6$ per mil). Such a strong reliance on marine foods is unlikely because of the relatively higher costs of marine fishing and collecting in relation to horticulture (Keegan 1989d). An alternative interpretation is that the higher $\delta^{13}C$ values indicate that maize was being consumed in substantial quantities during at least part of the year.

The isotopic analysis confirms the presence of the three proposed diets. A temporal dimension is imputed as a hypothesis to account for the variability observed in the bone collagen isotopic values of Lucayan individuals and is the subject of ongoing research. For the present, the isotopic analysis stands as an indication of differences in food consumption practices among Lucayans.

Nitrogen Isotope Distributions

Nitrogen isotope values are more difficult to interpret because the ranges for marine and terrestrial food sources overlap (Keegan and DeNiro 1988). The nitrogen isotope values of bone collagen may, however, provide a means for refining carbon isotope analyses.

The average $\delta^{15}N$ values for the various food sources have been calculated from the values listed in table 6.2 as: +7.5 per mil for land animals; +7 per mil for cultivated roots and tubers; +10 per mil for maize (DeNiro and Hastorf 1985); +1.5 per mil for *Codakia orbicularis*; +3 per mil for marine mollusks; +7.5 per mil for reef fishes; +9.5 per mil for secondary carnivores; and greater than +12 per mil for pelagic fishes and marine mammals (Schoeninger and DeNiro 1984). The distribution of nitrogen isotope values indicates that collagen $\delta^{15}N$ values cannot be used to distinguish the contributions of terrestrial animals, cultivated roots and tubers, maize, and reef fishes in the Lucayan diet because consumption of each of these foods would produce very similar $\delta^{15}N$ values, with an average value of about +8 per mil. When the $\delta15N$ values of Lucayan diets as estimated from bone collagen values are compared to this average, with a range of ±1 per mil allowed to account for the variability in the $\delta^{15}N$ value for diet estimated in this way (DeNiro and Epstein 1981), 76 percent of the individuals ($n=13$) fall within this range.

Deviations from this average diet $\delta^{15}N$ value of $+8\pm1$ per mil can be explained with reference to the lower $\delta^{15}N$ values of mollusks and the higher $\delta^{15}N$ values of pelagic fishes and marine mammals relative to other dietary components. One individual from Crooked Island (#4694, table 6.3) has a diet $\delta^{15}N$ value of +9.4 per mil, which suggests that animals with relatively higher $\delta^{15}N$ values comprised a larger component of his diet and that mollusks made a relatively minor contribution. The location of this burial in an area where the barrier coral reef approaches the shore and where the reef flat has a restricted range places this individual in the vicinity of marine habitats that are the most likely sources of such a dietary combination (Keegan 1982c, 1986a). The high diet $\delta^{15}N$ value for this individual also raises the possibility that pelagic fishes and marine mammals provided a substantial portion of the diet for some Lucayans.

The three individuals with diet $\delta^{15}N$ values that are lower than the average diet $\delta^{15}N$ range probably reflect a stronger reliance on mollusks, and perhaps a corresponding reduction in the consumption of higher-order carnivorous fishes than the majority of the samples. All three of these individuals are from islands with extensive *Thalassia* seagrass meadows (Grand Bahama Island and Great Abaco on the Little Bahama Bank, and Providenciales on the Caicos Bank). These shallow banks provide access to extensive mollusc populations while restricting access to reef-associated fishes (Wing and Reitz 1982; Wing and Scudder, 1983; Keegan 1986a). Two of the individuals are less than 0.6 per mil below the average range, which suggests a very minor increase in mollusc consumption on the order of less than 10 percent of total consumption. The other is 2.4 per mil below the average range which suggests a far greater reliance on mollusks and possibly other marine invertebrates, approaching 40 percent of the diet.

Summary and Conclusions

The preceding examination of Lucayan diet has drawn together evidence from a variety of sources. The economic model presented at the beginning of this chapter provided the logical structure in which the data were ordered. On a general level, the empirical findings are consistent with the expectations derived from the formal model. There is every reason to believe that the Lucayans were efficient, even optimal, horticulturalists (Keegan 1986b).

At the level of realism, the Lucayan diet can be described as follows. As is the case with modern tropical horticulturalists, life revolved around garden cycles (Malinowski 1978; Johnson 1983). Garden plots of about one hectare per household were cleared at regular, possibly annual intervals. Clearing involved the use of stone axes imported from the Greater Antilles, shell tools, or both to slash brush, fell trees, and girdle large trees so they would drop their leaves. After clearing, the brush was left to dry and was then burned, releasing the nutrients stored in the vegetation.

Planting was done with a sharpened digging stick. Manioc was planted in small mounds of loose earth in the Greater Antilles; similar *montones* may have been used in the Bahamas. The gardens were weeded, mature crops harvested, and replantings were made on a continuous basis until the garden was abandoned. Unlike temperate gardens, which die in the winter, tropical gardens can be maintained for years. After a few years, garden production is reduced to certain tree crops, and new gardens must be prepared. The old garden is left to fallow until covered by at least secondary forest, at which time it may again be cleared. The importance of this cycle is represented in the court at site MC-6, which has stones aligned to chart the summer solstice along with the risings of stars that were important in Native American agricultural calendars (Sullivan 1981).

The Lucayans probably cultivated as many as 50 different plants. These cultigens included numerous varieties of sweet and bitter manioc, sweet potatoes, cocoyams, beans, gourds, chili peppers, corn, cotton, tobacco, bixa, genip, groundnuts, guava, and papaya (Sturtevant 1961; Keegan 1987). The carbonized remains of corn, chili peppers, palm fruits, and an unidentified tuber are among the plant remains identified in West Indian sites (Lee Newsom, personal communication 1990). A variety of noncultivated plants would have also been eaten, for example, sea grapes and pigeon plums (Sullivan 1981).

In addition to garden plots there were house gardens around the dwellings. House gardens contained new varieties of cultigens, herbs and spices, medicinal and narcotic plants, vegetable dyes, fruit trees, and other cultigens that require special attention or are needed frequently in small quantities (Lathrap 1977, 1987).

Lucayan cultigens grew and matured at different rates. In this way the Lucayan diet was continuously changing with the seasons. Sweet manioc and the other root crops would have been available throughout the year. Boiling was the usual method of cooking. Bitter manioc, so called because it contains toxic levels of cyanide, had to be grated and squeezed. The juice releases its toxins when cooked so it is used as a base for stews, pepper pot, and manioc beer. The pulp is dried for use as starch (flour) or is toasted to make farina. The reward for so much additional processing effort is the only food in the Lucayan diet that could be stored for long periods of time (up to six months). Water is added to the starch to make pancakelike cassava bread, which is baked on large, round, pottery griddles. The stable-isotope analysis indicates that at least 50 percent of the diet came from plant foods (Keegan and DeNiro 1988).

A meal would not have been complete unless it contained meat. Marine turtles, which would have been highly prized for their meat and eggs, were available seasonally. The few land animals (hutia, iguana, and crabs) were also highly prized but were available in limited quantities. The marine environment provided a variety of vertebrates and invertebrates. Parrotfish, grouper, snapper, bonefish, queen conch, urchins, nerites, chitons, and Codakia clams are all found in substantial numbers in Lucayan sites (Wing and Reitz 1982; Wing and Scudder 1983). Finally, it is possible that grubs and other insects were eaten (see Johnson and Baksh 1987).

Meats were roasted in the fire or were barbecued (*barbecue* is derived from a Taino word). Sullivan (1981) has suggested that the Lucayans used another traditional form of tropical forest cooking called the "pepper pot". Pepper pots are stews made from bitter manioc juice that is kept simmering over a low fire for days, with meats and vegetables added to replenish the pot. The large thick clay pots that the Lucayans made are well suited to this type of food preparation.

With regard to the number of different ways individuals could satisfy their hunger, the Bahamas are noteworthy for the surfeit of options. It is difficult to imagine that anyone ever went hungry, and the preliminary examination of human skeletal remains indicates that the Lucayans enjoyed good health and nutrition (Keegan 1982b). They certainly did not suffer from the nutritional and diet-related disorders of other prehistoric horticulturalists in the West Indies (Budinoff 1987) or elsewhere (Cohen and Armelagos 1984). Yet the Lucayans' selectiveness in their food choices proves that they were careful consumers who based their subsistence practices on the cost-efficient capture of nutritional currencies.

Appendix

Following sample preparation, all of the samples are combusted (Stump and Frazer, 1973; Northfelt, DeNiro, and Epstein 1981). The volumes and

isotopic ratios of the resulting CO_2 and N_2 are then determined by ma-
nometry and mass spectrometry respectively. The volumes of CO_2 and N_2
are used to calculate C/N ratios (DeNiro 1985). The isotope ratios measured by mass spectrometry relate the sample to a standard and are expressed in the δ notation:

$$\delta^{13}C = \left[\frac{(^{13}C/^{12}C)_{sample}}{(^{13}C/^{12}C)_{standard}} - 1 \right] \times 1000 \; 0/00$$

$$\delta^{15}N = \left[\frac{(^{15}N/^{14}N)_{sample}}{(^{15}N/^{14}N)_{standard}} - 1 \right] \times 1000 \; 0/00$$

with Peedee belemnite (PDB) carbonate from South Carolina used as the
$\delta^{13}C$ standard and atmospheric nitrogen (AIR) as the $\delta^{15}N$ standard.

The precision of the measurements is evaluated through the replicate
analysis of a single sample performed intermittently throughout the study.
The gas collection and measurement techniques developed by DeNiro
have a precision of measurement of +.2 0/00 for $\delta^{13}C$ and +.4 0/00 for $\delta^{15}N$
values (DeNiro and Epstein, 1981; Schoeninger and DeNiro, 1984).

7

Population and Procreation:
Lucayan Demography

Population movements and migrations figure prominently in all culture histories, but nowhere have questions concerning population movements been more heatedly contested than in studies of lowland South America and the West Indies (Steward 1947; Meggers and Evans 1957, 1983; Ford 1969; Lathrap 1970; Rouse 1986, 1989b). Moreover, culture historical sequences in the region have alternated between migration and local development as the sufficient explanation (Meggers 1954; Carneiro 1960, 1961; Lathrap 1970, 1987; Gross 1975; Roosevelt 1980; Rouse 1986; Roe 1989).

To a large degree previous explanations of demographic behavior have relied on oversimplified versions of population trends under varying conditions of resource supply (fig. 7.1). In this chapter a more formal model of population growth and dispersal is deduced from the Verhulst-Pearl logistic equation, the equation from which the concept of carrying capacity was originally borrowed. By using the logistic equation it is easier to integrate the evidence from settlement patterns and economic analysis described in previous chapters with evidence of population trends.

The model presented here was developed to explore the relationship between economy and demography, with this relationship examined at long-term and short-term time scales. Long-term changes in demand at the group level reflect the net balance of birth and death rates. A positive net increase in population numbers is often taken as the independent prime mover of cultural change (Cohen 1977; Johnson and Earle 1987). In

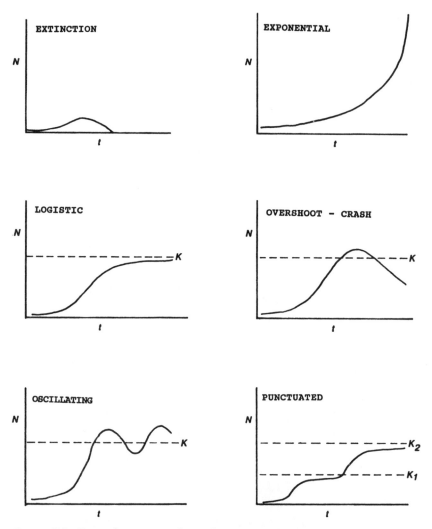

FIGURE 7.1. General patterns of population growth. Where N is population size, K is carrying capacity, and t is time.

the words of the classical economists, populations increased due to the "unbridled passion of the sexes" (Malthus 1959). This belief in the independence of reproduction assumes that offspring are produced without regard to their economic consequences.

More recent investigations have recovered ample evidence to the contrary. It is increasingly clear that people exert substantial control over their behavior such that reproduction (procreation) and production are interdependent (Cowgill 1975; Hassan 1981; Nardi 1981; Handwerker 1983). Along this line, demographic behavior is here viewed as the demand side of a supply/demand equilibrium. In sum, producing offspring is a reflection of the short-term economic potential for supporting additional offspring, and the factors that promote or constrain reproductive behavior are apparent in social relations that influence coital frequency and its timing relative to ovulation.

Short-term changes in demand include recruitment, or in-migration, and emigration. These behavioral responses to short-term production possibilities reflect attempts to balance economic return rates within a region. Recruitment should be apparent in the aggregation of population in a region or in evidence for alliance relations that are based on economic interdependence. An often cited example is exchange between areas with different sets of resources (Rathje 1971; Carneiro 1979). Emigration should be apparent in the wider distribution of population within a region and should reflect the integrative features of social organization (Davanzo 1981). Finally, household demand is manipulated with regard to the ratio of consumers to workers (Chayanov 1966; Tannenbaum 1984). Such manipulation should be apparent in changes in household size and in the number of households in an area.

This type of model building is useful for two purposes. First, since it is impossible to identify with certainty the first settlement in a region, population movements must be studied as the outcome of cultural processes. In turn, cultural processes must be described in simplified forms as specific relationships among variables (i.e., models). By developing models of how such processes are likely to have unfolded it is possible to generate testable hypotheses about past human behavior. Second, a logically integrated network of theories and models facilitates generalizations and comparative studies. These simplified versions of reality raise new questions, direct attention to variables that would otherwise be ignored, and improve our understanding of past cultures in ways that the empirical accumulation of knowledge can never achieve.

The initial colonization of the Bahamas was selected as an appropriate case for evaluating the utility of the population dispersal model. The model has been used to organize the largely circumstantial evidence that was available from previous studies (see chapter 3), and to identify additional data that were needed to reconstruct Taino population expansion. These included information on population distribution, described in chapter 4, and population size, discussed in this chapter.

This chapter begins with a detailed discussion of the population expansion model. In essence, the model describes population movement as falling along a continuum between the extremes of push and pull. On the one hand, people may find themselves pushed out of a region as pressure on the resource base increases. On the other, abundant resources in an area may attract colonists from other areas, even if those colonists are not under severe pressure where they are already living. The theoretical explication of these phenomena is important because the continuum between push and pull affects all human populations; it has proved essential in efforts to explain island colonization (Keegan and Diamond 1987; Siegel 1991).

Following the discussion of the model, the techniques used to estimate population numbers are discussed, beginning with a consideration of historical texts and their interpretation as a method for determining the size of West Indian populations at the time of European contact. Next, archaeological techniques for determining population size are discussed. Working from the contact-period population estimates generated with those techniques the discussion turns to the rate at which the population grew and the way in which the growing population distributed itself across the landscape.

Population Expansion Model

The Verhulst-Pearl Logistic Equation

Despite the possibility of an infinite number of equations that describe a process of density-dependent population growth, the Verhulst-Pearl logistic equation has survived as a central concept in population biology (Pianka 1974; Vandermeer 1981). The logistic equation has been known since the work of the Belgian mathematician P. F. Verhulst in the middle of the last century. It is a mechanical rate equation that describes the consumption of an unspecified fixed input. It is worth remembering that the equation is not inherently demographic; it also describes the rate at which a catalyst is consumed in a chemical reaction, the economic concept of diminishing returns (Hirshleifer 1980; Schultz 1981), and it recently has been used to describe the rate at which innovations are adopted (Rindos 1984; Braun 1987).

The logistic equation generates an S-shaped curve that describes population growth as beginning slowly as opportunities for growth become available, as gathering momentum as the power of population to grow exponentially when unimpeded is expressed, and as slowing down as the limits in resource availability are approached (fig. 7.2). This scenario recognizes that as population size increases, more of the finite resource base is allocated among existing members and fewer new members can be sustained throughout their lives. The result is a decline in the growth rate by the linear factor 1/K for every new individual. The population continues to grow until the growth rate equals zero (r=0) when population size (N) equals carrying capacity (K).

One simplification in the equation is the assumption that the relationship between population growth and resource capture is linear. This

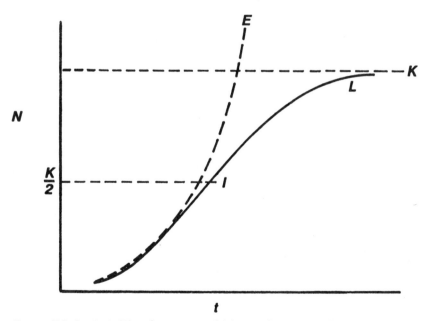

FIGURE 7.2. Logistic (L) and exponential (E) growth curves. Where N is population size, K is carrying capacity, t is time, and I is the inflection point in the curve (where $d/dN \times dN/dt = 0$).

assumption has been criticized as too simplistic (Pianka 1974:83–84; Freedman 1980). Although a fixed ratio between inputs and outputs may occur in the short run, economic studies that employ techniques such as linear-programming analysis have demonstrated that, due to averaging, such fixed relationships are unlikely to characterize long-term resource capture (Reidhead 1980:144; Johnson and Behrens 1982; Keegan 1986b). Because actual populations are likely to violate the linearity assumption, it is important that the logistic equation be restricted to understanding the general relationship between population growth and resource supply.

That caveat brings us to a consideration of the carrying capacity concept. Carrying capacity is defined as the theoretical maximum number of a species that can be supported in a habitat throughout their lives (Pianka 1974). As such it sets an absolute limit to the size of any population. The major problem with anthropological applications of the concept derives from a failure to recognize that carrying capacity is a constant that takes the place of food procurement and other economic variables in the logistic equation. The equation addresses the question, What is the pattern of population growth in a habitat of constant economic potential? This scenario involves the microeconomic conditions of inelastic supply and inelastic demand, where neither supply nor demand can be changed and which generate the S-shaped curve.

Most anthropologists view carrying capacity as susceptible to cultural manipulation and have reworked the concept in innumerable ways (Hayden 1975; Dewar 1984). Yet our understanding of the relationship between demography and economy will not be advanced by those post hoc justifications for a lack of conformity between actual and predicted carrying capacity. Carrying capacity must be viewed as a parameter of the more general logistic equation which can only be operationalized by developing lower-order models in which the relations between economic and demographic variables are specified (Orians 1980; Schultz 1981; Keegan, Johnson, and Earle 1985). The advantages of such formal models is that they require clarity of thought and that they are more easily falsified. The dispersal model described below is an example of a formal middle-level model, linking abstract concepts to empirical measures.

Equilibrium Points

When the logistic equation is plotted as a discrete model of population change, two equilibrium points can be identified (Vandermeer 1981). These points exist where the population density function, F(N(t)), crosses the 45° line at K and A (fig. 7.3). The former occurs when population density is equal to carrying capacity. This stable equilibrium point has been the subject of most population studies. The other equilibrium point, A, corresponds to the inflection point of the continuous logistic curve where the growth rate, r, changes from monotonically increasing to monotonically decreasing (where the second derivative equals zero: $d/dN \times dN/dt = 0$). Vandermeer (1981:10–11) notes that such use of both discrete and continuous models helps to clarify the equation's general meaning and behavior. It is interesting to note that the inflection point occurs at one-half of carrying capacity in the logistic equation. A number of anthropologists have noted that actual population sizes are often 40 to 60 percent of the average short-term estimate of carrying capacity (Birdsell 1957; Lee and De Vore 1968; Hassan 1981:166–167). These values have been interpreted as reflecting a population's conservatism with respect to long-term fluctuations in the resource base (Hayden 1975). An alternative explanation, discussed below, is that these values approximate an unstable, optimal equilibrium.

The equilibrium point A, which I have termed the *optimal equilibrium*, is asymptotically unstable (Vandermeer 1981; Sibley 1983). Populations can follow several trajectories from this point. First, the point may reflect

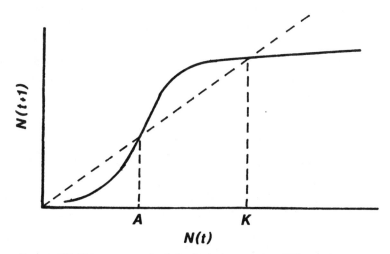

FIGURE 7.3. Discrete graph of the logistic equation. Where N is population size and t is time. Equilibrium points A and K exist where the dashed 45° line crosses the curve.

the critical density of an Allee effect: the population cannot grow and will eventually become extinct if it falls below this density. Second, above such a critical density the population may continue to grow at an exponential rate until it is subjected to density dependence and stabilizes at carrying capacity. This second trajectory is the long-term outcome of logistic growth.

Finally, when the population is able to regulate its density, the equilibrium point may reflect an optimal population density. This density is optimal with regard to the potential for further population increase because it occurs at the point at which density dependence first occurs. In other words, it defines the maximum potential increase in population numbers with respect to time (max dN/dt occurs when $d/dN \times dN/dt = 0$). The equilibrium point is unstable because it occurs at the point of maximum potential increase. Thus, the population will grow beyond the equilibrium point with every subsequent unit of time unless there is some mechanism for removing the excess population (Sibley 1983). Such is the dilemma of wildlife biologists who define this point as the maximum sustainable yield and then must determine what percentage of a population should be culled to maintain this equilibrium value (Pianka 1974).

When opportunities for dispersal are available, we would expect groups to have population sizes that oscillate around the equilibrium value. An increase in population numbers is promoted by the population-maximizing characteristics in effect before this point (i.e., density independence), while intragroup competition for resources (i.e., density dependence) would promote fissioning, dispersal, and the reduction of local group size to the equilibrium value after the point is reached. Furthermore, the shift from an unstable equilibrium to a stable equilibrium would be promoted by intergroup competition for resources within a region.

Implications of Equilibrium Analysis

The two equilibrium points can be viewed as reflecting the population values expected for r-selected and K-selected life-history strategies (MacArthur and Wilson 1967), an analogy that a number of archaeologists have found useful. The unstable equilibrium at A approximates the point at which density-dependent constraints initiate a divergence of the exponential and logistic curves (fig. 7.2). Up to this point the population is regulated largely by density-independent factors. Kirch (1984) has noted that the logistic equation assumes that density-dependent constraints are in effect even during this initial sequence of growth. These constraints, summed as the linear factor $1/K$, have a negligible effect on the growth rate when carrying capacity (K) is large relative to population size. The difference between true exponential growth and density-independent-logistic growth is minimal.

In an uncrowded environment natural selection favors growth rate via fecundity, early breeding, dispersal, rapid development, and small body size at the expense of greater sensitivity to environmental changes (Horn 1978:414). These characteristics tend to maximize the growth rate, r, so species that exhibit these characteristics have been called "r-selected" (MacArthur and Wilson 1967; Pianka 1974). Since r-selection should lead to the rapid filling up of uncrowded habitats, r-selected species typically are colonists who are successful at reaching habitats that other species find difficult to reach (e.g., islands), or are pioneers who rapidly occupy habitats that were vacated by environmental perturbations (Diamond 1977a, b).

The other extreme describes reproduction in a crowded environment in which density-dependent constraints act through competition to limit the maximum sustainable population in an area. Changes in the growth rate under these conditions are termed "K-selected," with K derived from the symbol for carrying capacity. K-selected species are adapted for the efficient conversion of a limited resource base into offspring (MacArthur and Wilson 1967:149). These species exhibit a higher tolerance for crowding via survival, competitive ability, and predator escape expressed in their larger body size, delayed and reduced breeding, and greater investment in parental care (Horn 1978).

The r/K dichotomy has obvious attractions for students of plant, animal, and human distributions. For instance, Diamond (1977a, b; Keegan and Diamond 1987) has commented on the striking similarities in the distribution of r-selected "Supertramp" birds and human cultures in Oceania, and Kirch (1980) once recognized the r-selected characteristics of Polynesian colonists. Kirch (1984:86) has since concluded that "the r/K selection model is itself too simplistic to explain Polynesian adaptation to the reproductive challenge of colonization." I agree. Furthermore the r-selection and K-selection life-history strategies are not directly applicable to humans because humans are a K-selected species. However, the r/K dichotomy can serve as a useful analog, a general model of reproductive strategies that require complementary models that specify the relationship between production and reproduction (procreation). The A-type and K-type dispersal models make such specifications.

A-type and K-type Dispersal Patterns

The equilibrium points of the Verhulst-Pearl logistic equation can be used to define two distinct patterns of population dispersal. It is here that the link between economy and demography is forged. The first, A-type dispersal, approximates the population-maximizing equilibrium point, at which access to resources is maximized under the constraints of travel time, long-term capital investments, and minimum colonizing group size. Population growth approximates an exponential rate and the population is dispersed at low and equal densities. The ultimate product is a *steady-state distribution* of population at equal densities throughout a region. Resource use emphasizes the highest-ranked resources in the optimal set.

The second, K-type dispersal, occurs at a slower rate due to the reduced rate of population increase, and access to resources reflects satisficing behavior: the next suitable, but not necessarily maximizing, habitat is occupied. The ultimate product of K-type dispersal is a *weighted distribution* in which the core area has higher densities than the expanding periphery. A broad-spectrum use of resources is characteristic. The K-type pattern of expansion has been described previously as the "wave of advance" model (Ammerman and Cavalli-Sforza 1973) and as patterns of predatory expansion (Sahlins 1961; Bettinger and Baumhoff 1982). K-type expansion is most likely to occur when one culture encroaches upon the territory or home range of another. Under this condition, intergroup competition favors larger groups that are able to outcompete the population that occupies the territory into which the colonists are expanding.

In examining the Lucayan case, the rate at which the population grew and the manner in which the population expanded through the archipelago will determine which distribution best characterizes reproductive output.

A Historical Perspective on Lucayan Demography

Perhaps the most volatile issue in early contact-period studies concerns the sizes of the native populations. These studies have tended to focus on the population of Hispaniola because it was the base of Spanish operations, and a great deal was written about Spain's first colony. They are useful for attempts to specify the Lucayan population because they point out strengths and weaknesses in the contact-period documents. With Hispaniola as a guide, it is possible to develop a reasonable estimate of the Lucayan population at contact.

Working from different assumptions about the quality of the data for Hispaniola, researchers have reached two opposing conclusions. On the one hand there are those who believe that Bartolomé Colón made a census of the native population of Hispaniola in 1496 and counted 1,130,000 people. On the other are those who do not believe that this count took place, and who number the native population at around 100,000. Today, the number 10 million is bandied about by those who seek to remind us of the devastating impact the Europeans had.

It will never be possible to give an exact count of natives in 1492. However, we can certainly define a probability range that is narrower than 100,000 to 10 million.

The first scholar to investigate the pre-Columbian demography of Hispaniola was Angel Rosenblat (1954), whose work in historical demography dates back to the 1930s. Rosenblat undertook a detailed review of the historic documents and concluded that the population of Hispaniola numbered 100,000 to 120,000. He (1976:44) rejected Bartolomé de Las Casas's claim that 3 or 4 million Tainos were living in Hispaniola as simply ammunition for Las Casas's ardent plea for the Indian and because it was not based on statistical evaluation. His conclusion is at least partially supported by Las Casas's discussion of Lucayan mortality, which he portrayed as a river of dead bodies between the Bahamas and Hispaniola, with the number of dead placed at 500,000.

Higher population numbers were proposed by Sherburne Cook and Woodrow Borah (1971a, 1974, 1979) in their three-volume *Essays in Population History*. Cook and Borah (1971b) used mathematical methods to transform contact-period estimates into demographic projections. They began with the disputed census of 1496, doubled that number to 2,260,000 because they concluded that only half of the island had been counted, then added another 40 percent to account for children and older people who they believed were not counted because they could not be used as slaves. Finally, they used their work in central Mexico as a guide in proposing 30 to 40 percent mortality per year due to diseases and other causes. They concluded that "the aboriginal population [was in 1496]

4,070,000. This is the number claimed by Las Casas as his upper estimate or near it. It is also the minimum number which we can accept without completely discarding the 1496 count. The most probable number [for 1492] may be put at 7–8,000,000. This is the order of magnitude obtained if we assume that the Columbus count was relatively accurate" (p. 408).

The strongest support for high population numbers has come from the study of diseases and their effects (Crosby 1972, 1986; Dobyns 1983; Ramenofsky 1987). Native Americans presented "virgin soil" conditions to infectious European parasites. Documented cases of virgin soil epidemics, in which the population lacks all immunity to the infectious parasites, have resulted in 30 to 100 percent mortality. In this vein, much of the case for high population numbers throughout North America has involved enumerating epidemics and identifying probable pathogens. Ramenofsky (1987:140) mentions chickenpox, influenza, measles, mumps, rubella, smallpox, pneumonia, scarlet fever, pertussis, yellow fever, anthrax, bubonic plague, epidemic typhus, and malaria as Old World diseases that were imported to the New World before A.D. 1700. In return, the Old World received a more virulent strain of syphilis.

Those favoring the higher population numbers for Hispaniola also find support for a massive reduction of population in a famine reported for most of 1495 and 1496. The famine was probably caused by the abandonment of fields and the early consumption of manioc tubers (Wilson 1990a). That the famine was limited to the central part of the island is indicated by the uninterrupted operation of cacicazgos in the east and west.

Despite evidence to the contrary, Cook and Borah (1971b:404) proposed an islandwide decline in population that exceeded 30 percent per year up to 1504. Such high mortality during this period is not consistent with the anthropological evidence. While all of Hispaniola was supposedly undergoing this massive genocide, totaling more than 3 million persons in the Cook and Borah projections, the cacicazgo of Xaragua, basically the part of the island now known as Haiti, continued to function and to pay tribute until after 1502 when the rulers were massacred by Governor Nicolás de Ovando. It is not possible that the cacicazgo of Xaragua could have survived intact while undergoing such massive depopulation. In fact, Ovando's actions in killing the rulers suggests that the Spaniards viewed the Xaraguan cacicazgo as a threat.

Furthermore, even though other European diseases are known to have caused considerable mortality elsewhere, the most virulent disease, small-pox, is not reported as an epidemic until 1517. It now appears that before the smallpox epidemic of 1517, by which time only 16,000 Tainos re-mained, the effects of diseases on Hispaniola were localized. It is certain that a major decline in population occurred, but the magnitude and dif-ferential effects of depopulation require more specific investigation. A somewhat clearer picture emerges if we look at what was happening in the Bahama Islands at the same time.

With the rapid decline of native populations on Hispaniola, the Span-ish officially directed their attention to the Bahama Islands in 1509 (Sauer 1966; Granberry 1980). Peter Martyr (1970) reported that 40,000 Lucayans were captured and exported to Hispaniola at a rate that left the Bahamas depopulated by the time of Ponce de León's voyage in 1513 (Sauer 1966: 160). Although the Spanish are known for their exaggerated estimates of native populations (Steward and Faron 1959:51), and Las Casas bemoaned the extinction of "500,000" Lucayan souls in *Tears of the Indians*, the 40,000 estimate is probably less biased than other population estimates. The number is based on the physical removal of Lucayans for use as la-borers, and the practice by missionaries of exaggerating the number of souls they had saved was not applicable at this time. As Sauer (1966:65) notes: "There was neither reason of vanity nor of practical ends to inflate the native numbers."

Because the counting of Lucayans dates to 1509, we need to consider whether the native population was substantially larger in 1492. It is rea-sonable to apply the Cook and Borah methodology to this question be-cause the Lucayans also experienced sporadic contacts with Europeans between 1492 and 1500, most notably with Amerigo Vespucci's and Vi-cente Yáñez Pinzón's expeditions of 1499–1500. There is every reason to expect that mortality levels paralleled those projected for Hispaniola.

To apply Cook and Borah's technique, the 40,000 persons in the 1509 census are used as the baseline. Cook and Borah have argued that such accountings do not included young children and old people because they could not be used as laborers. The census is therefore doubled to take ac-count of that group. To calculate the 1492 population, the 1509 popula-tion of 80,000 is multiplied by 99.9928, which represents the percentage of decline between 1492 and 1509 in Cook and Borah's projections. Esti-mated in this way the projected population of the Bahamas exceeded 8 million. Even if the number 40,000 is retained as the total for 1509, the projection still yields a population in excess of 4 million. Neither of these numbers is reasonable.

It is patently clear that the mindless projection of annual rates of decline is not an appropriate research strategy. The exercise is instructive, however, because it suggests that mortality could not have been as high or as widespread before 1496 as Cook and Borah suggest. This conclusion is also supported in the documents that describe mortality due to disease and warfare as occurring in relatively restricted areas on Hispaniola. Following this line of reasoning, the values 1 to 2 million for Hispaniola (Zambardino 1978:410) and 40,000 to 80,000 for the Bahamas seem to be quite reasonable and worthy of further evaluation.

One avenue by which such evaluation can be pursued is the use of cross-cultural anthropological data. In their overview of cultural evolution, Allen Johnson and Timothy Earle (1987:314,324) reported that chiefdoms typically have communities comprised of 200 to 500 people and polities of 1,000 to 100,000 people and are distributed at population densities of more than 4 persons per square kilometer. Archaeological and ethnohistoric evidence have indicated that the Lucayans were organized into simple chiefdoms and that the Tainos in Hispaniola were organized in more complex chiefdoms (Keegan and Maclachlan 1989; Wilson 1990a). Historic documents also describe communities and polities in the size ranges given by Johnson and Earle.

The total land area of the Bahamas archipelago is 13,456 square kilometers, excluding uninhabited small cays. If a population of 40,000 was evenly distributed over the area it would have a density of only 2.97 persons per square kilometer. Archaeological surveys indicate that the population was not evenly distributed and that some areas were never settled. A more representative or effective density is obtained by excluding islands that were not densely settled (e.g., Grand Bahama, Great Inagua). This yields a density of 3.83 persons per square kilometer (hence rounded to four) on an effective territory of 10,450 square kilometers.

The comparison of these estimates with modern population densities in the Bahamas gives meaning to those values. With the exception of the most developed islands, whose populations are today supported by trade and tourism (e.g., New Providence/Nassau, Grand Bahama/Freeport), population densities in the Bahamas range from 2 to 30 per square kilometer (Bahamas Ministry of Education 1976). The lower end of this range characterizes an economy based largely on subsistence production, while the higher densities are from islands that receive larger inputs of imported capital. The similarities between modern and prehistoric economies indicate that a prehistoric population density of 4 persons per square kilometer is reasonable.

Settlements in Cuba and Hispaniola were described by the Spanish as substantially larger than those in the Bahamas. Yet to achieve even simple parity with the Bahamas, a density of four persons per square kilometer on the 75,548-square-kilometer island of Hispaniola would require a population of 302,192. It should also be noted that Samuel Wilson (1990b) has projected a 1492 population of 380,976 for Hispaniola based on the censuses of 1508 and 1514. Given its substantially larger prehistoric population, is not inconceivable that the Taino population of Hispaniola was 1 to 2 million people at contact, the majority of whom, as in most growing populations, were younger than age fifteen.

This brief review of historical demography suggests that the Spanish may have been fairly accurate in their size estimates for the native populations of the northern West Indies. The next task is to determine whether archaeological evidence conforms to these ethnohistoric values. For purposes of comparison a population density of 4 persons per square kilometer and a total population of 40,000 are assumed to be accurate, subject to falsification.

Archaeological Retrodiction of Lucayan Population Numbers

Community Size

Site surface areas are commonly used to estimate prehistoric population numbers (Hassan 1981). In her study of catchment areas in the Caicos Islands, Elizabeth Wing calculated a population density value of 30 persons per effective hectare of a two-kilometer site catchment (see Sullivan 1981; Wing and Scudder 1983). Archaeological sites on Middle Caicos did not completely match expectations based on Wing's community density value. However, the lack of conformity could be explained as resulting from the intrusion of Tainos from Hispaniola at one of the sites she examined. The first objective test of the 30 persons per hectare of site value is made in this analysis.

A second person per site area value was developed by Anna Roosevelt (1980) in her study of prehistoric population expansion on the Orinoco River. Because the Saladoid peoples that she studied are related to the first colonists of the Antilles, her results can be usefully employed in the present study. Roosevelt came up with a population density value of 75 persons per hectare based on data collected among the Yanoama by Smole (1976).

The dimensions of 107 Lucayan sites have been measured as having a total area of 55 hectares. An additional 50 sites have been identified, but their dimensions could not be measured. If the measured sites were occupied at the densities suggested by Wing and Roosevelt (i.e., 30 to 75 persons per hectare of site), then the known sites can account for a Lucayan population of only 1,650 to 4,125 persons. If the 50 sites whose areas were not measured were similar in size to the others, then the estimated population is increased to between 2,421 and 6,053.

These estimates are well below the 40,000 persons suggested on the basis of historic documents. An island-by-island comparison, in which the total population on each island is calculated with both the regional density value (four persons per square kilometer) and the site area densities (30 to 75 persons per hectare times site area) is presented in table 7.1. These comparisons indicate that the site area density calculations are 47 percent to 88 percent less than the regional density estimate.

This comparison suggests that one or both of the techniques is flawed. For the moment, it is assumed that the regional estimate is more likely to be accurate because it is based on a conservative estimate of total population. With regard to site area estimates there are a number of potential sources of inaccuracy. The thoroughness with which an island was surveyed is one, and problems with measuring sites is another. However, these types of inaccuracy cannot overcome such substantial underestimates. Moreover, the thoroughness of archaeological surveys makes it very unlikely that sites at which only 12 percent to 47 percent of the population resided have been located. It is more likely that the assumptions on which the Wing and Roosevelt estimators were based are violated in the Bahamas.

When additional factors are considered, such as unknown values, unsurveyed areas, and unsettled areas, there is a consistent difference of about 60 percent between site area and regional density estimates. A possible reason for this consistent underestimate when using the Roosevelt

TABLE 7.1 Comparison of Population Densities Based on Regional and Site-Area Calculations

Island	Site area (m²)	Island area (km²)	Measured sites	Unmeasured sites	Observed population[a]	Expected population[b]	Percent expected accounted for by observed
Crooked Island	20,981	238	8	1	63 to 157	952	16
Acklins Island	97,080	389	23	7	291 to 728	1556	47
Long Island	81,150	448	20	11	244 to 609	1792	34
Exuma Islands	33,920	186	12	0	102 to 254	744	34
Mayaguana	20,660	285	9	1	62 to 155	1140	14
Cat Island	125,775	389	18	1	377 to 943	1556	61
Eleuthera	53,356	518	13	3	160 to 400	2072	19
Rum Cay	12,550	78	4	7	38 to 94	312	30

[a]Site area multiplied times .003 and .0075 (population per site-area values), rounded to the nearest tenth.
[b]Island area multiplied times 4 (population density per island area value).

area estimator is the inclusion of unoccupied plaza areas in Smole's (1976) original calculation of persons per site area among the Yanoama. A similar problem may affect Wing's area estimator, which was developed on the only island on which Lucayan sites have plazas (Sullivan 1981). Because sites in the Bahamas typically have a linear arrangement, unoccupied plaza areas would not be defined by artifact scatters. Further, at linear coastal settlements, activities are focused on the beach, which would reduce the dispersion of artifacts toward the interior.

It would seem that a more accurate method for calculating the population density of linear communities could be obtained by reconstructing the number of houses per site length along with the average number of persons per house. This linear estimator is constructed from several different sources of ethnohistoric and archaeological evidence for Lucayan and Cuban Taino settlements.

First, Columbus observed Lucayan villages on San Salvador, Long Island, and Crooked Island (Fox 1882; Keegan 1984a). He reported that villages ranged in size from 1 to 15 houses and was explicit about the maximum number. In a well-defined case he described a peninsula on San Salvador as having 6 houses. This point, today called Cut Cay, is 200 meters long. The density of settlement on this cay is 1 house per 33 meters. Since the shore along Columbus's route has been thoroughly surveyed by archaeologists, it is unlikely that any major villages were missed. It may therefore be inferred that the largest site (CR-14) is the one described as having the maximum number of houses. These 15 houses are on a site whose longest linear dimension is 560 meters (Keegan 1988), which gives a density of 1 house per 37 meters. The results from both locations are virtually identical.

A second source of evidence is differences in site size (see figure 4.1). As was reported, site length measurements exhibit a series of modes and peaks at 30-meter increments. Such regularity in site length suggests that architectural features are the cause, the inference being that each house resulted in a 30-meter increase in site length. This gives a density of 0.03 houses per meter or 1 house per 33 meters. Modes in the site length measurements at 100 meters and 200 meters may indicate that spacing was sometimes reduced to 1 house per 25 meters or may reflect a propensity by investigators to round estimates to the nearest hundred.

Semipit houses with stone foundation walls at site MC-6 on Middle Caicos provide a final source of evidence. Although MC-6 exhibits strong

Classic Taino affiliations (Sullivan 1981), the spacing of houses can be measured directly so the calculations are worth considering. There are 4 houses on both sides of the 120-meter long central plaza, or 1 house per 30 meters.

Additional information on community size can be obtained from ethnohistoric descriptions, from ethnographic analogy, and by evaluating the spatial needs of households. With regard to the first, Lucayan houses were described as tent-shaped and were compared to the *alfanque*, a round Moorish tent (Sauer 1966:62). The size of Lucayan houses was not reported, but more complete descriptions were provided for similar houses in Cuba. The Cuban houses were also described as alfanques, but they were reported to be somewhat larger. Houses were constructed of pole and thatch with a large unchambered interior. Las Casas reported that the houses in Cuba were 10 to 13 meters in diameter and contained 10 to 15 households (Sauer 1966:62). When married couples and an average number of dependents are assigned to each household, the number of persons per house would have ranged from 40 to 60. These figures come from the contact period when villages contained up to 3,000 residents (Cook and Borah 1971b), and the number of households in these communities would have required a more dense packing of the population. Furthermore, the large number of persons per house may reflect Spanish influences. Allotments of Indians to individual Spaniards resulted in the aggregation of native peoples in central places. Displaced persons would also have sought refuge with their relatives in other villages.

In lowland South America the tropical forest pattern of settlement is for houses to contain complete lineage sections or even entire villages (Steward and Faron 1959:298–299; Maybury-Lewis 1974; Murphy and Murphy 1974:116; Gregor 1977; Chagnon 1983). The identification of Cuban houses as composed of 10–15 households is consistent with the evidence for other tropical forest societies. In the prehistoric Bahamas, native communities were smaller than those in Cuba. However, because the Cubans and Lucayans had similar economic and social organizations it is likely that the Lucayan communities were simply scaled-down versions of the Cuban settlements. The noted Cuban archaeologist José Guarch (1974) has suggested that a more conservative number of 20 persons per house more accurately characterizes precontact Cuban villages. This number is a reasonable estimate for Lucayan household size as well.

A house with a diameter of 10 meters also fits the evidence for Lucayan sites. In fact, the location of sites atop coastal dunes would have prevented a significant increase in house width beyond 10 meters, which may account for the increase in the number of houses per site rather than an increase in house size as the Lucayan population increased. The spacing of houses at 30-meter intervals is reasonable because this would allow for small house-gardens around the houses. A similar distance is reported for the spacing of household clusters in Oaxaca, Mexico, during the Formative period (M. Winter 1976).

All of the evidence on community size, drawn from such disparate sources as Columbus's diario, overall Lucayan site dimensions, site MC-6, and precontact settlement in other regions, gives a consistent figure of one house per 33 meters of site length (0.03 houses/m) with 20-member households occupying each house. Thus community size can be retrodicted by multiplying the length of the site by 0.6 persons per meter (i.e., 20 persons per house times 0.03 houses per meter of site length).

The comparison of population estimates based on site lengths (i.e., 0.6 persons per meter of site length) with those obtained with the regional density estimate of 4 persons per square kilometer reveals a close conformity. The linear estimator accounts for more than 80 percent of the expected population (based on the regional estimate) for the four islands for which the best evidence is available (table 7.2). Moreover, for islands with obvious reasons for the differences between observed and expected values, adjustments resulted in a closer fit, exceeding 100 percent in three cases.

It would be possible to achieve conformity on the islands for which survey data are available by slightly adjusting the number of occupants per house or by reducing the spacing of houses. It should also be noted that two of the largest islands were excluded from the regional density calculation of four persons per square kilometer because archaeological surveys suggested that these islands were settled at lower overall densities. Prehistoric settlements on these islands would bring the total population closer to the 40,000 total reported by the Spanish.

It should also be kept in mind that the key island with regard to archipelago-wide population numbers is Andros. Andros Island has more than half of the surface area used in the regional estimate (5,957 km²) and would therefore have supported more than half of the population. To date, little archaeology has been done on Andros (Goggin 1939; Keegan and Sealey 1988). However, there is no reason to believe that Andros was

TABLE 7.2 Comparison of Population Densities Based on Regional and Site-Length Calculations

Island	Site length (m)	Observed population[a]	Expected population[b,c]	Percent expected accounted for by observed[c]
Cat Island	2540	1524	1556	98
Long Island	2715	1629	1792	91 (103)
Exuma Islands	1125	675	744	91
Acklins Island	2115	1269	1556	82
Rum Cay	320	192	312	62 (106)
Crooked Island	968	557	952	58 (117)
Eleuthera	1313	788	2072	38
Mayaguana	632	379	1140 (664)	33 (57)
Great Inagua	940	564	6176 (984)	9 (57)

[a]Site length multiplied times 0.6 persons per meter.

[b]Regional density estimate (total island area multiplied by 4 persons per square kilometer).

[c]Percentages in parentheses reflect post hoc modifications based on the following: There are 11 sites of undetermined length on Long Island, 7 on Rum Cay; the observed population was doubled to account for the unsurveyed south coast of Crooked Island; 42 percent of Mayaguana and 84 percent of Great Inagua were apparently unsuited for settlement.

any less densely occupied than the islands for which survey data are available.

The purpose of this exercise was to determine whether known sites could reasonably account for a total population of 40,000. The conclusion is that they can when due consideration is given to undiscovered sites, restricted settlement on some islands, and unknown site dimensions. These estimates could be refined, and they probably gloss over local variations. However, given our knowledge of Lucayan settlement patterns, they serve to indicate that settlement evidence is consistent with a terminal period population of 40,000.

Lucayan Population Growth Rate

The dispersal model indicates that the long-term population growth rate provides important information about the initial processes of dispersal. If the population grew rapidly, approaching an exponential rate, then a steady-state distribution is likely to result. If a slow rate of growth obtained, then a weighted distribution is more likely.

The long-term (average) population growth rate is calculated with the exponential growth formula $[r = ln(N_2/N_1) \div t]$, where r is the growth rate, t is elapsed time between population censuses, and population sizes N_1 and N_2 are initial and terminal sizes respectively (Hassan 1981:139). The exponential growth formula, rather than the logistic equation, is used because a colonizing population would not approach carrying capacity until late in the terminal period (Kirch 1984:101; Keegan and Diamond 1987).

Starting with an initial population of 50, a terminal-period population of 40,000 could have been achieved in 800 years at an exponential growth rate of 0.84 percent (80,000 at 0.92 percent). This growth rate is less than that estimated for population growth in the prehistoric Hawaiian Islands (Kirch 1980, 1984). The Hawaiian Islands were colonized shortly before A.D. 500 and had achieved a total population of about 300,000 by A.D. 1300. These numbers produce an exponential growth rate of 1.09 percent (Keegan, Johnson, and Earle 1985). A Hispaniola population of 1 million could have been achieved at a growth rate of 0.90 percent, while 380,000 would have had a growth rate of 0.81 percent.

The above estimates differ significantly from Hassan's (1981) conclusion that the maximum prehistoric rate of increase was 0.52 percent. The estimated growth rates for the Greater Antilles, Hawaiian Islands, and Bahama Islands also involve long-term averaging, which makes these conservative estimates. In other words, the actual growth rate at particular times and places could have been substantially higher. In comparison with other prehistoric populations, the prehistoric populations of the West Indies approached an exponential rate of growth. An exponential growth rate is to be expected of populations pursuing A-type dispersal.

Population Growth and Dispersal

Population growth in a region is equal to the sum of births plus immigrants minus the sum of deaths and emigrants. When migration is not possible, the growth rate is a measure of reproductive potential. However, because migration is known to have occurred in the Bahamas, the effects of migration on the rate of population growth must be examined. For instance, a high rate of growth on one island prior to the colonization of the others would produce a staggered pattern of growth. In other words, there would be many people on one island and many fewer on the others.

Differences in timing would reduce the total population to well below the number that could be achieved given true exponential growth. It is possible that the growth rate for the Bahamas was closer to that estimated for Hawaii and the Greater Antilles, but that migration between islands in this linear archipelago reduced the potential expression of exponential growth. The point is that one large group will increase in size more rapidly than will several small groups, even if their total numbers are equal.

The settlement patterns and subsistence practices described in chapters 4 and 6 suggested that the Bahama archipelago was colonized at a rapid rate. Information on the population growth rate presented above is consistent with that conclusion. Moreover, interisland comparisons of settlement densities identified a general decline from south to north. The inference was that differences in the timing of settlement were responsible. In addition, there is an area that exhibits the expected steady-state distribution within this regional pattern, where the similar person per land-unit densities indicate that the population was originally distributed at low densities. It has been proposed that a colonizing group would move to an unoccupied island when the potential person per land-unit ratio was equal to that for the occupied island. The motive for such rapid expansion at low densities was the greater availability and rapid depletion of high-ranked terrestrial prey following the start of human predation.

The expansion process that produced the observed distributions is inferred to reflect the drift method of segmentation or group fissioning (Fox 1967). A simple version of this type of fissioning, designed to examine group-level or aggregate phenomena, assumes that population grew at a constant rate, and that expansion events occurred when the population had doubled. Expansion events are then simulated as reflecting the process of population doubling using the doubling-time equation from population biology ($Dt = .6931/r$) (Hassan 1981:140).

The predictions of the growth and expansion model are tested with settlement evidence for Rum Cay. Rum Cay was selected because it is located in the central zone of steady-state values, and because its coastline has been thoroughly surveyed (Mitchell and Keegan 1987). Given the prediction that an island will be settled when its person per land-unit ratio is less than or equal to that of the island that supplies the colonists, the first task is to measure the size of Rum Cay in relation to Long Island (the source of colonists). Long Island is 5.7 times larger than Rum Cay, so Rum Cay would have been colonized after 6 settlements were established on Long Island (i.e., 6 sites per 448 square kilometers = 1 site per 78 square kilometers).

Next, the sequence of expansion is reconstructed beginning from the first island colonized in the archipelago (Great Inagua). There are two possible outcomes with each doubling of population. Either a new settlement is established on the occupied island, or the next island in the sequence is colonized. The outcome selected will depend upon the density relationship between adjacent islands. New settlements will continue to be established on the occupied island until the colonizing group could achieve a lower density on the next island. It should be noted that the population of every settlement doubles at each doubling time (Dt_n). This produces a geometric growth in population density.

From the initial settlement on Great Inagua (Dt_0), Acklins Island would have been settled after the first doubling of population (Dt_1). This results in one settlement on each island. Long Island would have been settled next (Dt_2). After two population doublings (Dt_4) [Long Island: $n=2$, Dt_3; $n=4$, Dt_4] Cat Island would have been settled by one of the Long Island doublings and three settlements would have remained on Long Island. The next doubling (Dt_5) results in six settlements on Long Island (as the three on Long Island doubled) and the colonization of Great Exuma. This leaves five settlements on Long Island, because one moved to colonize Great Exuma. San Salvador and Rum Cay would have been colonized following the next doubling of population (Dt_6). This initial settlement on Rum Cay would then double three (Dt_9) or four (Dt_{10}) more times before Spanish contact.

The growth of population was terminated after 10 doublings because the terminal population size was reached $(r=.0084)$. In this simulation 410 years would have been required to establish one settlement on each of the 16 main islands, assuming that every settlement contained an equal number of persons.

Returning to the Rum Cay example, a total of 6–12 sites of settlements of equal size would have been produced by colonization at Dt_6 and continued exponential growth to Dt_9–Dt_{10}. These settlements would have supported a population of 300–600 persons. A total of 11 sites have been found during archaeological surveys, and the total population is estimated at 312 persons (i.e., 78 square kilometers times 4 persons per square kilometer).

The growth and dispersal model illustrates how the observed distribution of population could have been produced. In the central subarea, Acklins Island was the first island settled. Following the colonization of Long Island, additional growth would have been restricted to Crooked and Acklins Islands because these lacked additional outlets. In contrast, Long Island had four outlets for population growth. By supplying colonists to Cat Island, Great Exuma, Rum Cay, and San Salvador, the density of settlement in this zone would have been lower than that for Crooked and Acklins Islands. At the same time, if these islands were settled at equivalent densities, a steady-state distribution would obtain. Finally, expansion to the north of Cat Island would have resulted in a continuation of the weighted distribution because there are two outlets for expansion from Eleuthera (New Providence and Great Abaco). By supplying colonists to two islands, the density would have been reduced below that for Cat Island, which supplied colonists only to Eleuthera.

In sum, the observed distributions fit the predictions of the model exactly. Under conditions of a high rate of population growth and A-type dispersal the Lucayan population spread rapidly through the entire archipelago. An overall weighted or K-type dispersal pattern is also observed but as an artifact of geographical constraints to northward migration in this branching archipelago. The steady-state distribution was retained in the central Bahamas, whose land areas and coastline lengths more closely approximate ideal conditions.

Summary and Conclusions

This chapter began with the global Verhulst-Pearl logistic equation and identified two population equilibrium points. These equilibrium points were then used to operationalize the concepts r-selection and K-selection with regard to episodes of human dispersal. By specifying the parameters of the general models of population change, a middle-level predictive model was deduced. The two types of dispersal, A-type and K-type, corresponding to the equilibrium points in the logistic equation, provide a framework for organizing otherwise disparate sources of data for the logical evaluation of colonization processes.

The model was developed to examine population expansion in the prehistoric Bahamas. Models of this type are necessary because present archaeological techniques and preservational biases preclude direct answers to most distributional questions. Moreover, it is physically and financially impossible to obtain a sufficient number of radiocarbon dates from the 250 known Lucayan sites, and using a two-sigma standard deviation for such dates would make them of limited value in an archipelago that was occupied for only about 800 years. Modeling the dispersal process provides a means for evaluating alternative interpretations.

The analysis of prehistoric population expansion in the Bahama archipelago was shown to conform to that expected for A-type dispersal. In this chapter that conformity was demonstrated by reference to the estimated long-term aggregate growth rate and to settlement distributions. In addition, the evidence for changes in subsistence practices that was presented in the last chapter is consistent with the conclusion that the rapid dispersal of population occurred to maximize access to the highest-ranked resources, within limits imposed by the kinship system (Keegan and Maclachlan 1989).

8

Christopher Columbus
and the City of Gold

Christopher Columbus, Admiral of the Ocean Sea, the Great Navigator, renowned as the champion of the belief that the earth was round; the man who sought the riches of the Far East by sailing to the west, and who happened instead upon a New World; the man who "discovered" America. Removed from Hispaniola in chains in 1500 and wrongly persecuted in his later years, Columbus typifies the tragic heroic figure. Yet how accurate is the portrait of Columbus that is painted today? How much of that portrait is the product of the deification of a long-dead hero whose personal attributes have been touched up to reflect the greatness of his discoveries (Varela 1987)? Would we accept less than a Great Man as the discoverer of America?

When one lifts the shroud of myth that today surrounds Columbus we find in his portrait more the likeness of a period of history than of an individual man. For example, Columbus is often credited with being the first to believe that the earth was round, a fact first proved by the Greek mathematician Pythagoras in the sixth century B.C. and generally accepted in Europe by the thirteenth century. What was not agreed upon was the earth's circumference. Yet when faced with contradictory navigational readings off the coast of South America during his third voyage in 1498, Columbus quickly abandoned his round earth theory. Instead he suggested that the earth was not round but rather shaped like a pear with a rise "something like a woman's breast," on the nipple of which was located the "Terrestrial Paradise," the Garden of Eden, to which no man could sail without the permission of God (Morison 1942:557; Pohl 1966: 46). Although his actions pushed him toward the Renaissance, his sensibilities were still firmly rooted in the Middle Ages (Fuson 1987).

We are well advised to remember that Christopher Columbus did not discover America; America discovered him. Stretching in an almost unbroken line between the north and south poles the Americas presented an enormous barrier in the way of westward passage to Asia. Furthermore, the continents were not uninhabited. They had been settled by peoples who crossed the Bering Straits at least 15,000 years ago, and the descendants of these first settlers had built fabulous civilizations throughout the Americas. The Americas were the home of civilizations whose presence would confound Europeans for centuries.

It must also be remembered that, closer to home, there is archaeological evidence for a Norse (Viking) presence in North America almost 500 years before Columbus's first voyage, and others have also laid claim to the "discovery" of America (Severin 1978; McGhee 1984).

Columbus rightly deserves recognition for his skills as a mariner (but see Sale 1990). He succeeded in crossing the Atlantic Ocean and, more important, he *returned* safely. The presence of at least islands to the west was suspected by others (e.g., the Martin Behaim globe of 1492); the Portuguese attempted several crossings before Columbus's first voyage, and British seamen from Bristol were fishing off the coast of northern North America in the 1490s. John Cabot, sailing for England, may have landed in North America in 1494 and did explore as far south as New England by 1497.

Earlier voyages in the middle latitudes failed because the winds ceased a short distance out into the Atlantic. Based on his sailing experiences in the Mediterranean and in northern Europe, possibly including a voyage to Iceland, Columbus postulated that his passage to Asia and back would be a large oval course before the trade winds. On the southwesterly portion of the route his ships would be carried by the northeast trades and on a northerly return he would receive the assistance of the westerlies. In other words, he recognized the clockwise circulation of winds and currents that characterize the North Atlantic. We can infer this conclusion because he had the lateen sails on his ships replaced with square sails. The triangular lateen sail was developed for sailing into the wind (much like the modern jib), while square sails are suited only for courses that follow the wind (figure 8.1).

FIGURE 8.1. Lateen-rigged caravels featured on the Juan de La Cosa map, 1500.

Columbus was fortunate to have possessed such skills as a navigator because his understanding of geography (cosmography, as it was then practiced) could have otherwise proved fatal. Columbus believed that he had discovered a western passage to "Asia," that he had discovered the land of Middle Eastern legend inhabited entirely by women (Matinino, the land of the Amazons), and that he had discovered the "Terrestrial Paradise" (Garden of Eden). In sum, he discovered more fiction than fact.

The story seems to begin with Columbus seeking financial sponsorship for a voyage to Asia and the Indies. But was Asia really Columbus's objective? Henry Vignaud (1905) and others have maintained that Columbus pursued more personal goals. In support of Columbus's stated objective, Samuel Eliot Morison (1942), following the lead of Columbus's son Fernando, has directed attention to Paolo dal Pozzo Toscanelli's geographic interpretations of Marco Polo's travels. Toscanelli, a fifteenth-century physician and humanist, concluded that mainland China was about 5,000 nautical miles due west of Portugal. Columbus sailed an estimated 3,600 nautical miles to reach the coast of Cuba, which Morison interpreted as ample distance to support Columbus's contention that Cuba was mainland China.

Columbus's actions, however, contradict his stated objective. Although Toscanelli's interpretations supported Columbus's course, Robert Fuson (1987) has suggested that Columbus was unaware of Toscanelli's geography. Fuson goes on to suggest that Fernando Columbus actually in-

vented the correspondence between his father and Toscanelli to show
scholarly support for his father's actions. With or without Toscanelli's
advice, Columbus must have believed that the earth has a substantially
smaller circumference (about 25 percent smaller).

At the time, the geography of Ptolemy still held precedence. Ptolemy
placed the entrance to the Sinus Magnus, the sea passage to the Indies, at
8.5° south of the equator. Columbus's failure to seek the Sinus Magnus at
the appropriate latitude may be what prompted Amerigo Vespucci, the
man after whom the Western Hemisphere was named, to explore the east
coast of South America (Pohl 1966).

Many questions remain unanswered. Upon reaching the islands Columbus spent two weeks searching for gold in the Bahamas. Why did he
waste time in the Bahamas when his stated objective lay a short distance
to the southwest? Why did Columbus bring trinkets for trade if the gold
of the Grand Khan (in Latin, "king of kings") was his primary objective?
Why did Columbus claim lands for the Spanish Crown, and himself as
the Crown's representative, if these belonged to an Asiatic kingdom? Why
is there no mention of Asia or the Indies in the titles awarded to Columbus by his royal sponsors?

Evidence that he had not discovered the China of Marco Polo must
have been overwhelming. The native Tainos lacked large cities, wore little clothing, possessed few "riches," had no knowledge of iron, and so on.
But perhaps the most telling action occurred when Columbus reported
that he was "only about 100 leagues from Zayton and Quinsay," the two
great seaports of China that Marco Polo had visited. Then, for no apparent reason, he turned his vessels and sailed in the opposite direction. Yet
he was so confident that Cuba was China, he made his crew sign letters
confirming this conclusion during his second voyage (Harrisse 1961;
Sauer 1966).

The ease with which Columbus was distracted from his mission, his
adoption of a "radical" geographical interpretation, his practice of claim-
ing islands for the Spanish Crown, his obsession with gold and other
riches, and his apparent satisfaction with Hispaniola as his reward raise
the question of whether he actually sought a route to the Indies or
whether he was motivated by more personal goals. In reconstructing Columbus's voyage through the West Indies it is important to consider
these motives, for it was these goals that influenced the course of his
explorations.

Columbus the Chronicler

To the Spanish humanist Ramón Iglesia, Columbus seemed to be writing the promo-
tion literature of a tourist bureau which he did with Italian exuberance. (Sauer
1966:29)

Columbus's personal record, prepared as a report to his royal sponsors, has not survived to the present. Accounts of the voyage that have survived include a postvoyage interview with the priest Andres Bernaldez by Pietro Martire d'Anghiera (Peter Martyr); general histories by Oviedo and Francisco López de Gomara; Fernando Columbus's discussions of the voyage; and a transcription of Columbus's personal record (diario) in the hand of Bartolomé de Las Casas. Las Casas, who arrived at Hispaniola in 1502, was the first priest ordained in the New World in 1510 and was the author of the most complete history of his day, which was completed in 1552.

Recent reconstructions of Columbus's first voyage begin with the Las Casas transcription of the diario. The Las Casas transcription was made from a copy of the original that was made by an unnamed scribe. Thus, the record of Columbus's first voyage that is used today is a third-hand sixteenth-century manuscript that has been translated into modern languages by perhaps twenty different translators (Judge 1986). All of the translations differ in certain, sometimes critical details (Fuson 1987). Recently, a transcription and juxtaposed English translation was prepared by Oliver Dunn and James E. Kelley, Jr. (1989). Their book presents a complete transcription of the Las Casas folios including the gaps, margin notes, and all alterations to the text.

Even if every translation exactly duplicated the Las Casas transcription, there are still questions concerning the accuracy of that transcription (Fuson 1983, 1987). Consuelo Varela (1984) has recently suggested that the transcription be used with extreme caution. From her work with documents from this period in the archives in Seville, she has concluded that Las Casas was at times a sloppy copyist. His works contain numerous erasures along with notes in the margins intended for later inclusion in the text or as notes to himself. Documents that Las Casas claimed to be exact quotations, however, seem to be an important exception. When these have been compared to the originals, any errors are usually very minor. In the diario, Las Casas begins to quote Columbus *after* Columbus arrived on the island called Guanahani by the natives, renamed by him San Salvador.

Varela has also pointed out that Las Casas seems to hesitate when transcribing three words: *entrar* (to go in, to enter), *salir* (to go out, to leave), and *partir* (to depart). In their sixteenth-century variants, the Spanish and Italian languages assigned nearly opposite meanings to these words. It is therefore possible for significant errors to arise unexpectedly.

David Henige's (1991) critical analysis of the diario raises more serious questions. Henige's textual critique suggests that the diario is not a sufficiently accurate or complete record of events and cannot be used to identify Columbus's first landfall and subsequent route. While the author shares Henige's concerns, I disagree with his final assessment. Used with caution, the various sources of information in the diario unveil a route that converges on one island, San Salvador.

Perhaps Varela's most significant point is that Columbus almost certainly recorded distances in geometric miles (Kelley 1983; Charlier 1987). Most distances in the diario are given in leagues, which only later became the Spanish standard measure. Therefore, either Las Casas or the scribe who preceded him converted the original distance estimates into leagues. Moreover, either Las Casas or the unnamed scribe exhibits a predisposition toward the use of leagues. In twelve cases Las Casas crossed out the word *leguas* (leagues) and replaced it with *millas* (miles); there are no cases in which the opposite occurs.

The question of whether Columbus used miles or leagues is of critical importance. The major problem with the track proposed by Samuel Eliot Morison (1942) is that the second island was recorded as 5 leagues by 10 leagues in the diario, while Morison's second island, Rum Cay, measures approximately 5 miles by 10 miles. Yet this problem is almost certainly one of transcription. In the half-dozen places where distances in the Bahamas are reported, two standards often seem to be in use. The first is the quite accurate description of distances between islands in leagues. The second is an apparently shorter unit of measure for distances along coasts. Morison invented an "alongshore league" to account for these differences, but even his most ardent supporters have had difficulty accepting this invention. Kelley (1983, 1987) has demonstrated that along Cuba some of the differences result from currents, tidal flows, or both, making a passage seem longer or shorter than it actually was.

On two occasions Columbus provides estimates both before and after the crossings between the first-and-second and second-and-third islands. He first estimated the distance he would travel as he departed the island and then corrected this estimate after the crossing had been completed. For example, after his crossing to the second island Columbus stated, "[A]nd as the island was farther than five leagues, rather about seven, and the tide detained me, it was about noon when I reached said island" (Dunn and Kelley 1989:77).

The most accurate results are obtained when one accepts that miles and leagues were, on occasion, confused during transcription. If one is willing to examine each distance estimate on a case-by-case basis to determine which of these measurement units is applicable, complete conformity with the diario can be obtained. For the passages between islands, as in the quotation above, it was possible for the transcriber to check which measurement unit was being used because the time required for the crossing is also reported. Such seems to be the case for the transatlantic crossing in which most of the corrections from leagues to miles occur. Such cross-checking would also explain why the second island was described in terms of leagues; Columbus had led the transcriber to believe he was describing "large" islands.

In other cases it was not possible to check which unit of measure was more appropriate. As suggested above, because the transcriber was predisposed to use leagues as the unit of measure, cases in which miles should have been used are obscured. It will be shown below that the neo-Roman mile (4,888 feet) is the measurement unit that was used for distances along the coasts of the Bahamas (also see Charlier 1987).

The question of what measurement unit was in use is important for a second reason. In the transcription, Las Casas stated (in 23 places) that Columbus reported less progress than he reckoned "so that the men would not be frightened if the voyage were long" (Kelley 1987:127). This so-called double accounting or two logs is, in fact, an invention of Las Casas. Remember, first, that this portion of the diario is a summation by Las Casas and not a direct quotation of Columbus. Second, Kelley (1983, 1987) has demonstrated that the difference between the distances recorded by Columbus and those reported to his crew are equal to the conversion from the geometric league to the Portuguese league. In other words, Columbus was used to thinking in terms of a unit of measure that was six-fifths of the unit used by his crew. The situation is similar to that which occurs when a person accustomed to thinking in kilometers converts distance estimates to miles for someone used to the English system. Even if Columbus did try to hide the facts from his crew, he could not have succeeded for long because of the close quarters aboard ship and the number of experienced mariners and pilots on the three vessels.

In dispensing with the two logs we should also dispense with the notion that Columbus's crew was constantly on the verge of mutiny. As Sauer (1966:20) points out, both crew and officers aboard the *Niña* and *Pinta* were neighbors and kinsmen with maritime experience.

> Columbus, being on the *Santa María* heard the whining of landlubbers [convicts and criminals] which he dramatized to contrast with his own courage. [Las Casas may be partly responsible.] The seasoned seamen, the men of Palos and Moguer, led by their own capable navigators, had no cause to be dismayed by a prosperous voyage that may have been somewhat longer than they had been on, but from which they were confident that they would know how to return. Columbus had originated and promoted the idea of the voyage; Spanish seamen made it possible and carried it through.

Finally, we should note that Columbus was given to overestimating the dimensions of his "discoveries." As Angel Rosenblat (1976) documented, Columbus estimated that the area of Hispaniola was equal to all of Spain from Catalonia to Fuenterrabia, that Hispaniola was larger than England, that Hispaniola was larger than Portugal, that the province of Cibao alone seemed as big as the kingdom of Portugal, that the coast of Hispaniola was greater than that of Spain, and that Jamaica was bigger than Sicily. In fact, Hispaniola has 76,286 square kilometers with less than 2,000 kilometers of coastline, and Jamaica 10,859 square kilometers. England has 142,588 square kilometers, Portugal has 92,082 square kilometers, Spain has 494,946 square kilometers and 3,318 kilometers of coastline, and Sicily has 25,461 square kilometers. Columbus either exaggerated or was a poor judge of geography. However, James Kelley (personal communication) has countered that Columbus's exaggerated estimates are consistent with the cartography of the day. In other words, the geographic representations of Europe are close to the sizes one would expect working backward from Columbus's comparisons with the West Indies. Was Columbus exaggerating, or do his estimates reflect the knowledge and perceptions of his day?

Columbus as Ethnographer

As interest in Columbus's first voyage has grown in anticipation of the five-hundredth anniversary of this event the most frequently asked question has been, Why is it important to identify which island is Guanahani (Columbus's San Salvador)? Because the first-landfall question has attracted scholars and avocationalists, sailors (often admirals) and landlubbers, oceanographers, geologists, archaeologists, geographers, poets, historians, and so forth, the question would undoubtedly elicit a wide variety of responses. In general, the answers have touched upon two main themes: the lure of an unsolved mystery and the pursuit of historical accuracy.

From an anthropological perspective, the identification of Guanahani is important because it is the key to using Columbus's descriptions of the islands and their inhabitants. Columbus was the only European to record first-hand observations of Lucayan lifeways. Although additional information is available in later summaries (e.g., Las Casas 1951; Martyr 1970), the Bahamas was never a permanent base of Spanish operations, and there were few opportunities to observe the Lucayans, who were exterminated by 1520. Columbus's diario is thus our only first-hand source of information about the Lucayans at contact.

Retracing the First Voyage

If Columbus was uncertain of his landfalls with regard to the world of 1492, investigators who during the past 150 years have attempted to retrace the route of his first voyage are equally uncertain. After nearly 500 years, debate still rages over where Columbus first landed. It is agreed that Columbus's first landfall, Guanahani, is located in the Bahama Islands (used generically to include the Turks and Caicos Islands). That, however, is where agreement ends. No fewer than 10 different islands (out of about 25 possible candidates) have been identified as Guanahani, and more than 30 different routes crisscross the Bahamas from those initial landfalls (see Parker 1983, Fuson 1987, and Taviani 1987, for reviews of the major theories).

Following the publication of Samuel Eliot Morison's book, *Admiral of the Ocean Sea*, in 1942, the landfall debate was largely considered settled, and Guanahani came to be identified as Watling Island, today known officially as San Salvador. Opposing viewpoints continue to be suggested (e.g., Link and Link 1958; Sadler 1972; Molander 1982, 1983; Larimore 1988; Winslow 1991), but none have seemed to capture much attention (see Parker 1983). Then, in the November 1986 *National Geographic*, senior editor Joseph Judge began his campaign to convince the public that Morison was wrong and that Judge's reconstruction of Columbus's first voyage is correct.

An entire book would be required to provide the details of each track, the assumptions that make them plausible, and the problems that prevent their widespread acceptance. After seven years of trying to prove otherwise, I am now convinced that San Salvador Island is the island the Lucayans called Guanahani. What follows are my reasons for this belief. For the most part I will restrict my comments to the Watling track. However, because the *National Geographic* enjoys such enormous readership (estimated at 40 million worldwide) and because the conclusions published in the magazine were so recently and forcefully presented, it is necessary to point out several of the argument's fatal flaws (see Fuson 1987; Taviani 1987; Larimore 1988; Keegan 1989a).

That the Morison track was inaccurate in a number of places was no surprise to those familiar with the debate. It was these nagging problems that kept alive interest in the first-landfall question. In general outline, Morison's "Watling track" goes from San Salvador (Watling) to Rum Cay to northern Long Island to Crooked and Fortune islands and then to Cuba (map 8.1).

Beginning in 1982, Steven Mitchell, a geologist at California State University in Bakersfield, and I initiated a comprehensive research program designed to disprove, if possible, the Morison track (Keegan 1984a, 1988; Keegan and Mitchell 1987; Mitchell and Keegan 1987). The program involved collecting data with respect to three specific types of descriptions found in the diario: navigation-related reports of sailing directions and distances, descriptions of island physiography, and locations of the Lucayan villages that were visited or observed. Two additional categories of evidence have also been investigated: the reports of Spanish expeditions that followed Columbus, and the archaeological distribution of European trade goods that entered the native exchange network in the early contact period.

Careful use of the diario, with cross-checking among the different types of descriptions, provides a remarkably complete reconstruction of Columbus's passage through the Bahamas. In general, the proposed recon-

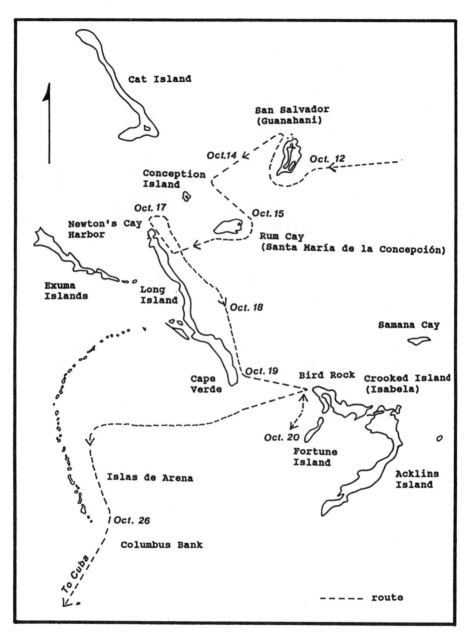

MAP 8.1. Route proposed for Columbus's first voyage.

struction matches the Morison track, although it differs in certain details to achieve better conformity with the diario. Such changes in detail result from recent archaeological, geological, and geographical studies that were not available to Morison.

The Transatlantic Crossing and Guanahani

In 1986, Luis Marden presented a simulation of the transatlantic crossing using values for *prevailing* winds and currents. Marden reached the conclusion that Columbus's track could only have ended in the vicinity of Samana Cay. These results were presented as irrefutable proof that Samana Cay was Columbus's first landfall.

Marden's study led Woods Hole oceanographers Philip Richardson and Roger Goldsmith (1987) to examine the transatlantic crossing in greater detail. They argued that using *prevailing* values overestimated by a factor of three the probable influences of winds and currents on Columbus's ships. They further demonstrated that by using values for *average* winds and currents the same crossing ended within sight (15 miles) of San Salvador Island. In comparison, the Marden simulation *overshot* Samana Cay by more than 300 miles.

Both simulations are based on reasonable assumptions. Their different conclusions indicate that both Samana Cay and San Salvador Island can be supported with this type of evidence, although Richardson and Goldsmith's end point within sight of San Salvador would seem to favor their conclusions (also see Kelley 1983, 1987). Richardson has since used the same techniques to prove that the crossing could have ended at Grand Turk (Marvel and Power 1991).

Another suggestion for the transatlantic crossing is that Columbus was a latitude sailor who followed the latitude from the Canary Islands. Working with modern maps, Arne Molander (1983) has shown that Egg Island, which is at the northern end of Eleuthera, is on line with the Canary Islands. Others have questioned whether it is appropriate to use modern maps. Maps from the sixteenth century tend to displace the latitude of the Bahamas far to the south in relation to the Canary Islands (Kelley 1989). Robert Power (Marvel and Power 1991) has shown that on the Juan de la Cosa map of 1500, the east-west line from Ferro in the Canaries passes through Grand Turk. Starting from the same basic assumption concerning Columbus as a latitude sailor, two conclusions have been reached, separated by almost 300 miles.

In the same vein, it is useful to recall that an angle of only 9 degrees from the Canary Islands defines an arc that encompasses all of the Bahamas and Turks and Caicos. Furthermore, questions still remain concerning navigational techniques, the accuracy of sandglasses that had to be turned every half hour to measure time, and rate-of-speed estimates based on the time it took a piece of flotsam to pass the length of the ship. Although Columbus may have been a superb navigator, even he was sometimes well off the mark, as when he recorded that navigational readings indicated that he was sailing uphill along the northeastern coast of Venezuela.

On Friday, October 12, 1492 (Julian calendar; October 21 in the modern Gregorian calendar), Christopher Columbus set foot on the island of Guanahani. As others, especially Morison (1942), have shown, present-day San Salvador has all of the physical characteristics described by Columbus: a large protected harbor, a central lagoon and much water, a peninsula that could be fortified and made into an island, and so forth (map 8.2) (Obregón 1987; Sealey 1987; Taviani 1987). In addition, recent archaeological investigations have identified the "two or three" Lucayan settlements that were observed during the longboat survey (it remains to be demonstrated that the sites were occupied in 1492), have located a Lucayan site near the peninsula where Columbus observed six houses, and have recovered European objects dating to this period from a Lucayan site near the proposed first-landing beach (Hoffman 1987b; J. Winter, per. com. 1985).

Although Spanish pottery has been found on other islands in Lucayan sites, the objects that Charles Hoffman has recovered on San Salvador are presently unique. These objects include green and yellow glass beads, a brass D-ring, and a belt buckle, as well as other objects that were mentioned in the diario (Hoffman 1987a; Brill et al. 1987). Unfortunately, it is presently impossible to prove that these objects were left on the island by Columbus's expedition (Keegan 1984a; Keegan and Mitchell 1987). Nonetheless, these are the types of objects one would expect to find in the vicinity of Columbus's landfalls.

Santa María de la Concepción

After leaving San Salvador, Columbus "saw so many islands" that he could not decide to which he should go first. The previous night he recorded that it was his intention to sail to the southwest to seek the vil-

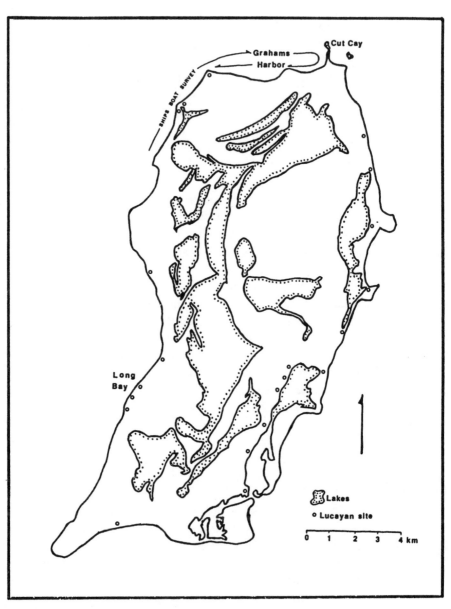

MAP 8.2. San Salvador Island, also known as Watling Island and *Guanahani*.

lage of the "King" who possessed much gold. Although Columbus did not record the direction in which he actually sailed when he left San Salvador, a west-southwest departure from the northern end of the island would bring many islands into view. By midcrossing, when his next diario entry was apparently made, Cat Island would have been visible to the west-northwest, Conception Island to the southwest, Rum Cay to the south-southwest, and Long Island (then or soon) to the west. Each of these islands would have appeared to be many as their high ridges rose above the horizon while the intervening swales lay below the horizon. On this course the hills of Rum Cay make it appear to be the largest island, the island toward which Columbus directed his ships.

This crossing is an excellent match for the account in Columbus's diario. First, Columbus "saw many islands." Second, he headed to the largest which "is about five leagues distant from this island of San Salvador, and the others of them [islands] some more, some less" (Dunn and Kelley 1989:77). Columbus later revised his estimate of the distance to the second island to "rather about seven" leagues. Rum Cay is about 21 miles (seven leagues) from San Salvador, and along this route Conception Island is closer, and Long and Cat islands more distant.

As mentioned previously, Rum Cay is one-third the size of the island described in the diario, but the mistranscription of leagues for miles accounts for this discrepancy. Rum Cay measures five by ten miles in the type of mile that Kelley (1987) suggests Columbus was using. In addition, Columbus "killed time" between the first two islands during the night and then sailed less than seven leagues between dawn and noon. If after reaching Rum Cay he sailed along the east and south coasts to anchor on the west cape, then he would have traveled a similar distance between noon and sundown. It is also clear from information about winds and drift that Columbus's anchorage was on the south side of the island, which matches the location proposed on this track (Dunn and Kelley 1989:79n.3). In sum, the small size of Rum Cay matches the sailing described in the diario.

Columbus did not describe in detail this second island, which he christened Santa María de la Concepción. He did not decide to visit the island until he was almost past, and his visit ashore was uneventful. The Lucayans "allowed us to go through the island," but he *does not* describe a Lucayan settlement (*contra* Judge 1986). The remains of Lucayan settlements are present on Rum Cay, and, as expected from the diario, none has been identified on the western cape where Columbus went ashore (map 8.3).

In contrast, it is assumed on the Samana track that Columbus really did write "leagues." To account for the full five by ten leagues he would have had to sail to the northeastern tip of Acklins Island. If he had done otherwise, he would not have seen the five-league north-south trending coast. Yet, Columbus had to sail almost due south to even view northeast Acklins, and topographic maps and ground surveys indicate that eastern Crooked Island, with its higher and more extensive ridge system, would have appeared as a larger target than northeast Acklins, most of which is less than twenty feet in elevation. Because Northeast Acklins is also the closest island to Samana Cay, where is the closer island?

There are additional aspects of the Samana track that do not conform to the diario. Two islands, Crooked and Acklins, must be all of the "many" islands that Columbus observed and did not know toward which he should go. Why did he not correct what would clearly be a misrepresentation after he had sailed along their north coasts? Also, after failing to sail seven leagues the previous afternoon and then sailing less than four leagues between noon and sunrise, Columbus somehow managed to more than double his speed to cover the remaining ten leagues (30 miles) between noon and sundown in order to anchor on the western end of Crooked Is-

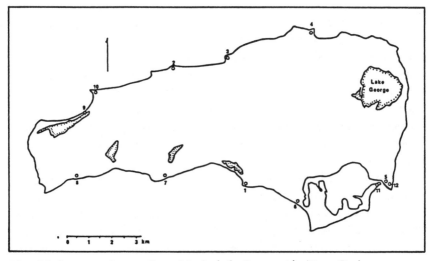

MAP 8.3. Lucayan sites on Santa María de la Concepción (Rum Cay).

land. In addition, Columbus could not have seen the large island to the west (Long Island) by the time it was described in his diario, and it was still out of sight when he began sailing to it from the western end of Crooked Island (Fuson 1987). Lastly, his anchorage at Crooked Island would have been on the north coast, even though the reported wind direction indicates a south coast anchorage.

Fernandina

When Columbus *arrived* at Santa María de la Concepción, he observed a large island to the west. With hills rising to 150 feet, and trees adding perhaps 50 feet more, Long Island would have been visible before Columbus anchored at Rum Cay. He estimated that the crossing was nine leagues and later revised it to eight, which is consistent with the impression obtained when approaching a relatively higher island. The actual distance is closer to seven leagues or about twenty miles. Two interesting points come to light during the crossing.

First, Columbus is quoted, "And it surely seems that it would have on this coast more than 28 leagues on this side." Kelley has pointed out that about seven leagues (or roughly 21 statute miles) was something of a mariner's standard for the distance one could see to the horizon from a ship. How then could Columbus have seen for more than 80 miles?

To my mind, the main cause of confusion is that Long Island is roughly that length. Before Lyon's (1986) translation for the *National Geographic* study, Columbus's second statement, that the island was longer than 20 leagues, was mentioned exclusively. Twenty leagues provides a good fit with Long Island's roughly 60-mile, as the crow flies, east coast. Thus, the island and the description *seemed* to match quite well. However, while it may be possible to make such a match with map in hand, no one could have seen the entire length of coastline, not even Columbus. If we again substitute miles for leagues, the problem is solved. From an offshore position at some distance from the end of the island it would have been possible to observe 28 miles of the coast (see Fuson 1987:86).

The second interesting occurrence was the interception of a Lucayan who was paddling his canoe in the same direction. Columbus had already developed a reputation for carrying off "interpreters" and "guides" against their will, so he ordered that the man be treated well and sent on his way. This strategy was apparently effective because the man "had given such good word of us that all this night there was no lack of canoes alongside the ship," and the next morning Columbus was brought to a village (map 8.4). This village was a major stumbling block for the Watling route before Mitchell and I completed our archaeological and geological surveys of the island in 1984. Until then it was thought that Long Island was nearly uninhabited in 1492 and that no windward coast was suited for permanent habitation (Sears and Sullivan 1978; but see Krieger 1937, 1938). Our surveys identified more than 40 Lucayan sites on Long Island, 16 of which are located on the windward east coast (Keegan and Mitchell 1984b). More importantly, two of the village sites are in locations that satisfy descriptions in the diario. In addition to the sites themselves, the physical characteristics of the coast match the descriptions in the diario.

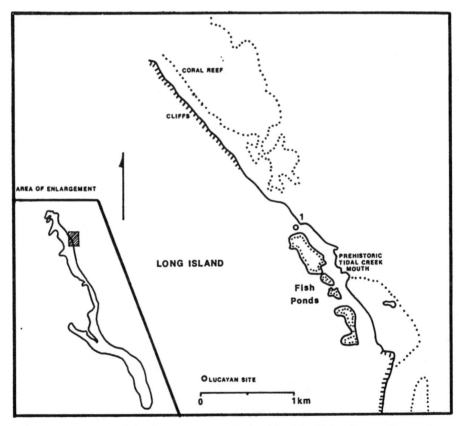

MAP 8.4. Location of the first Lucayan village visited by Columbus on Fernandina, northern Long Island.

Columbus's first stop on Long Island was at a village near present-day Fish Ponds. Here a "cape" projects where the coast shifts from a north-northwest to a northwest orientation. Columbus left this village at midday and stated that his intention was to sail to the south and southeast to reach Samoet. Martín Alonso Pinzón, captain of *Pinta*, interpreted native testimony to the effect that a southern course was more easily followed by rounding the island to the north-northwest. Columbus decided to follow the northwesterly course because the winds were more favorable for that direction. Only an anchorage at the northern end of Long Island can account for their conclusion that the best course to the south was achieved by rounding the island to the north. Moreover, this course may derive from a native practice. Canoe passage along the western lee shore of Long Island was certainly preferable to travel along the windward east coast and there is little difference in the distance one would travel to reach Crooked Island (this idea was suggested to me by William Dunwoody).

After leaving the first anchorage, Columbus sailed to the north until he came upon a harbor with two mouths. Here is an instance where Morison was wrong. Morison placed the harbor-with-two-mouths on the west side of the island. It is clear in the diario that this harbor is on the east coast (Keegan and Mitchell 1987). Its location was given as "two leagues before the cape [end] of the island." They followed a northwesterly course after leaving the first harbor, a direction of travel that would only fit an east coast location, "as far as the coast that runs east-west" (Dunn and Kelley 1989:95). The two mouths of the Newton Cay harbor are 1.68 and 2.02 neo-Roman miles from the northern end ("cape") of Long Island, where the coast runs east-west. Here is another case where the use of miles, rather than leagues, can be shown to provide a better fit to the diario description.

The harbor-with-two-mouths occurs where Long Island is capped by Newton Cay (map 8.5). Columbus described the harbor as appearing like the mouth of a river, but there are no true rivers in the Bahamas (Sealey 1985). The tidal creek that separates Newton Cay from Long Island flows into this harbor through a constriction in the Pleistocene Age limestone that channels the flow at its entrance into the harbor producing the appearance of a river. Columbus took on water at a Lucayan village, the remains of which, in association with a freshwater pond, have been identified on Newton Cay near the harbor.

Despite the close conformity between the northern end of Long Island

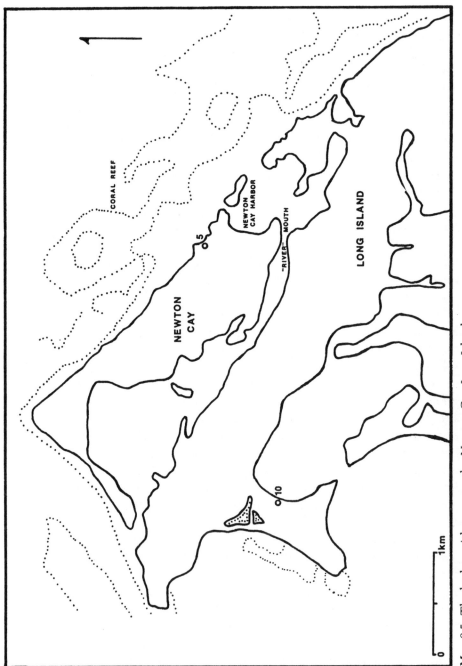

MAP 8.5. The harbor with two mouths, Newton Cay, Long Island.

and Columbus's descriptions, those favoring competing routes have pointed out that the northern end of Long Island has a southwest-northeast orientation, rather than the required east-west orientation (Judge 1986). However, when the northern east coast of Long Island is shifted to the north-northwest orientation described by Columbus, the top of Long Island obtains an orientation of about 247 degrees, or west-southwest. Given the compass terms used to describe the orientation of the coast, the description of the top of Long Island as having an east-west orientation is acceptable. In fact, there may be a technological justification for this conclusion. Kelley (1989) recently suggested that on early maps and navigational records of the area there may have been a 14-degree clockwise rotation of the islands deriving from undetected westerly magnetic variation. This magnetic variation would also account for the description of northern Long Island as trending north-northwest rather than simply northwest, and for the northern end to be called east-west.

Columbus left the Newton Cay settlement about dusk and sailed all night and all the following day until dusk. Although he may not have made much progress initially, because the wind was light and it rained heavily after midnight until daybreak, he sailed from daybreak until dusk "with the wind and went around the island as far as I could." During as many as 12 hours sailing with the wind he could easily have sailed from northern to southern Long Island. It is about 60 nautical miles from one end of the island to the other. Although Columbus would have had to sail somewhat farther to remain offshore, he may actually have sailed somewhat less. His directions of travel the following day indicate an east coast anchorage as far as 10 miles north of the southern end of the island (Morison 1942). In comparison, the next day, with the same following winds, his ships traveled about 30 nautical miles between dawn and midday (about 5 nautical miles per hour). Furthermore, Columbus did not sail around the southern end of the island. If he had, his courses the next morning, all trending toward the east, would have had to cross land. The word "around," as used by Columbus, can also be translated as "on a circuit." In this context it seems to be more appropriate to describe his course as "along" the island since he did not round the southern end of his circuit.

The next morning Columbus sent his ships to the east-and-southeast, to the south-southeast, and to the southeast, the course of a man who was looking for something that he knew was there but was unsure of its exact location. Before three hours they saw an island to the east, and they arrived there by midday. In all they sailed about 30 miles in less than six hours. This passage accurately describes a trip from southern Long Island to Crooked Island, Saomete, and the "Cape of the Small Island," the solid foundation upon which the revised Watling track is based. From here Columbus spent three days of seeking an audience with the "king" of Samaot on the island he renamed La Isabela. Failing in that quest he set sail for Cuba.

"Samaot . . . the island or city where the gold is"

Of the islands that he observed and visited, it is the fourth that Columbus described most completely. The Lucayan captives who were brought from the first and second islands called this island Saomete. Actually, four spellings appear in the diario (i.e., Samaot, Samoet, Saomete, Saometo), which suggests that Columbus had difficulty understanding native terms for locations (Keegan 1984a). It may be the case that Columbus heard correctly, and that one name or two similar names were being used to indicate slightly different locations. The use of one name in related contexts is fairly common in linguistic systems. It provides a means of denoting relationship (e.g., parent-child), ownership (e.g., landowner-parcel of land), and forms of political integration (e.g., headman-village). It is reported that this practice was common among the Classic Taino of Hispaniola (Fewkes 1907).

Fewkes states that the Classic Tainos's provinces were often designated by the name of the cacique (chief). Thus, Columbus may have been confused by the use of one name for both the island and the village of the paramount chief. Alternatively, two similar names with slight differences in word endings or in pronunciation might have been used. Much as we use *city* and *state* to distinguish between the two New Yorks, Samaot (Samoet) may refer to the village of the chief, while Saomete (Saometo) refers to the island(s) on which the settlement was located (i.e., the main province of the paramount chief). This interpretation is supported by Columbus's report that the population of Saomete resided further "inland" (away from the shore at which he was anchored). He goes on to state, "I believe that it [Cape Hermoso] is an island separate from Saometo and even that there is even another small one between."

The village of a king who had much gold was first mentioned on October 13 while Columbus was still on San Salvador. Samaot was first mentioned by name in the report for Wednesday, October 17, upon arrival at the third island, Fernandina. Columbus stated, "I set sail with a south wind to strive to go around the whole island and to keep trying until I find Samaot, which is the island or city where the gold is; for so say all these men who come here in the ship, and so told us the men of the island of San Salvador and of Santa María" (Dunn and Kelley 1989:87–89).

The significance of Samaot has been either ignored or missed by most investigators. It is usually assumed that Columbus made no plans concerning the island toward which he headed because he did not know where he was. To the contrary, there are explicit statements that Samaot was his objective, an objective he declared first on October 13 before he left San Salvador. He was directed toward this goal by his obsession with gold and riches (see Sauer 1966).

It is no surprise that proponents of the Samana Cay track have ignored the implications of Samaot because they reveal a fatal flaw in the Samana Cay argument. The quotation above describes a course that is contrary to that argument's placement of Columbus at the southern end of Long Island. Why would Columbus set out to sail 60 miles to the north so he could round the island when he was less than 4 miles from the island's southern end? The south wind that day would have been equally suited to sailing along the east or west coasts.

More importantly, how could the following sequence of events have been possible? (1) Columbus leaves the island of Santa María de la Concepción; (2) when he arrives at Fernandina the next morning he states that he will strive until he reaches Samaot; (3) he concludes that a course rounding the island to the north is the shortest route to the south, changes course because of a change in winds, and returns to the south; (4) he sends his ships toward the east along slightly different courses because he is searching for an island that he does not want to miss; (5) he succeeds in sailing to within ten miles of the location that he had left three days earlier; (6) the native captives from San Salvador and Santa María finally decide to tell him that this is the Samaot (Saomete) he has spent three days trying to reach.

Even if, as Judge and his supporters maintain, Fortune Island and Crooked Island do not appear to be the same island (an opinion that I do not share, based on first-hand observations), it is inconceivable that Columbus would have spent almost three days sailing around Fernandina only to find his objective within ten miles of his previous landing place. On the Samana track Columbus could see his previous anchorage, an anchorage from which he could have walked to Samaot and thus saved himself three days of sailing.

Three days were spent sailing up and down the western shore in an effort to gain an audience with the chief who lived at Samaot. Columbus anchored his ships at three capes along this shore: the Cape of the Small Island on the north coast, Cape Hermoso on the west coast, and Cape of the Lagoon at the southwestern end (map 8.6). The locations that elsewhere Columbus described as "capes" are the ends of islands or places where the coast is marked by a sharp bend. The capes identified here are consistent with that definition.

Columbus arrived first at the Cape of the Small Island, which he described as being in an east-west direction from Fernandina. He then wrote, "And the coast ran, after (this), from the small island to the west and extends 12 leagues up to a cape. And here I named the Cape Hermoso, which is on the west side." This quotation has given investigators considerable grief. Without punctuation, the sentence can be read to fit almost any direction of travel.

Most people read the quotation as stating that the coast ran from the cape of the small island for 12 leagues to the west. However, when read carefully, "the small island to the west" actually indicates the location of this island in relation to Cape Hermoso, the place from which the description is being made. In other words, the cape of the small island is to the west of Cape Hermoso.

The quotation encapsulates the following sequence of events. First, Columbus arrived at a "north point," which he named the Cape of the Small Island. Since the wind was still out of the north he would not have sailed along the north coast of the east-west trending Crooked Island because the winds would have pushed him onto the shore. Instead, he sailed along the west coast, which trends toward the southeast. By sailing about 12 miles to the southeast Columbus would have come to the end of Crooked Island (French Wells). There Crooked Island is separated from Fortune Island by a narrow strait. Replacing leagues with miles (for the reasons discussed previously), taking wind direction into account, and using Columbus's typical definition of a cape, it is apparent that the quotation describes a shore that does not run *to* the west but *from* the west; with from/to the west included to indicate the location of the Cape of the

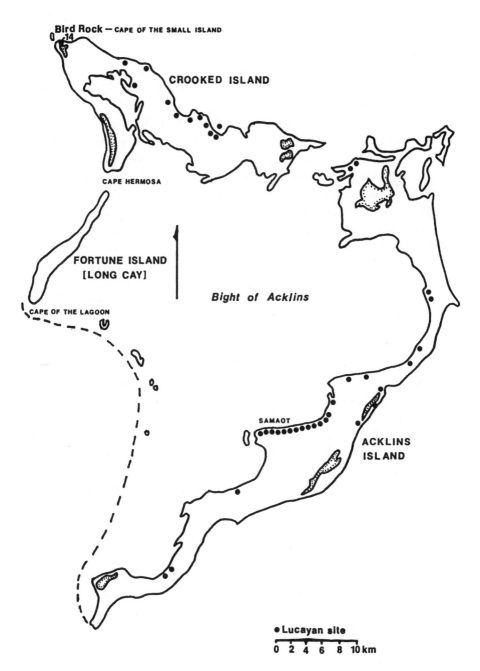

MAP 8.6. Crooked and Acklins islands, including Lucayan site locations.

Small Island *in relation to* Cape Hermoso. As mentioned above, the description was made at the Cape Hermoso anchorage.

Lyon's (1986) translation of the diario indicates that Columbus was fond of reporting travel in terms of both the direction toward which he was going and the direction from which he came. The quotation can thus be rewritten: "And the coast ran, after (this), 12 miles to the (south)east from the small island in the (north)west. And here I named the cape Hermoso, which is on the west side." Alternatively, this may be an example of a transcription error in which the word *sueste* (southeast) was replaced by *gueste* (west) (Dunn and Kelley 1989:99n3). In either case, the result is a perfect fit between the diario description and the configuration of western Crooked/Fortune islands.

Columbus next moved to the southwestern cape, the Cape of the Lagoon, which is here identified as Windsor Point, Fortune Island. From there he attempted to sail to the northeast and east, but he found the water too shallow. Windsor Point is the only cape on the west coast from which a northeast course is possible. The other option that Columbus considered was a course in the opposite direction, which he discarded as "a very long way around," the implication being that Samaot is close enough to sail to on a direct course, but too far away if he must sail around the shallows. The only location that matches this description is on the western coast of Acklins Island.

These descriptions paint a unique portrait that fits only one group of islands—Fortune/Crooked/Acklins, which are shaped like a horseshoe with Fortune and Acklins the projections and Crooked Island the crosspiece. The three surround the Bight of Acklins, an expanse of shallows that has changed little in the past five centuries and over which a conservative mariner would never consider sailing. Across the Bight of Acklins from the southwestern cape of Fortune Island are the remains of a Lucayan settlement. In contrast to other Lucayan settlements, which extend along the shore a maximum distance of 1 kilometer, this settlement is more than six kilometers long. Preliminary investigations begun in 1987 thus far support the identification of this settlement complex as Samaot, Columbus's village of the "King" (Keegan 1984a, 1988).

Columbus never reached Samaot, but he did visit a village near the Cape of the Small Island (map 8.7). Morison identifies the small island as Bird Rock, which lies just off the northwestern end of Crooked Island. There is a Lucayan site at the appropriate distance from an anchorage

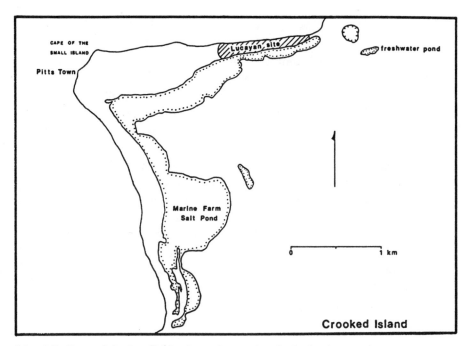

M AP 8.7. Cape of the Small Island, northwest Crooked Island.

near Bird Rock. Excavations conducted in 1987 indicate that this was a very large village that could have been occupied in 1492. Columbus found this village while searching for water, and a freshwater lake has been identified within about one kilometer of the site. In addition, Daniel McKinnen (1804:152), who visited the area in 1802–3, reported a freshwater spring at the head of the pond at Pittstown.

Columbus described capturing a 5.7-foot "serpent" (*sierpe*) in the lagoon; Martín Alonso Pinzón killed a second of similar size the next day. These were skinned, and their skins were brought back to Spain. Since Columbus wrote previously about snakes (*culebra*) and lizards (*lagartos*), the identity of this large serpent has long been a mystery. During excavations at the Lucayan site (CR-14) the leg bone (femur) of a crocodile (*Crocodylus* sp.) was recovered. This discovery was surprising because crocodiles were not previously reported for this time period in the Bahamas (Wing and Reitz 1982). Although it is highly unlikely that this bone is from the crocodiles captured by Columbus's crew, it demonstrates that large "serpents" were living in the appropriate area.

In the past, Columbus's serpent has always been identified as an iguana. Although iguanas are reported to have reached that size, there are no contemporaneous reports of giant iguanas. Further, the animal's behavior—it "threw" itself into the lake—is more typical of crocodiles than of iguanas. Iguanas will enter the water, but only as a last resort. Finally, crocodiles are sufficiently rare to warrant such special notice and attention (capture and skinning), and they survived in the area until the nineteenth century (McKinnen 1804:188).

In sum, all of the categories of evidence are satisfied by Fortune/ Crooked/Acklins Islands. Furthermore, no other island or combination of islands possesses these unique characteristics: three capes on a western coast, a huge expanse of shallows to the east of a southwestern cape across from which is the location of a "king's" village, a Lucayan village near the northern cape associated with a freshwater lagoon in which "serpents" resided, restricted Lucayan settlement on a lee coast, and a location that fits Columbus's arrival from the west, and from which the departure to Cuba matches the remainder of the passage.

Distribution of Fifteenth- to Sixteenth-Century European Artifacts

Columbus described, in some detail, the exchange of European objects for native Lucayan materials (Daggett 1980; Rose 1987). We would therefore expect to find European artifacts in the Lucayan villages that Columbus visited. At first glance, the discovery of European objects in a "pre-Columbian" site would seem proof positive that Columbus was there. Unfortunately, the situation is greatly more complicated.

In addition to the unique European objects that Charles Hoffman has recovered during excavations on San Salvador (Hoffman 1987a; Brill et al. 1987), European objects have been recovered from MC-6 in the Caicos Islands, including a brass nose ornament (Sullivan 1981), and Spanish earthenwares have been recovered from the surfaces of sites on Long Island, Little Exuma, and Acklins Island and from nonspecific contexts (isolated surface finds) on Conception Island and Samana Cay. It is certain that additional European materials will be recovered when these and other Lucayan sites are excavated.

Three mechanisms can be suggested to account for the recovery of

European objects in "pre-Columbian" sites. Two of these assume that the sites were occupied when the objects were introduced, and the third assumes that the objects are intrusive. The first mechanism is the direct exchange between Spaniard and Lucayan with the European object then deposited in the vicinity of the exchange. In addition to Columbus, the expeditions of Amerigo Vespucci and Vicente Yáñez Pinzón in 1499–1500, undocumented voyages (Harrisse 1961), shipwrecked sailors (Peterson 1974; Keith et al. 1984), and slaving expeditions could also have introduced European objects. This type of exchange should produce a distribution pattern similar to that recorded along the Hernando de Soto trail (Hudson et al. 1987: fig. 2). There is, however, the problem of deciphering which of the Spanish expeditions introduced the materials at any given site.

The second mechanism follows the first and involves the subsequent exchange of materials along the native exchange network (Daggett 1980). Through this mechanism materials can be moved tremendous distances. For instance, Rose (1987) reports that a piece of jadeite recovered from the Pigeon Creek site, San Salvador, has a trace-element composition indicating a Guatemalan source. For perhaps 20 years after the first arrival of the Spanish (1492–1518) opportunities for the exchange of European materials between Lucayan communities existed. In addition, European objects could have been obtained through native exchange with Hispaniola and Cuba, along the same networks that Taino pottery moved before the arrival of the Spanish. However, by 1520 the majority of Lucayans had been killed or enslaved, so the number of exchanges would have decreased dramatically by the end of this period.

The final mechanism is the deposition of European artifacts on Lucayan sites after the sites were abandoned. The presence of such materials would indicate nothing about initial contacts except, perhaps, the date by which they ceased. Between about 1502 and the final extermination of the Lucayans around 1520, an estimated 320 caravel loads of Lucayans (40,000 people) were removed from the Bahamas. There is a high probability that European objects were accidentally deposited in Lucayan villages at this time. Examples could include the Spanish olive jar fragment recovered on Samana Cay, which has been identified as middle-style dating to the mid-1500s, and the French Haitian earthenware vessel recovered from a cave on Great Inagua.

Until additional excavations are conducted it will be impossible to sort out the context(s) in which those European objects were deposited. One method that may answer some of the questions involves techniques for determining the original source of the European object (e.g., Brill et al. 1987). Such techniques may help to distinguish which explorer introduced the object by providing information about source or a refinement of chronological controls. For instance, Steven Mitchell (pers. com. 1987) has suggested that the earthenware jars on Columbus's voyage may have been manufactured in a different area of Spain than were the jars carried on subsequent voyages. Thus, by identifying source areas it may be possible to identify pieces from Columbus's cargo. Such sourcing studies are, however, only a partial solution to the problem because there is no way to tell how many exchanges took place between the source and the final resting place. For the present, additional research is needed before the distribution of European objects can contribute to the debate.

Finally, the careful scrutiny of documents concerning later voyages and maps produced during the sixteenth century are helping to identify where later explorers and cartographers believed Guanahani to be located (Kelley 1988; McGuirk 1989). These studies demonstrate that Guanahani is consistently depicted in the central Bahamas, which would tend to discredit the most northern (Egg Island) and southern (Turks and Caicos) routes. The maps can be read to support the identification of Watling as Guanahani (McGuirk 1989).

Summary

Despite the passage of nearly 500 years, the particulars of Christopher Columbus's first voyage remain the subject of intense debate. Leaving aside questions concerning Columbus's motives, which will never be adequately answered, I conclude by reviewing the landfall debate. The varying opinions concerning the first landfall and subsequent route of Columbus's first voyage are the product of different initial assumptions (e.g. latitude sailing, transatlantic crossing, descriptions of the first island), differences in emphasis regarding information contained in the diario, the mistranslation of key diario passages, and personal agendas.

Beginning fresh in the years just prior to the 500th anniversary it is now possible to be conclusive about where Columbus first landed. Many of the problems with the diario have been resolved through close scrutiny and debate, and the most complete and accurate rendering of the Las Casas folios was recently completed by Oliver Dunn and James Kelley, Jr. (1989). Questions concerning the transatlantic crossing have received a most thorough investigation in the computer simulations of Kelley (1983), Marden (1986), and Richardson and Goldsmith (1987). Attention has now been given to the appearances of the islands at first contact through the geological reconstruction of coastlines (Mitchell and Keegan 1987), archaeological investigations of Lucayan settlements (Keegan 1984a, 1988; Hoffman 1987b; Keegan and Mitchell 1987; Keegan, Williams, and Seim 1990), and paleobotanical studies of the tropical forests that once grew on these islands. Materials analysis of European trade goods recovered in archaeological sites has helped to identify their sources (Brill et al. 1987).

The landfall debate is not simply an exercise aimed at solving a historical mystery. The debate has served to refine the reconstruction of Columbus's voyage for the purpose of determining where his descriptions of native peoples were made. Because these are the only first-hand observations of Lucayan lifeways, they provide important clues in efforts to reconstruct the past.

9

Las Islas de Lucayos,
1499-1520

Columbus was awarded the title "Admiral of said islands and mainland which you may thus discover and acquire, and shall be our Admiral and Viceroy and Governor therein, and shall be empowered henceforward to call and entitle yourself *Don Cristóbal Colón,* and his heirs and successors forever may be so entitled" (Morison 1942:105). By analogy to the Admiral of Castile (the title was not restricted to seamen), Columbus pressed his claim for exclusive rights to both the passage to and products from the Indies. He was to receive a percentage of the proceeds from all commerce and was therefore interested in maintaining a monopoly. In sum, Columbus enjoyed a legal stranglehold with respect to access to the Indies.

As the only person with a legal right to sail to the Indies, it is sometimes assumed that Columbus was, in fact, the only person who did so before 1499, an assumption supported in the official record by the absence of chartered expeditions before that date and by the caveat that accompanied later patents and charters: "keep away from shores that pertain to the King of Portugal and do not trespass on any land that has been discovered by Columbus" (Sauer 1966:107). It was only after the magnitude of Columbus's discoveries was appreciated, or after the promise of riches continued unfulfilled, that Spain began to legally sanction other expeditions.

There are reasons to believe that Columbus was not the exclusive explorer of the Indies before 1499. First, the Portuguese had previously attempted crossings, but they failed to follow the winds and therefore got only a short distance from the coast. Given Columbus's success it is difficult to believe that the Portuguese simply abandoned their interest. Second, during his second voyage (1493-94), Columbus discovered the remains of a European shipwreck on the island of Guadeloupe. It is usually assumed that these "ship's timbers" floated across the Atlantic (Morison 1942) as does so much flotsam today.

Finally, on the Juan de la Cosa map of 1500, Cuba is represented as an island, and a mainland to the west of the Bahamas is depicted. These representations occur despite Columbus's assertion in 1494 that Cuba was the mainland, despite Cuba not being (officially) circumnavigated until 1508, and despite credit being given to Juan Ponce de León's expedition of 1513 for the discovery of La Florida, itself described that year as an island. Harrisse (1961) has suggested that others sailed the Indies in secrecy during these early years.

John Cabot, sailing for England, may have reached North America in 1494 and had certainly cruised near New England in 1497. The first British vessel sighted by Spaniards in the West Indies dates to 1526 (an earlier sighting may have taken place in 1519), and the French were taking cargoes of dyewood in Brazil by 1506. The impression that Columbus alone was the exclusive explorer between 1492 and 1499 may not be correct; within a quarter-century, explorers from around Europe were everywhere.

Challengers of Columbus, 1499

> The contemporary perspective on Columbus was informed and fair. The chroniclers took pride in his discovery that gave Spain title to the New World but they saw also his limitations and failures. The seven years of Columbus's government were a continuing and growing series of disappointments and deficits. The extravagant prospectuses of promised wealth went on but revenues did not materialize. Nor did Columbus know how to govern men. Fonseca and Ferdinand . . . decided that if the affairs of the Indies were to be rescued Columbus would have to go. (Sauer 1966:104-105).

Although the Spanish crown was peripatetic, the affairs of the Indies were managed from the beginning at Seville (Sauer 1966:106). At the time of Columbus's second voyage, Juan Rodríguez de Fonseca, then archdeacon of the cathedral of Seville, was assigned as the manager of New World explorations. Fonseca began his attempts to rehabilitate the Indies in 1499 with the appointment of Francisco de Bobadilla as governor and judge "of all the islands and mainland of the Indies" (supplanting Columbus), and with the licensing of independent expeditions (Sauer 1966:105).

At least four expeditions were licensed by Fonseca in 1499. They were led by Alonso de Hojeda and Amerigo Vespucci, Vicente Yáñez Pinzón, Peralonso Niño, and Diego de Lepe. These explorers set out independently, and all charted their initial course to the Gulf of Paria on the Venezuelan coast. Only the first two expeditions are important for the present discussion as they passed through the Bahama Islands at the end of the voyages. First, a brief digression into the life of Amerigo Vespucci is warranted to resolve certain continuing misconceptions and to examine the motives behind his four-month voyage through the Bahamas.

Amerigo Vespucci

Amerigo Vespucci is best known as the man after whom the New World, Tierra Firme, was named. This honor was bestowed by Martin Waldseemuller, professor of geography at the College of Saint-Die, who applied the name *America* to the southern continent on his 1507 map of the world (Pohl 1966:170). *America* was applied to the northern continent later in the century on Mercator's maps.

With the exception of that honor, Vespucci has received little of the credit he is due for his major contributions to the study of New World geography. In part, Vespucci's contributions were overshadowed by the deification of Christopher Columbus that Columbus's son Fernando initiated in response to the growing discontent with Columbus's administration of the Indies (Taviani 1985; Fuson 1987). But the major reason for Vespucci's lack of recognition comes from the wide circulation of fraudulent letters that were attributed to him. As Pohl (1966:147) reports: "By forged quotation, by libelous exaggeration, he was made to appear as a boaster, a liar, a quack navigator. Thus, excess of fame defamed him."

It is reported that when Waldseemuller learned that Vespucci had not made a voyage to South America in 1497, the year before Columbus's "discovery" of the continent, he unsuccessfully sought to remove Vespucci's name from the map. Pohl (1966:170) notes that *America* as a variant of the German *Amalrich* (which glosses as "rich through work"), along with its being so euphonious a name and parallel with Asia, Africa, and Australia, resulted in its rapid adoption and spread into universal usage. What Waldseemuller had given, he was unable to take away.

The first of the forgeries, *Mundus Novus* (New World), appeared in August 1504 and was purported to be a letter from Vespucci to his patron, Lorenzo di Piero Francesco de' Medici. The second was published in September 1504 as *Letter from Amerigo Vespucci to Piero Soderini, Gonfaloniere, the Year 1504;* since it provides accounts of four voyages, it is frequently mentioned by its more descriptive title, *Four Voyages.* Of the four voyages, the first is certainly false and was apparently created to give Vespucci priority over Columbus for the discovery of the South American mainland. The fourth voyage is possible but has never been documented.

The accounts of each voyage contain obvious embellishments that make the entire work unusable as a scholarly document. Although the forgeries were apparently recognized as such in Spain and Portugal, the truth concerning Vespucci's voyages was not known in Italy, France, the Low Countries, and Germany where the pamphlets were being printed (Pohl 1966:157). Even today, publications concerning "The Four Voyages of Amerigo Vespucci" far outnumber those that consider the actual records of Vespucci's voyages. Failures to recognize the forgeries as such have compounded inaccurate interpretations of Caribbean ethnohistory (e.g., Myers 1984).

Amerigo Vespucci was born to a wealthy family in Florence, Italy. He was well-educated and was personally acquainted with the leading Florentine scholar, Paolo dal Pozzo Toscanelli. In 1483, Vespucci became *maestra di casa* (manager of the firm) of the Cadet branch of the Medici. In their service he proved to be a successful trader and businessman. He was married in Spain and established residence there in 1492 while continuing in the service of the Medici (Pohl 1966). Vespucci was among the first to recognize that Tierra Firme was a new continent and not the Asiatic shore, as Columbus maintained. In the final years of his life (1508–12), he served the Spanish Crown as the first pilot major responsible for the office of navigation and coast survey in the *Casa de Contratación de las Indias* (Sauer 1966).

Pohl (1966:46) suggests that Vespucci was stimulated to conduct his own expedition by Columbus's report from his third voyage that he had approached the "Terrestrial Paradise" (Garden of Eden) near the northeastern tip of Venezuela (Morison 1942:556–558). Columbus wrote that he could not sail further toward the Terrestrial Paradise because the waters were not navigable, so he turned north and cruised along the northern coast of South America.

While Columbus maintained the belief that he would reach the Asiatic mainland by sailing to the west of the Indies, Vespucci sought to test Ptolemy's proposition that the Cape of Catigara, which formed the headlands above the Sinus Magnus that separated India Extra Gangem from Indochina, was located at 8.5° S latitude (map 9.1). From the perspective of Vespucci, Columbus had not sailed far enough to the south to reach the straits that led to India (Pohl 1966).

The Voyage(s) of Alonso de Hojeda and Amerigo Vespucci

Under license from Fonseca, the expedition set sail from Cádiz, Spain, on May 18, 1499. Vespucci set out in the company of Hojeda and Juan de la Cosa, both· of whom had sailed with Columbus on previous voyages (Sauer 1966). La Cosa is also known for his map of 1500, which in addition to depicting the geographical knowledge of the day also has contributed Lucayan place names to our knowledge of aboriginal geography. During the Atlantic crossing, Vespucci, with his two ships, set out independently of the rest of the fleet. It is apparent that he and Hojeda sought different ends. Whereas Hojeda's primary motivation appears to have been the profits to be made on the pearl coast of northern Venezuela, Vespucci sought the passage to India.

The particulars of their explorations along the South American coast are reasonably well documented. During these explorations Vespucci developed a technique for longitude reckoning, which did not, however, solve the problem of determining longitude; that problem was not solved until the chronometer was developed in the seventeenth century. Until then mariners would have to estimate their east-west distances by dead reckoning, which involves a periodic estimate of vessel speed. Such estimates would be accomplished by counting the time it took for an object to float the length of the ship. The time required for the vessel to pass an object that was dropped into the water at the bow provides a fairly accurate measure of speed. In addition, a half-hour sandglass was used to mark time. Columbus's successes were at least partly due to his abilities at dead reckoning.

In his attempts to solve the problem of longitude reckoning Vespucci

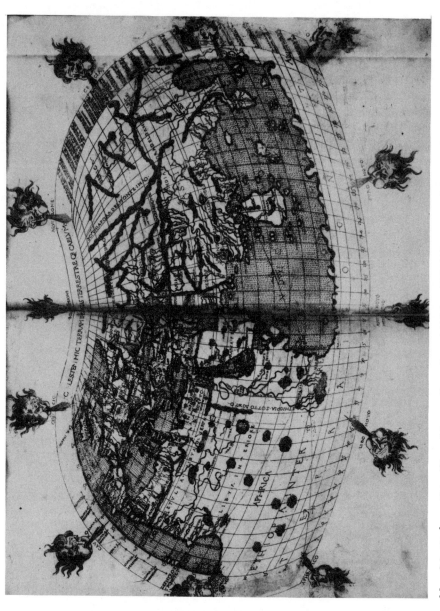

MAP 9.1. Ptolemy-Crivelli world map, Rome?, ca. 1480 (ca. 1590). Courtesy of the Newberry Library.

hit upon the idea of measuring the moon's conjunction with major planets (Pohl 1966:62-68). Using this technique, Vespucci calculated his longitudinal distance from Cádiz at his farthest west along the north coast of South America as about 66.5° of Cádiz (72.5° W of Greenwich) (Pohl 1966:67). Pohl (1966:68) concludes that with the means available in the late fifteenth century, western longitude could be reliably estimated to within about 2 degrees (circa 140 miles). Vespucci's efforts at measuring longitude also help to define his actions while cruising the Bahamas.

On September 5, Hojeda and La Cosa arrived in Hispaniola. Hojeda landed at Yaquimo (Jacmel) and attempted to secure a cargo for his return. He became involved in a bloody dispute with Columbus's administration and unsuccessfully attempted to incite a revolt against Columbus (Sauer 1966). Vespucci arrived at Hispaniola about three weeks later (September 23). He apparently avoided the ongoing hostilities.

Vespucci in the Bahamas

After repairing and provisioning his vessels, Vespucci sailed to the Bahamas in late November. The complete report of his Bahama explorations reads: "We agreed together to go in a northern direction, where we discovered more than a thousand islands and found many naked inhabitants. They were all timid people of small intellect; we did what we liked with them. This last region that we discovered was very perilous to our navigation because of the reefs and shoals which we found in it. We often ran the risk of being lost. We sailed in this sea for two hundred leagues towards the northward" [Vespucci's letter from Seville, 1500; translated and quoted in Pohl (1966:87)]. After almost a year at sea, Vespucci and his crew left the Bahamas for Spain in March 1500. Before leaving, they "went to certain islands and took by force two hundred and thirty-two persons" (Pohl 1966:87).

This chronicle, covering almost four months of exploration, is surprisingly short and vague, albeit typical of sailing logs of the day. To speak of "discovering" more than 1,000 islands is an exaggeration, and it ignores the prior discoveries by Columbus of which Vespucci was certainly aware. Furthermore, Pohl (1966:75) reports that by Vespucci's own reckoning he had gone "further west by a degree and a half among the islands north of Hispaniola then he did along the coast of the great land to the South." A degree and a half west would place him at 74° longitude, which, interpreted literally, means that Vespucci did not explore further west than Acklins Island. Even allowing for the possibility of a two degree error in his calculations, this would only take him as far west as the meridian connecting western Great Exuma and little San Salvador (between Cat Island and Eleuthera).

One explanation for the discrepancy between his previous reports of the South American mainland and his terse description of his explorations in the Bahamas is that he maintained his practice of careful exploration and experimentation with longitude reckoning, and that he changed reporting style due to the secrecy associated with this portion of his voyage. The evidence for this conclusion is based first on the instructions from Fonseca that all expeditions were "not to trespass on any land that had been discovered by Columbus" (Sauer 1966:107; emphasis added). Vespucci had clearly violated those instructions by sailing to the Bahamas. However, he clouds that fact by exaggerating the number of islands he discovered and by placing his westernmost position just east of Columbus's landfalls on San Salvador and Crooked Island. It therefore appeared that he had simply explored a southeastern extension of Las Islas de Lucayos that Columbus had never visited.

We might further ascribe some intrigue to Vespucci's voyage. It is reasonable to assume that Fonseca, as the crown's manager of New World affairs, sought expert testimony concerning Columbus's discoveries, especially in light of the variance between promised and realized revenues. The voyages to South America accomplished part of this goal, and they were approved by narrowly defining Columbus's discoveries in that area (Sauer 1966: 107–108). Such a narrow definition of Columbus's Bahamian interests was less easily accomplished since the admiral was at the time actively overseeing his interests from a base on Hispaniola.

Finally, it is difficult to accept that 232 slaves provided adequate compensation for the four months this experienced businessman and trader spent sailing around the Bahamas. A more reasonable conclusion is that Vespucci made a careful inventory of Bahamian waters, that he visited the islands that Columbus reported visiting, and that he may even have established temporary bases on some of these islands. Four months is a long time to spend at sea without careening a vessel for cleaning and repair. Archaeological investigations may someday recover material evidence of Vespucci's expedition.

The World Map of 1500

The most conclusive evidence for an extensive survey of the northern islands is the world map of 1500. One of the earliest world maps to depict the New World, it is a brightly colored 3-foot by 6-foot map on oxhide (vellum) that is dated to 1500 and is attributed to Juan de la Cosa. As with many documents from this period, there are disagreements concerning when the map was actually drawn. In addition, it has been maintained that two different persons by the name of Juan de la Cosa took part in the early events of Spanish exploration. One la Cosa was the owner and master of the *Santa María*, who accompanied Columbus on his first two voyages and who accompanied Hojeda and Vespucci on theirs. The other la Cosa is presumed to have been the mapmaker.

Antonio Ballesteros y Baretta may be responsible for the notion of two la Cosas, an opinion he set forth in his book *Historia de America y de los Pueblos Americanos* (1936). Samuel Eliot Morison (1942) accepted and promoted that view. The two la Cosas were not reunited until 1954, when Ballesteros recanted his earlier opinion in the book *La Marina Cantabra y Juan de la Cosa*. It now seems certain that there was but one Juan de la Cosa. The accuracy with which the New World shores are depicted is testimony to their being drawn by a man who had made firsthand observations.

The World Map of 1500 contains a wealth of information concerning explorations and opinions about the New World. For purposes of illustration, the World Map of Johannes Ruysch, Rome 1507, is reproduced here (map 9.2). First, at least twelve islands are represented, ten of which are named, in the Bahama archipelago. If Columbus were the sole explorer of these islands we would expect no more than four named islands, the total number that he visited. Second, Cuba is represented as an island; Columbus maintained that Cuba was the mainland. Third, named places along the coast of South America can be directly attributed to Vespucci's voyage of 1499 (Pohl 1966). Fourth, there is a mainland to the northwest of Cuba with named landmarks. Attempts to correlate these names with features of the Asiatic, North, and even Central American coastlines have been unsuccessful. Harrisse (1961) has suggested that the North American mainland had been discovered by this time, although the absence of wealth caused it to be ignored until Juan Ponce de León's 1513 expedition to colonize La Florida. Finally, there is no mention of Cathay (China), Ci-

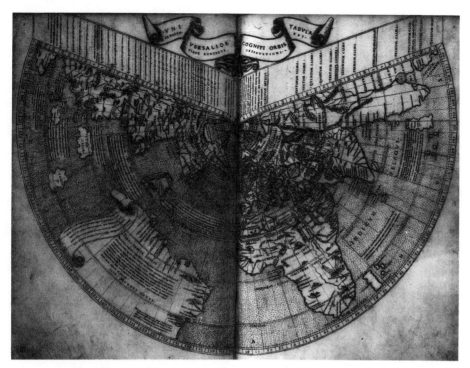

MAP 9.2. World map of Johannes Ruysch, Rome, 1507. Courtesy of the Edward E. Ayer Collection, Newberry Library.

pango (Japan), or other Asiatic landmarks whose positions Columbus believed he had established.

One need not have firsthand knowledge to accurately represent a landmass on a map. One need only have expert testimony. It is clear, however, that the New World was drawn by someone who had a clear vision of its parameters, someone who is likely to have developed that vision through personal experience. A better use of his cartographic opinions can therefore be obtained by considering where la Cosa is likely to have traveled.

It cannot be determined with certainty whether or not la Cosa accompanied Vespucci to the Bahamas. Sauer (1966:112) and Morison (1974) assume that the expedition remained together, but this was clearly not the case during the Atlantic crossing or during explorations along the South American coast. Pohl (1966:72–74) suggests that Vespucci and Hojeda did not rejoin forces in Hispaniola, and that Hojeda, if not la Cosa, remained in Hispaniola until the spring when he returned to Spain.

Although many people have discounted the utility of maps and navigation records from the sixteenth century, recent careful scrutiny has demonstrated that these are accurate renditions of geographical knowledge. To some degree such knowledge must be "translated," for example, Kelley (1989) has suggested that a 14-degree westerly compass variation has tilted the depictions of the islands and that the islands are elongated due to errors in reckoning latitude. Although it is too early to report conclusive results, such studies promise to make substantial contributions toward the reconstruction of the routes of early voyages (Kelley 1988; McGuirk 1989).

Early Sixteenth-Century Spanish Shipwrecks

The ships of exploration were general-purpose cargo vessels (investors were reluctant to risk first-class ships). They were uncomfortable and were not made for the business of discovery, yet their maneuverability, their flexibility of rigging, and their ability to travel more than 100 miles per day under favorable conditions and to sail in shallow water gave them a major role in voyages of exploration. In the words of Roger Smith, underwater archaeologist for the State of Florida, caravels were the "Mercury spacecraft of a long line of transoceanic vessels" (Smith 1986:7). It was only after the major discoveries of the sixteenth century had been completed that a new vessel was created for transoceanic commerce, the famed galleon. Designed in response to the need for speed and security, galleons combined the cargo capacity of the *nao*, the sleek water lines of the galley, and the sail patterns and rigging of the caravel.

The extensive shallow banks and coral reefs in the vicinity of most Caribbean islands present hazards to navigation that were immediately appreciated by the Spanish explorers (G. Fox 1882; Pohl 1966; Sauer 1966). These dangers were compounded by violent tropical storms and hurricanes that appeared without sufficient warning, and by the unseaworthy character of vessels that had spent months cruising in shipworm-infested waters (Morison 1942; Sauer 1966). Despite the explorers' exercising what must have seemed due caution, there is an extensive list of shipwrecks (map 9.3). Columbus himself lost nine ships: *Santa María*, which was wrecked near Haiti on Christmas eve of his first voyage; *Niña* and three other vessels at La Isabela in 1495 (Lyon 1989); and the entire fleet of his fourth voyage—*Vizcaina* and *Gallega* off the coast of Central America

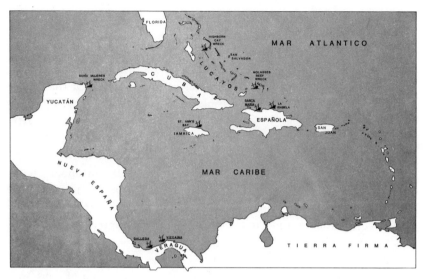

M AP 9.3. Fifteenth- and sixteenth-century Caribbean shipwrecks under investigation by Ships of Discovery and the Texas A&M Institute of Nautical
Archaeology. Courtesy of Ships of Discovery.

in 1503 and *Capitana* and *Santiago* in Puerto Santa Gloria, Jamaica, 1504.

In addition to vessels that passed through the Bahamas on slaving expeditions, vessels returning to Spain from the New World colonies frequently passed near the Bahamas. In part this was due to the position of
these islands in relation to Spain's northern Caribbean settlements, but it
also reflected the practice of sailing to the north where easterly trending
winds facilitated the return voyages. Vespucci's report that he sailed 200
leagues to the northward on his return to Spain in March 1500 is an example of a practice that began with Columbus.

Archaeologists have only recently begun to investigate historic shipwrecks in the New World (Keith and Thompson 1985; Keith 1987; R.
Smith 1987). To date, only two early sixteenth-century wrecks have been
excavated in the Bahamas. In 1966 and 1967, a wreck near Highbourn
Cay was salvaged by its discoverers (Peterson 1974; Smith et al. 1985), and
a wreck on Molasses Reef near West Caicos has been the site of ongoing
investigations by the Institute of Nautical Archaeology since 1980 (Keith
et al. 1984; Keith and Simmons 1985; Keith 1987). Both wrecks were at
one time identified as Pinzón's *Pinta*, although these identifications have
since been questioned and deemphasized (Peterson 1974; Keith et al. 1984).

Shipwreck archaeology is providing information that is available from
no other source. For example, because there is little mention of weapons
in the earliest chronicles, most naval historians have concluded that the
ships were not well armed. The work of Donald Keith, director of Ships of
Discovery, and other nautical archaeologists, has challenged that view.
Keith reports that the earliest Caribbean shipwrecks have well-formed
batteries of armament. For example, the Molasses Reef wreck, a late
fifteenth- to early sixteenth-century Spanish wreck in the Turks and
Caicos Islands, carried "ship-killing" wrought-iron cannons called *bom-
bardetas* and a *cerbatana*; three types of *versos*, swivel guns mounted on
the "gunwale" (hence the name) that were useful for raking the decks of
enemy ships or keeping unfriendly canoe-borne Indians at bay; smaller
swivel guns called *harquebuts*, which could be mounted on the ship's
boats during amphibious assaults; and a variety of portable arms including rifles (*arquebuces*), crossbows, lances, swords, and even hand grenades
(fig. 9.1). These weapons show a sophisticated appreciation of guns and
a range of shot that formed a key element in the conquest of the Americas (Keith 1987).

Given the relative isolation of many Bahama islands, especially with
regard to diver support facilities, it is probable that many additional
wrecks from this time await discovery. The wrecks are significant in that
they provide our best available material culture record of early Spanish
explorations in the Bahamas. By obtaining dates for these, and other,
early Spanish shipwrecks, the introduction of European artifacts into or
onto prehistoric sites can be more completely documented. Such evidence
would improve our understanding of contact-period relations between the
Spaniards and the Lucayans as well as facilitate the identification of the
probable sources of European artifacts encountered in aboriginal sites. In
addition, evidence for contact with the Lucayans may be found in other
forms; for instance, Palmetto Ware sherds were recovered from the Molasses Reef wreck.

Slaving Expeditions and the Lucayan Genocide, 1509-1512

The concept of capturing native Antillean peoples as slaves was part
of the earliest ideology brought to the New World. During his second

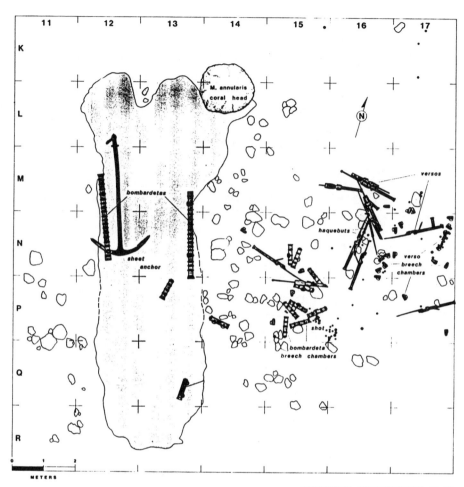

ORDNANCE DISTRIBUTION PLAN

FIGURE 9.1. Molasses Reef wreck. Courtesy of Ships of Discovery.

voyage (1493), Columbus proposed a slave trade to be conducted along the lines of the Portuguese trade in African slaves (Sauer 1966:77). In 1495, this proposal was realized in the shipment of 550 men and women from the Macorix cacicazgo in the northeastern Dominican Republic to Spain on February 17, 1495 (Sauer 1966:88). Sauer suggests that this number reflects the capacity of four caravels, which also carried passengers, a figure that is consistent with Vespucci's removal of 232 Lucayans on two ships.

Whatever abilities Columbus may have had as an explorer, he proved to be an incapable administrator. His promise of great wealth went unfulfilled, and the economy of Hispaniola required continuous support from Spain. By 1498–99, Spanish colonists were in open revolt, the collapse of the native social structure and excessive demands had reduced the flow of tribute, and gold production had dwindled. In an attempt to reorganize the failing economy Columbus conceived a two-part program for generating profits based on the export of brazilwood (dyewood) and slaves (Sauer 1966).

At that time the Spanish Crown did not look favorably upon the export of native peoples as slaves. In part this was based on their religious commitment to saving souls, but it may have also reflected the pragmatic recognition that the Tainos did not make good laborers due to their inability to adapt to Spain's colder climate along with their high mortality from European diseases (Crosby 1987). Columbus never got the opportunity to implement his plan. Overwhelmed by revolts and the growing dissatisfaction in Spain with his administration, he was removed from Hispaniola in June 1500. The new governor, Francisco de Bobadilla, changed the focus of Spanish-native relations from an emphasis on exporting slaves to one of using the native population as laborers, especially in the gold fields and in provisioning ships. By the time the call for slaving expeditions came again, the demand was for a supply of local labor and not for an export commodity.

On May 3, 1509, King Fernando ordered the governor of Hispaniola "to import all the Indians that could be obtained from the neighboring islands in the manner 'in which they have been brought on other occasions, so that those needed shall be placed in our enterprises and the others be given in allotment in the manner that has been used until now' " (Sauer 1966:159).

Fernando's order came in response to Governor Ovando's statements that there was a shortage of native labor. This shortage of native labor was both real and apparent. The total population of Hispaniola had dwindled from as many as 2 million to about 61,000 by 1509, of whom 30,000 to 40,000 were *indios de servicio,* men and women older than fourteen years (Cook and Borah 1971b).

The impact of importing natives from neighboring islands is apparent in Cook and Borah's (1971b) population projections, which show an increase of total population in 1510 to a figure of 68,800. This increase occurred despite an estimated net mortality rate approaching 35 percent. Given that estimated net mortality rate, and a negligible increase in population through procreation, it is estimated that 25,760 persons were imported in 1510, most of them probably taken from the Bahama. Las Casas reported,

> Therefore when permission came from King Ferdinand to bring to this island of Hispaniola the people who were living in the islands we are accustomed to call Lucayos, there gathered together ten or twelve citizens of the city of la Vega or Concepcion and the town of Santiago, who raised between them 10 or 12,000 gold pesos, with which they bought two or three vessels and hired fifty or sixty men—sailors and the rest— to go and attack the Indians who were living carefree in the peace and security of their native land. . . . Brought to this island and disembarked, especially at Puerto de Plata and Puerto Real, which are on the north coast facing the Lucayos themselves, men and women, young and old, were divided into groups. (Quoted in Granberry 1979–81:15)

The number of Spanish slaving expeditions has not been determined. Using the simplifying assumptions that a complete complement of captives $(n=125)$ was carried on each caravel that plied the Bahamas for slaves, that none of these vessels were wrecked, and that the total number of captives removed was 40,000; then at least 320 vessel loads were required to remove those people. This estimate is not meant to imply that a single large fleet plied the Bahamas for slaves. Rather, the estimate indicates the level of activity required to depopulate the Bahamas. The magnitude of this number, and our relatively conservative assumptions, documents the extreme difficulty of assigning European artifacts to the voyage of a particular explorer.

Initially, the Lucayans were sold for four gold pesos and no more. However, once it was learned that they were physically well-suited to the rigors of pearl diving, they were exported to the pearl fisheries near the island of Cubagua off the north coast of Venezuela. Las Casas continues,

> The Spanish began to sell the Lucayan Indians to gather pearls, because they are in general all excellent swimmers . . . for which reason they were sold, usually in public, not at 4 pesos as had been ordered at the start, but at 100 and 150 gold pesos and more . . . and it was a miracle if, after a few days, a single Lucayan could be found on this island of

Hispaniola. The course which through necessity must be taken from this island to the Isle of Cubagua is around 300 long leagues, and they carried them all there in vessels by that route. (Quoted in Granberry 1979–81:16)

By 1511, many of the southern Bahamas seem to have been depopulated. The rapid and complete depopulation of the Bahamas is apparent in the reports of the 1520 slaving expeditions of Francisco de Gordillo and Lucas Vásquez de Ayllón. Their combined expedition did not succeed in obtaining slaves until they reached the coast of Florida (Swanton 1946: 36–37; cf. Granberry 1979–81). Within a generation of the arrival of the Spanish, the Lucayans ceased to exist as a people. Their proximity to Cuba and to Hispaniola and their abilities in the water made them too valuable to leave unmolested.

The Empty Islands: Juan Ponce de León, 1513

Juan Ponce de León is an explorer of renown for his search for the fabled "fountain of youth," a quest that may have been inspired by Taino beliefs. Henry Dobyns (1983: 255–256) has suggested that migrations of Tainos to Florida from Cuba, perhaps from Puerto Rico and Jamaica, and even from Hispaniola, were inspired by a pan-Taino millenarian movement; a response to Spanish atrocities. As William Marquardt (1987) recounts, "Escalante Fontaneda, a Spaniard held captive by the Calusa Indians from circa 1550 to 1567, relates that 'many Indians from Cuba entered the [southwest Florida] province of Carlos's in search of a mystical river reputed to bestow youth and renew vigor to those who bathed in it.'"

Having made his fortune during the Spanish colonization of Puerto Rico (1508–12) by appropriating more than was his right, and faced with the prospect of losing his position, Ponce de León sought and was granted a contract to settle the island of Bimini, at that time the name for the southern coast of Florida. In the *Libro de Asientos*, September 17, 1514, Ponce de León's right "to settle the island of Bimini and the island of Florida [northern part of the coast] which he had discovered" is acknowledged (quoted in Sauer 1966:190).

Ponce de León departed from San Juan in March 1513 and sailed slowly along the eastern side of the Bahamas (Davis 1935). Landfalls were apparently made on the Caicos, at Rum Cay, San Salvador, Cat Island, Eleuthera, and Grand Bahama before this northwestern trek was concluded with his landing in the vicinity of St. Augustine, Florida, on April 2 (Davis 1935; Sauer 1966; Granberry 1979–81; Molander 1984). From there he turned south and either explored the southern and western coasts of Florida (Davis 1935) or returned to the Bahamas and explored the Little Bahama Bank around Grand Bahama and Abaco Islands (Molander 1984).

The problem of determining Ponce de León's exact course results from the loss of his journal. The information that survives today is contained in secondhand reports, most noteworthy among these being Antonio de Herrera y Tordesillas's (1601) *Historia General de los Hechos los Castellanos, en las Islas y Tierra-Firme de el Mar Oceano*. Although the details of his voyage are not available in their original form, the significance of his voyage to the present discussion rests in his limited and intermittent contact with Lucayans.

As the geographer Carl O. Sauer (1966:160) reminded us, "The Lucayan Islands were the first part of the New World to become wholly depopulated, for which the date 1513 seems acceptable. The 'discovery' of Florida by Ponce de León in 1513 was, in fact, an extension of slave hunting beyond the empty islands."

10

After the End: Reflections
on a Paleoethnography

Most academics like to coin new terms or use existing terms in new ways. I accept the blame for two terms—*allochthonous* and *autocatalysis*—which were foisted upon archaeology in collaborative efforts with scientists from other disciplines (Keegan and Mitchell 1986; Keegan and Diamond 1987). Given this track record it should come as no surprise to find at least one new term in this book (new in the sense that I have not seen it used, although I suspect it has been used before). I am referring to *paleoethnography*, which I define as a portrait of a past society built up from traditional ethnographic categories.

Having reached the end of this book, the reader may have found little difference between what I am calling a paleoethnography and the culture histories that are the mainstay of the discipline. I have decided, however, to use this term to distinguish the present study from previous West Indian culture histories. In those previous studies the emphasis has been on pottery styles arranged according to chronological and spatial relationships in what are called time-space diagrams (Rouse 1972, 1986). In contrast, the present study has a very weak handle on time, and spatial organization is the primary basis for comparisons and inferences. In addition, this book has very little to say about pottery styles. Where pottery is discussed it is in reference to studies conducted elsewhere in the West Indies or in the context of exchange relations between the Bahamas and the Greater Antilles. The result is that this study more closely resembles

ethnological accounts of an "ethnographic present" than it does a chronological history of events.

The point of these distinctions is that studies with a cultural-historical
perspective need not adhere to the notion that archaeologists rebuild past
societies by using a ladder of inference or levels of interpretation (Hawkes
1954; Rouse 1977). Far too often these methodological constructs have
led to narrow particularistic studies and the pigeonholing of "cultures" in
time-space boxes. In some ways this challenge to traditional modes of inquiry is a product of critiques generated by the emerging postmodern archaeologies that seek a more interpretive product (Hodder 1985, 1991;
Earle and Preucel 1987; Preucel 1991). Yet, postmodern archaeologies have
yet to develop an adequate research strategy, and they continue to be
overshadowed by processual or holistic archaeologies that claim stronger
grounds for their inferences (Maclachlan and Keegan 1990; Roosevelt
1990).

Some compromise between processual and postprocessual perspectives
is likely to emerge in the future (Preucel 1991). As Wylie (1990) recently
noted, both perspectives share certain common grounds. In any archaeological program the investigator, viewing the past as reflected and re-
fracted in material remains, must begin by deciding what is *real.*

What is Real?

When Christopher Columbus arrived in the Bahama archipelago after
his first transatlantic crossing, he encountered native peoples who gave
him all that they possessed—including cotton thread, parrots, spears, and
"other little things too tiresome to write down"—with the expectation of
almost nothing in return. One man, according to Columbus, gave 12 kilograms of cotton for the equivalent of a Castilian *blanca* (less than three
cents; Fuson 1987:71), while others accepted pieces of bowls and broken
glass cups (Dunn and Kelley 1989:71). While such behavior might seem
irrational to formalist economists, Columbus viewed this as appropriate
treatment for himself and his crew. For according to Columbus, the Lucayans who boarded his ships called to the others: "Come see the men
who came from the heavens. Bring them something to eat and drink."
More likely, the Tainos viewed Columbus and his crew as men from hell.

When Columbus arrived in America he was expecting to find the Caniba, literally the people of the Grand Khan (Dunn and Kelley 1989:217). Instead he encountered the Tainos who believed in Caribes. The similarity in names is responsible for some of the confusion of real people and mythical beings. Caribes were, at least partly, mythical beings associated with the underworld (thus my allusion to hell) who, among other things, consumed human flesh (Antonio Stevens-Arroyo, personal communication 1990, has pointed out that for the Tainos "consumption" may have referred equally to sexual activities). Columbus (Dunn and Kelley 1989: 167), and later Frey Ramón Pané (Arrom 1974), reported that the Tainos, at least initially, identified the Christians as Caribes (i.e., as the incarnation of myth).

The interplay of cultures on West Indian beaches in 1492 shares remarkable parallels with Marshall Sahlins's (1985) depiction of how the interplay of native Hawaiian cultural categories with those of Captain James Cook led to Cook's death. In both contexts, the direction of travel was significant. Cook's circuit of Hawaii matched that expected of the god Lono; while Columbus's route, from west to east, was toward the land of the Caribes. Cook came to be identified as Lono and was killed because he violated mythical prescriptions when his ship returned to Hawaii. Similarly, Columbus's expedition came to be identified as Caribes, and the 39 men that founded the settlement of La Navidad may have been killed because this settlement violated similar mythic proscriptions. In other words, mythical beings were not supposed to stay permanently.

The usual explanation for the killing of these men is that they violated local behavioral rules (e.g., they stole, looted, raped, and otherwise pillaged). Yet if such local violations were the cause, then the local cacique, Guacanagarí, should have done the killing. It is clear in the documents that Guacanagarí was not blamed for killing these men (Sauer 1966; Wilson 1990a). Blame and retribution centered on Caonabo, a cacique at the acme of the Taino political hierarchy. The five caciques at this paramount level could take unilateral actions so long as these were prescribed by supernatural sanctions.

Mythological proscriptions do not, however, provide a complete explanation for the demise of the 39 Spaniards. In terms of regional politics, the principal caciques could not permit a second-level cacique to harbor a garrison of well-armed Europeans. The Europeans had to be eliminated because they upset the established balance of power. Hawaii again offers similar circumstances, with the exception that Hawaiian politics were not truncated by introduced diseases as quickly as diseases decimated the West Indian populations. With the help of European ships and weapons, King Kamehameha I became the first to achieve political control of the entire Hawaiian archipelago (Kirch 1984).

What of these past events is real? We know that 39 men lost their lives, but were their crimes political, mythological, personal, or some combination? The same question arises repeatedly when we confront the problem of identifying different cultural perspectives. It must be admitted that a number of different answers are correct, and that the interplay of cultures had different meanings for the different individuals and groups of actors. Arguments over whose meaning is significant will not advance our knowledge. A more important question is, what is scientific?

A Processual Methodology

Whether it is called a culture history or a paleoethnography, an archaeological report involves storytelling and narrative (Terrell 1990). What makes some "just so" stories (named for Rudyard Kipling's stories), others postmodern narratives (Gero 1991), and others scientific theories? What separates science and myth (Maynard Smith 1988)? Although one usually spells out one's theory of knowledge (epistemology) at the outset, I have waited until the end because it is at this point that the reader is likely wondering—how does he know that? Given what I perceive as a break with previous West Indian culture histories, the how and why of the present study should make more sense now that the data and the interpretations have been presented.

Part of the difficulty with this study comes from its very complicated logic and its heavy reliance on theories and models. How can we know so much from so little evidence? In addition, these theories and models are drawn from evolutionary ecology, microeconomics, demography, and bone chemistry, fields of inquiry that have matured in the past decade and with which many people have only a limited acquaintance. To make matters even more difficult, simplifications in the theories have been the subject of critiques as investigators work to strengthen the theories. If one were to read only the critiques, several inescapable conclusions would emerge. For instance, neo-Darwinian evolutionary theory is null and void (Maynard Smith 1988), the physical universe is unknowable (Hawking

1988), and the human sciences can only progress by reveling in their subjectivity (Marcus and Fischer 1986). Scientific approaches reject those conclusions, and proceed through the continuous reevaluation of theory in relation to empirical reality.

The present study has adopted the epistemology of cultural materialists and most natural scientists (M. Harris 1979; Maynard Smith 1988; Keegan 1991a). The culture materialist paradigm recognizes that *one* approach is to impose the categories of the investigator on observations ("etic") and to pursue falsification as the means for improving the conformity between theories and observations. Although theories can never be proved, those that are contradicted by observations can be rejected in favor of alternatives that better fit the observations.

The application of this philosophy is guided by Richard Levins's model of model building (fig. 10.1). Levins (1966:422) has suggested that it is "desirable to work with manageable models which maximize the qualities *generality, precision,* and *realism* toward the overlapping but not identical goals of *understanding, predicting,* and *modifying* nature" (emphasis mine). Because the model qualities are more continuous than discrete, it is neither possible nor necessary to completely separate them in the course of analysis. For a scientific research tradition to be adequate it must recognize similar qualities and goals.

ANALYTICAL LEVEL	MODEL QUALITY	SCIENTIFIC GOAL
GENERAL THEORY	GENERALITY	EXPLANATION/UNDERSTANDING
PREDICTIVE THEORY	PRECISION	PREDICTION
REALISM	DESCRIPTION	MODIFY BEHAVIOR
RECONSTRUCTION THEORY AND METHODS	RELATE MATERIAL CULTURE TO THE CULTURAL SYSTEM	TRANSFORMATION FROM STATIC TO DYNAMIC

FIGURE 10.1. Structure of a processual methodology.

The simplifying assumptions and different goals of models make the simultaneous maximization of all three model qualities impossible. It is impossible to be both general and specific at the same time, and there are fallacies of logic that result from assuming otherwise. In Levins's model the solution is to hierarchically arrange or "nest" models that maximize one or two of the model qualities. Nesting proceeds in such a way that each level provides an interpretation of the "sufficient parameters" of the next-higher level (Levins 1966:431). As one proceeds from higher to lower levels of abstraction the research methodology becomes less general and more realistic (see Winterhalder 1981).

The basis for the present study had little to do with the people whose lives provided the empirical tests. The logical first step was linking the production of food and the production of offspring as contingent, co-evolving variables. Past perspectives, in which production and procreation were identified as dependent and independent variables respectively (e.g., Malthus 1959; Boserup 1965; Cohen 1977; Johnson and Earle 1987; also see Hassan 1981), are here rejected as too simplistic to characterize the actual relationship between human population growth and food supply.

From the assumed interdependence of economy and demography the next step was to identify the possible implications of this linkage and to test these hypotheses in a cultural setting. Because human migration will have different outcomes under different sets of initial conditions, the Bahama archipelago was selected for study. In the course of study, economic, demographic, and social processes were used to predict patterning in the archaeological record. In sum, the approach has been to work from the general to the particular, with data feeding back in the opposite direction to improve the precision of the initial generalizations.

The effort throughout has been to develop "robust" generalizations of population expansion in general and of Lucayan society in particular. As Levins (1966:423) has stated: "We attempt to treat the same problem with several alternate models each with different simplifications but with a common biological assumption. Then, if these models, despite their different assumptions, lead to similar results we have what we can call a robust theorem." By attacking a generalization from different perspectives, the usefulness of the generalization can be continuously reevaluated. At the lowest level of analysis this procedure is embodied in multiple working hypotheses, mutually exclusive but nonetheless possible outcomes of a particular generalization. At a higher order this procedure is described by different theories of culture.

Creating the Lucayans

If all Lucayan sites represent settlements that were occupied at about the time of European contact, then this distribution was achieved through the rapid expansion of population at low and equal densities. A logical reason for such rapid spread at equalizing densities is that the Lucayans were attempting to maximize access to food resources.

If their behavior was based on the efficient capture of food, then a shift in diet should have occurred when the highest-ranked resources declined in availability due to human predation, and new food items were added to the diet to replace them. Such a shift along the predicted lines of diet-breadth expansion is apparent in the so-called crab/shell shift in the Antilles (Keegan 1989d). Variability in Lucayan diets that may also indicate such a shift has been noted (Keegan and DeNiro 1988), but the timing of these differences needs to be established before this conclusion can be taken as accurate.

Settlement patterns also conform to the predictions, but in a complicated way. Rather than the expected regular pattern of spacing between individual sites, there was a regular spacing of paired sites. A review of ethnohistoric and ethnological theory revealed logical reasons for the paired settlement pattern and for the violation of predicted maximizing dispersion and reiterated the assumption that settlements were contemporaneous. Finally, demographic evidence conformed to the expectation that the Lucayan population grew at a very rapid rate.

Each of those lines of investigation is linked, yet each retains certain degrees of freedom. By attacking the theory from all of these perspectives—economic, demographic, social—the logic of the theory is repeatedly subject to falsification. The result is a robust theory, along with a research program that is ongoing and adding new refinements of detail to the record of past human behavior.

BIBLIOGRAPHY

Aberle, D.F.
 1961 Matrilineal Descent in Cross-Cultural Perspective. In *Matrilineal Kinship*, edited by D.M. Schneider and K. Gough, pp. 655–727. Berkeley: University of California Press.
Adams, J.
 1973 *The Gitksan Potlach.* Toronto: University of Toronto Press.
Albury, Paul
 1975 *The Story of the Bahamas.* London: Macmillan.
Alegría, R.E.
 1979 Apuntes para el Estudio de los Caciques de Puerto Rico. *Revista del Instituto de Cultura Puertoriqueña* 85:25–41.
 1983 *Ball Courts and Ceremonial Plazas in the West Indies.* Yale University Publications in Anthropology, no. 79. New Haven: Yale University Press.
 1986 *Apuntes en Torno a la Mitología de los Indios Tainos de las Antillas Mayores y sus Origenes Suramericanos.* San Juan: Centro de Estudios Avanzados de Puerto Rico y el Caribe.
Allaire, L.
 1977 *Later Prehistory in Martinique and the Island Caribs: Problems in Ethnic Identification.* Ph.D. dissertation, Yale University. Ann Arbor: University Microfilms.
 1980 On the Historicity of Carib Migrations in the Lesser Antilles. *American Antiquity* 45:238–245.
 1984 A Reconstruction of Early Historical Island Carib Pottery. *Southeastern Archaeology* 3(2)Winter:121–133.
 1987 Some Comments on the Ethnic Identity of the Taino-Carib Frontier. In *Ethnicity and Culture*, edited by Reginald Auger, Margaret F. Glass, Scott MacEachern, and Peter H. McCartney, pp. 127–133. Archaeological Association, University of Calgary.
 1990 The Peopling of the Caribbean Islands: A Review of the Latest Evidence. Paper presented at the conference on Non-Imperial Polities

in the Lands Visited by Christopher Columbus during His Four Voyages to the New World, Smithsonian Tropical Research Institute, Panama.

1991   Understanding Suazey. In *Proceedings of the Thirteenth International Congress for Caribbean Archaeology*, edited by E.N. Ayubi and J.B. Haviser, pp. 715–728. Curacao: Reports of the Archaeological-Anthropological Institute of the Netherlands Antilles, no. 9.

Ambrose, S. H.

1987   Chemical and Isotopic Techniques of Diet Reconstruction in Eastern North America. In *Emergent Horticultural Economies of the Eastern Woodlands*, edited by W.F. Keegan, pp. 87–107. Center for Archaeological Investigations, Occasional Paper no. 7. Carbondale: Southern Illinois University.

Ammerman, A.J., and L.L. Cavalli-Sforza

1973   A Population Model for the Diffusion of Early Farming in Europe. In *The Explanation of Culture Change: Models in Prehistory*, edited by C. Renfrew, pp. 674–678. Gloucester Crescent: Duckworth.

Arrom, J.J.

1974   *Fray Ramón Pané, "Relación acerca de las Antigüedades de los Indios": el Primer Tratado Escrito en América.* Mexico City: Siglo XXI editores.

1986   Fray Ramón Pané o el rescate de un mundo mítico. *La Revista* 3:2–8.

Aveni, A.F., and G. Urton

1982   Ethnoastronomy and Archaeoastronomy in the American Tropics. *Annals of the New York Academy of Sciences*, vol. 385.

Bahamas Archaeological Team (B.A.T.)

1984   *Archaeology in the Bahamas.* Report for 1982/1983, Bahamas Archaeological Team, Nassau.

Bahamas Department of Archives

1980   *The Salt Industry of the Bahamas.* Nassau: Ministry of Education and Culture.

Bahamas Ministry of Education.

1985   *Atlas of the Commonwealth of the Bahamas.* Kingston, Jamaica: Kingston Publishers.

Bahamas National Trust

n.d.a   *A Field Guide to the Broad-Leaf Coppice.* Nassau: Bahamas National Trust.

n.d.b   *Reptiles and Amphibians of the Bahamas.* Nassau: Bahamas National Trust.

Ballesteros y Baretta, A.
 1936   *Historia de America y de los Pueblos Americanos.* Madrid: San-
        tander.
 1954   *La Marina Cantabra y Juan de la Cosa.* Madrid: Santander.
Beach, D.K., and R.N. Ginsburg
 1980   Facies Succession of Pliocene-Pleistocene Carbonates, Northwest-
        ern Great Bahama Bank. *American Association of Petroleum Geol-
        ogists Bulletin* 64:1634–1642.
Bellin, N.
 1768   *Description Geographique des Debouquemens qui sont au Nord de
        l'Isle de Saint Dominigue.* Paris.
Bender, M.M.
 1968   Mass Spectrometric Studies of Carbon-13 Variations in Corn and
        Other Grasses. *Radiocarbon* 10:468–472.
 1971   Variations in $^{13}C/^{12}C$ Ratios of Plants in Relation to the Pathway of
        Photosynthetic Carbon Dioxide Fixation. *Phytochemistry* 19:1239–
        1244.
Bender, M.M., D.A. Baerris, and R.L. Steventon
 1981   Further Light on Carbon Isotopes and Hopewell Agriculture. *Amer-
        ican Antiquity* 46:346–353.
Berg, C.J., Jr., J. Krzynowek, P. Alatalo, and K. Wiggin
 1985   Sterol and Fatty Acid Composition of the Clam, *Codakia orbicu-
        laris,* with Chemoautotrophic Symbionts. *Lipids* 20:116–120.
Berreman, Gerald D.
 1978   Ecology, Demography and Domestic Strategies in the Western Hima-
        layas. *Journal of Anthropological Research* 34:326–368.
Bettinger, R.L., and M.A. Baumhoff
 1982   The Numic Spread: Great Basin Cultures in Competition. *Ameri-
        can Antiquity* 47:485–503.
Birdsell, J.B.
 1957   Some Population Problems Involving Pleistocene Man. *Cold Spring
        Harbor Symposium on Quantitative Biology* 22:47–69.
Bjorndal, Karen A.
 1981   The Consequences of Herbivory for the Life History Pattern of the
        Caribbean Green Turtle, *Chelonia mydas.* In *Biology and Conserva-
        tion of Sea Turtles,* edited by K.A. Bjorndal, pp. 111–116. Proceed-
        ings of the World Conference on Sea Turtle Conservation. Wash-
        ington, D.C.: Smithsonian Institution Press.
Black, Stephen
 1978   Polynesian Outliers: A Study in the Survival of Small Populations.

In *Simulation Studies in Archaeology*, edited by I. Hodder, pp. 63–76. Cambridge: Cambridge University Press.

Boomert, Arie
1986   The Cayo Complex of St. Vincent: Ethnohistorical and Archaeological Aspects of the Island Carib Problem. *Anthropologica* 66:3–68.
1987   Gifts of the Amazons: "Green Stone" Pendants and Beads as Items of Ceremonial Exchange in Amazonia and the Caribbean. *Anthropologica* 67:33–54.

Boserup, Ester
1965   *The Conditions of Agricultural Growth*. Chicago: Aldine.

Botkin, Steven
1980   Effects of Human Exploitation on Shellfish Populations at Malibu Creek, California. In *Modeling Change in Prehistoric Subsistence Economies*, edited by T.K. Earle and A.L. Christenson, pp. 121–139. New York: Academic Press.

Braun, D.P.
1987   Coevolution of Sedentism, Pottery Technology, and Horticulture in the Central Midwest, 200 B.C.–A.D. 600. In *Emergent Horticultural Economics of the Eastern Woodlands*, edited by W.F. Keegan, pp. 153–181. Center for Archaeological Investigations, Occasional Paper no. 7. Carbondale: Southern Illinois University.

Brill, R.H., I.L. Barnes, S.S.C. Tong, E.C. Joel, and M.J. Murtaugh
1987   Laboratory Studies of Some European Artifacts Excavated on San Salvador Island. In *Proceedings of the First San Salvador Conference, Columbus and His World*, edited by D.T. Gerace, pp. 247–292. San Salvador Island: CCFL Bahamian Field Station.

Brooks, W.C.
1888   On the Lucayan Indians. *National Academy of Science, Memoirs* 4:215–233.

Budinoff, Linda
1987   An Osteological Analysis of the Human Burials Recovered from an Early Ceramic Site on the North Coast of Puerto Rico. Paper presented at the Twelfth International Congress for Caribbean Archaeology, Cayenne, French Guiana.

Bullen, Ripley P.
1964   The Archaeology of Grenada, West Indies. *Contributions of the Florida State Museum, Social Sciences*, no. 11. Gainesville.

Burleigh, R., and D. Brothwell
1978   Studies on Amerindian Dogs, 1: Carbon Isotopes in Relation to

Maize in the Diet of Domestic Dogs from Peru and Ecuador. *Journal of Archaeological Science* 5:535–538.

Butt, Audrey J.
1977   Land Use and Social Organization of Tropical Forest Peoples of the Guianas. In *Human Ecology in the Tropics*, edited by J.P. Garlick and R.W.J. Keay, pp. 1–17. London: Taylor and Francis.

Byrne, Bryan T.
1990   Help the Data Speak: A Formal Procedure for the Retrodiction of an Ancient Kinship Terminology System. Manuscript in possession of the author.

Campbell, David G.
1978   *The Ephemeral Islands*. London: Macmillan.

Carbone, V.A.
1980a   The Paleoecology of the Caribbean area. *Florida Anthropologist* 33(3):99–119.
1980b   Some Problems in Cultural Paleoecology in the Caribbean Area. In *Proceedings of the Eighth International Congress for the Study of the Pre-Columbian Cultures of the Lesser Antilles*, edited by S.M. Lowenstein, pp. 98–126. Arizona State University, Anthropological Research Papers.

Carneiro, R.L.
1960   Slash and Burn Agriculture: A Closer Look at its Implications for Settlement Patterns. In *Man and Cultures: Selected Papers of the Fifth International Congress of Anthropological and Ethnological Sciences*, edited by A. Wallace, pp. 229–234. Philadelphia: University of Pennsylvania Press.
1961   Slash-and-Burn Cultivation among the Kuikuru and Its Implications for Cultural Development in the Amazon Basin. In *The Evolution of Horticultural Systems in Native South America: Causes and Consequences, a Symposium*, edited by J. Wilbert, pp. 47–68. Sociedad de Ciencias Naturales La Salle, Supplement Publication, no. 2. Caracas: Editorial Sucre.
1979   A Theory of the Origin of the State. *Science* 169:733–738.

Carr, Archie
1981   Notes on the Behavioral Ecology of Sea Turtles. In *Biology and Conservation of Sea Turtles*, edited by K.A. Bjorndal, pp. 19–26. Proceedings of the World Conference on Sea Turtle Conservation. Washington, D.C.: Smithsonian Institution Press.

Carr, Robert, and Sandra Riley
1982   An Effigy Ceramic Bottle from Green Turtle Cay, Abaco. *Florida Anthropologist* 35:200–202.

Castellanos, R.
1981   La Plaza de Chacuey, un Instrumento Astrónomico Megalítico. *Boletin del Museo del Hombre Dominicano* 16:31–40.

Chagnon, Napolean A.
1983   *Yanomamö: The Fierce People.* 3d ed. New York: Holt, Rinehart and Winston.

Chang, Kwang–Chih, ed.
1968   *Settlement Archaeology.* Palo Alto: National Press Books.

Chanlatte Baik, Luis A.
1991   Doble Estratigrafia AGRO–II (Saladoide). In *Proceedings of the Thirteenth International Congress for Caribbean Archaeology,* edited by E.N. Ayubi and J.B. Haviser, pp. 149–161. Reports of the Archaeological-Anthropological Institute of the Netherlands Antilles, no. 9, Curacao.

Chanlatte Baik, Luis A., and Yvonne M. Narganes
1980   La Jueca Vieques: Nuevo Complejo Cultural Agroafarero en la Arqueología Antillana. In *Proceedings of the Eighth International Congress for the Study of the Pre-Columbian Cultures of the Lesser Antilles,* pp. 73–95. Arizona State University, Anthropological Research Papers no. 22.

Charlier, G.A.
1987   Value of the Mile Used at Sea by Christóbal Colón during His First Voyage. In *Proceedings of the First San Salvador Conference, Columbus and His World,* edited by D.T. Gerace, pp. 115–120. Fort Lauderdale, Fla.: CCFL Bahamian Field Station.

Charnov, E.L., and G.H. Orians
1973   Optimal Foraging: Some Theoretical Explanations. MS, Department of Biology, University of Utah.

Chayanov, A.V.
1966   *The Theory of Peasant Economy,* edited by D. Thorner, B. Kerblay, and R.E.F. Smith. Homewood, Ill: American Economic Association.

Cherry, J.F.
1981   Pattern and Process in the Earliest Colonization of the Mediterranean Islands. *Proceedings of the Prehistoric Society* 47:41–68.
1985   Islands Out of the Stream: Isolation and Interaction in Early East Mediterranean Insular Prehistory. In *Prehistoric Production and*

Exchange: The Aegean and East Mediterranean, edited by A.B. Knapp and T. Stech, pp. 12–29. UCLA Institute of Archaeology, Monograph 25. Los Angeles.

Chisholm, B.S., D.E. Nelson, and H.P. Schwartz
  1982   Stable-carbon Isotope Ratios as a Measure of Marine versus Terrestrial Protein in Ancient Diets. *Science* 216:1131–1132.

Clough, Garrett C.
  1972   Biology of the Bahamian Hutia, *Geocapromys ingrahami. Journal of Mammology* 53:807–823.

Cohen, M.N.
  1977   *The Food Crisis in Prehistory.* New Haven: Yale University Press.

Cohen, M.N., and G. Armelagos, eds.
  1984   *Paleopathology at the Origins of Agriculture.* New York: Academic Press.

Conklin, Harold S.
  1968   An Ethnoecological Approach to Shifting Agriculture. In *Man in Adaptation: The Cultural Present,* edited by Y.A. Cohen, pp. 126–131. Chicago: Aldine.

Cook, S.F. and W. Borah
  1971a *Essays in Population History,* vol.1. Berkeley: University of California Press.
  1971b The Aboriginal Population of Hispaniola. In *Essays in Population History.* Vol. 1: *Mexico and the Caribbean,* edited by S.F. Cook and W. Borah, pp. 376–410. Berkeley: University of California Press.
  1974   *Essays in Population History,* vol. 2. Berkeley: University of California Press.
  1979   *Essays in Population History,* vol. 3. Berkeley: University of California Press.

Cosculluela, J.A.
  1946   Prehistoric Cultures of Cuba. *American Antiquity* 12:10–18.

Cowgill, George L.
  1975   On Causes and Consequences of Ancient and Modern Population Changes. *American Anthropologist* 77:505–525.

Craton, Michael
  1986   *A History of the Bahamas.* 3d ed. Waterloo, Ontario: San Salvador Press.

Crosby, A.
  1972   *The Columbian Exchange.* Westport, Conn: Greenwood Press.
  1986   *Ecological Imperialism: The Biological Expansion of Europe, 900–1900.* Cambridge: Cambridge University Press.

Cusick, James G.
   1989   *Change in Pottery as a Reflection of Social Change: A Study of Taino Pottery Before and After Contact at the Site of En Bas Saline, Haiti.* Master's paper, University of Florida, Gainesville.

Daggett, R.E.
   1980   The Trade Process and the Implications of Trade in the Bahamas. *Florida Anthropologist* 33:143–151.

Dalleo, Peter, ed.
   1979   Documents: A Look into the Past Maricuana. *Journal of the Bahamas Historical Society* 1:17.

Davanzo, J.
   1981   Microeconomic Approaches to Studying Migration Decisions. In *Migration Decision Making,* edited by G.F. DeJong and R.W. Gardner, pp. 90–129. New York: Pergamon Press.

Davis, Dave D.
   1988a   Calibration of the Ceramic Period Chronology for Antigua, West Indies. *Southeastern Archaeology* 7:52–60.
   1988b   Coastal Biogeography and Human Subsistence: Examples from the West Indies. *Archaeology of Eastern North America* 16:177–185.

Davis, Dave D., and R. Christopher Goodwin
   1990   Island Carib Origins: Evidence and Non-Evidence. *American Antiquity* 54:37–48.

Davis, T.F.
   1935   *History of Juan Ponce de León's Voyages to Florida.* Jacksonville.

Deagan, Kathleen
   1987a   *Artifacts of the Spanish Colonies of Florida and the Caribbean: 1500–1800.* Vol. 1: *Ceramics, Glassware, and Beads.* Washington, D.C.: Smithsonian Institution Press.
   1987b   Initial Encounters: Arawak Responses to European Contact at the En Bas Saline Site, Haiti. In *Proceedings of the First San Salvador Conference,* edited by D. Gerace, pp. 341–359. Fort Lauderdale, Fla.: CCFL Bahamian Field Station.
   1988   The Archaeology of the Spanish Contact Period in the Circum-Caribbean region. *Journal of World Prehistory,* 2:7–12.

DeBooy, Theodoor
   1912   Lucayan Remains in the Caicos Islands. *American Anthropologist* 14:81–105.
   1913   Lucayan Artifacts from the Bahamas. *American Anthropologist* 15: 1–7.

deFrance, Susan D.
1988   *Zooarchaeological Investigations of Subsistence Strategies at the Maisabel Site, Puerto Rico.* Master's research project, Department of Anthropology, University of Florida, Gainesville.

Delwiche, C.C., and P.L. Steyn
1970   Nitrogen Isotope Fractionation in Soils and Microbial Reactions. *Environment, Science and Technology* 4:929–935.

Delwiche, C.C., P.J. Zinke, C.M. Johnson, and R.A. Virginia
1979   Nitrogen Isotope Distribution as a Presumptive Indicator of Nitrogen Fixation. *Botanical Gazette* (Suppl.) 140:565–569.

DeNiro, M.J.
1985   Postmortem Preservation and Alteration of In Vivo Bone Collagen Isotope Ratios in Relation to Palaeodietary Reconstruction. *Nature* 317:806–809.

DeNiro, M. J., and S. Epstein
1978   Influence of Diet on the Distribution of Carbon Isotopes in Animals. *Geochimica et Cosmochimica Acta* 42:495–506.
1981   Influence of Diet on the Distribution of Nitrogen Isotopes in Animals. *Geochimica et Cosmochimica Acta* 45:341–351.

DeNiro, M.J., and C.A. Hastorf
1985   Alteration of $^{15}N/^{14}N$ and $^{13}C/^{12}C$ ratios of Plant Matter during the Initial Stages of Diagenesis: Studies Utilizing Archaeological Specimens from Peru. *Geochimica et Cosmochimica Acta* 49:97–115.

Dewar, R. E.
1984   Environmental Productivity, Population Regulation, and Carrying Capacity. *American Anthropologist* 86:601–614.

Diamond, J.M.
1977a Colonization Cycles in Man and Beast. *World Archaeology* 9:249–261.
1977b Distributional Strategies. In *Sunda and Sahul: Prehistoric Studies in Southeast Asia, Melanesia, and Australia,* edited by J. Allen, J. Golson, and R. Jones, pp. 295–315. New York: Academic Press.

Divale, W.
1974   Migration, External Warfare and Matrilocal Residence. *Behavior Science Research* 9:75–133.

Dobyns, H.
1983   *Their Numbers Become Thinned.* Knoxville: University of Tennessee Press.

Doran, Edwin, Jr.
  1955   *Landforms of the Southern Bahamas.* Austin: University of Texas
          Press.
  1958   The Caicos Conch Trade. *Geographical Review* 48:388–401.
Driver, H.E., and W.C. Massey
  1957   Comparative Studies of North American Indians. *Transactions of
          the American Philosophical Society* 47:165–456.
Dunn, Oliver, and James E. Kelley, Jr., eds.
  1989   *The Diario of Christopher Columbus's First Voyage to America
          1492–1493,* abstracted by Bartholomé de Las Casas. Norman: Uni-
          versity of Oklahoma Press.

Earle, T.K.
  1976   A Nearest Neighbor Analysis of Two Formative Settlement Sys-
          tems. In *The Early Mesoamerican Village,* edited by K.V. Flannery,
          pp. 196–223. New York: Academic Press.
  1980   A Model of Subsistence Change. In *Modeling Change in Prehis-
          toric Subsistence Economies,* edited by T.K. Earle and A.L. Chris-
          tenson, pp. 1–29. New York: Academic Press.
  1985   Prehistoric Economics and the Evolution of Social Complexity: A
          Commentary. In *Prehistoric Production and Exchange: The Aegean
          and Eastern Mediterranean,* edited by A.B. Knapp and T. Stech, pp.
          106–111. Monograph 25, UCLA Institute of Archaeology, Los An-
          geles.
  1987   Chiefdoms in Archaeological and Ethnohistorical Perspective. *An-
          nual Review of Anthropology* 16:279–308.
Earle, Timothy K., and Andrew L. Christenson, eds.
  1980   *Modeling Change in Prehistoric Subsistence Economies.* New York:
          Academic Press.
Earle, T.K., and R.W. Preucel
  1987   Processual Archaeology and the Radical Critique. *Current Anthro-
          pology* 28:501–538.
Ehrlich, Paul R.
  1975   The Population Biology of Coral Reef Fishes. *Annual Review of
          Ecology and Systematics* 6:211–247.
Ember, M.
  1974   The Conditions That May Favor Avunculocal Residence. *Behavior
          Science Review* 9:203–209.
Ember, M., and C.R. Ember
  1971   The Conditions Favoring Matrilocal Versus Patrilocal Residence.
          American Anthropologist 73:571–594.

Farnsworth, P., J.E. Brady, M.J. DeNiro, and R.S. MacNeish
  1985   A Re-evaluation of the Isotopic and Archaeological Reconstruc-
         tions of Diet in the Tehuacan Valley. *American Antiquity* 50:102–
         116.

Fewkes, J.W.
  1907   The Aborigines of Porto Rico and Neighboring Islands. *Twenty-fifth
         Annual Report of the U.S. Bureau of American Ethnology, 1903–
         1904*, pp. 35–281. Washington, D.C.

Flannery, Kent V.
  1976   Evolution of Complex Settlement Systems. In *The Early Mesoameri-
         can Village*, edited by K.V. Flannery, pp. 162–173. New York: Aca-
         demic Press.

Ford, J. A.
  1969   A Comparison of Formative Cultures in the Americas: Diffusion or
         the Psychic Unity of Man. *Smithsonian Contributions to Anthro-
         pology*, no. 2, Washington, D.C.

Fox, G. V.
  1882   Methods and Results: An Attempt to Solve the Problem of the First
         Landing Place of Columbus in the New World. *United States Coast
         and Geodetic Survey, Report for 1880*, Appendix no. 18. Washing-
         ton, D.C.

Fox, R.
  1967   *Kinship and Marriage.* New York: Cambridge University Press.

Freedman, J.L.
  1980   Human Reactions to Population Density. In *Biosocial Mechanisms
         of Population Regulation*, edited by M.N. Cohen, R.S. Malpass, and
         H.G. Klein, pp. 189–207. New Haven: Yale University Press.

Fry, B., R. Lutes, M. Northam, P.L. Parker, and F. Ogden
  1982   A $^{13}C/^{12}C$ Comparison of Food Webs in Caribbean Seagrass Mea-
         dows and Coral Reefs. *Aquatic Botany* 14:389–398.

Fry, B., and E.B. Sherr
  1984 $d^{13}C$ Measurements as Indicators of Carbon Flow in Marine and
         Freshwater Ecosystems. *Contributions to Marine Science* 27:13–47.

Fuson, Robert H.
  1983   The *Diario de Colón*: A Legacy of Poor Transcription, Translation,
         and Interpretation. *Terrae Incognitae* 15:51–75.
  1987   *The Log of Christopher Columbus.* Camden, N.J.: International Ma-
         rine Publishing Company.

Garrett, Peter, and Stephen Jay Gould
    1984   Geology of New Providence Island, Bahamas. *Geological Society of America Bulletin* 95:209–220.

Gero, Joan
    1991   Experiencing Change: Who Knew What in Prehistory? In *Processed and Postprocessual Archaeologies: Multiple Ways of Knowing the Past*, edited by R.W. Preucel, pp. 126–139. Center for Archaeological Investigations, Occasional Paper no. 10. Carbondale: Southern Illinois University Press.

Gifford, Charles A.
    1962   Some Observations on the General Biology of the Land Crab, *Cardisoma guanhumi* (Latreille) in South Florida. *Biological Bulletin* 123:207–223.

Gillis, W.T.
    1977   Biogeography and Vegetation. In *Land Resources of the Bahamas: A Summary*, edited by B.G. Little, D.K. Buckley, R. Cant, P.W.T. Henry, A. Jefferiss, J.D. Mather, J. Stark, and R.N. Young, pp. 13–23. Ministry of Overseas Development, Land Resources Study no. 27, Surrey, England.

Glazier, Stephen D.
    1978   Trade and Warfare in Protohistoric Trinidad. In *Proceedings of the Seventh International Congress for the Study of the Pre-Columbian Cultures of the Lesser Antilles*, pp. 279–283. Montreal: Centre de Recherches Caraibes.
    1991   Impressions of Aboriginal Technology: The Caribbean Canoe. In *Proceedings of the Thirteenth International Congress for Caribbean Archaeology*, edited by E.N. Ayubi and J.B. Haviser, pp. 149–161. Reports of the Archaeological-Anthropological Institute of the Netherlands Antilles, no. 9, Curacao.

Glynn, Peter W.
    1973   Aspects of the Ecology of Coral Reefs in the Western Atlantic Region. In *Biology and Geology of Coral Reefs*, Volume II: *Biology I*, edited by O.A. Jones and R. Endean, pp. 271–323. New York: Academic Press.

Goggin, J. M.
    1937   *1937 Bahamas Field Notes*. MS, P.K. Yonge Library, University of Florida, Gainesville.
    1939   An Anthropological Reconnaissance of Andros Island, Bahamas. *American Antiquity* 5:21–26.

1952   *1952 Bahamas Field Notes.* MS, P.K. Yonge Library, University of Florida, Gainesville.

González, Nancie L.
1988   *Soujourners of the Caribbean: Ethnogenesis and Ethnohistory of the Garifuna.* Urbana: University of Illinois Press.

Goodenough, W.H.
1955   Residence Rules. *Southwestern Journal of Anthropology* 12:22–37.

Goodwin, R. C.
1978   The Lesser Antilles Archaic: New Data from St. Kitts. *Journal of the Virgin Islands Archaeological Society* 5:6–16.
1979   *The Prehistoric Cultural Ecology of St. Kitts, West Indies: A Case Study in Island Archaeology.* Ph.D. dissertation, Arizona State University. Ann Arbor: University Microfilms.
1980   Demographic Change and the Crab-Shell Dichotomy. In *Proceedings of the Eighth International Congress for the Study of the Pre-Columbian Cultures of the Lesser Antilles,* pp. 45–68. Arizona State University, Anthropological Research Papers no. 22.

Granberry, Julian
1956   The Cultural Position of the Bahamas in Caribbean Archaeology. *American Antiquity* 22:128–134.
1957   An Anthropological Reconnaissance of Bimini, Bahamas. *American Antiquity* 22:378–381.
1978   The Gordon Hill Site, Crooked Island, Bahamas. *Journal of the Virgin Islands Archaeological Society* 6:32–44.
1979–   Spanish Slave Trade in the Bahamas, 1509–1530: An Aspect of the
81   Caribbean Pearl Industry. 3 parts. *Journal of the Bahamas Historical Society,* 1, 2, and 3.
1980   A Brief History of Bahamian Archaeology. *Florida Anthropologist* 33:83–93.
1987   Antillean Languages and the Aboriginal Settlement of the Bahamas: A Working Hypothesis. Paper presented at the conference "Bahamas 1492: Its People and Environment," Freeport, Bahamas.

Gregor, Thomas
1977   *Mehinaku.* Chicago: University of Chicago Press.

Gross, D.R.
1975   Protein Capture and Cultural Development in the Amazon Basin. *American Anthropologist* 77:526–549.

Guarch, J.M.
1974   *Ensayo de Reconstrucción Etno-histórica del Taino de Cuba.* Serie Arqueológica no. 4, Havana, Cuba.

Gumerman, G.
    1986   The Role of Competition and Cooperation in the Evolution of Is-
            land Societies. In *The Evolution of Island Societies*, edited by P.V.
            Kirch, pp. 42–49. New York: Cambridge University Press.
Halkitis, M., S. Smith, and K. Rigg
    1980   *The Climate of the Bahamas*. Nassau: Bahamas Geographical Asso-
            ciation.
Hames, Raymond B., and William T. Vickers
    1982   Optimal Diet Breadth Theory as a Model to Explain Variability in
            Amazonian Hunting. *American Ethnologist* 9:357–378.
Handwerker, W. Penn
    1983   The First Demographic Transition: An Analysis of Subsistence
            Choices and Reproductive Consequences. *American Anthropolo-
            gist* 85:5–27.
Harrington, M.R.
    1921   *Cuba before Columbus*, vols. 1 and 2. Indian Notes and Mono-
            graphs, Museum of the American Indian. New York: Heye Founda-
            tion.
Harris, David R.
    1965   *Plants, Animals and Man in the Outer Leeward Island, West Indies:
            An Ecological Study of Antigua, Barbuda and Anguilla*. Berkeley:
            University of California Press.
Harris, M.
    1979   *Cultural Materialism: The Struggle for a Science of Culture*. New
            York: Random House.
Harrisse, H.
    1961   *The Discovery of North America* [1892]. Amsterdam: N. Israel.
Hassan, F.A.
    1981   *Demographic Archaeology*. New York: Academic Press.
Haviser, J.B., Jr.
    1990   Geographic, Economic and Demographic Aspects of Amerindian
            Interaction Between Anguilla and St. Martin–St. Maarten. Paper
            presented at the 55th Annual Meeting of the Society for American
            Archaeology, Las Vegas.
    1991   Preliminary Results of Test Excavations at the Hope Estate Site, St.
            Martin. *Proceedings of the Thirteenth International Congress for
            Caribbean Archaeology*, edited by E.N. Ayubi and J.B. Haviser, pp.
            647–666. Reports of the Archaeological-Anthropological Institute
            of the Netherlands Antilles, no. 9, Curacao.

Hawkes, Christopher
1954 Archaeological Theory and Method: Some Suggestions from the Old World. *American Anthropologist* 56:155–168.

Hawking, Stephen
1988 *From the Big Black Holes: A Brief History of Time.* New York: Bantam.

Hayden, B.
1975 The Carrying Capacity Dilemma: An Alternate Approach. *American Antiquity Memoir* 30:11–21.

Heinrich, Bernd
1979 *Bumblebee Economics.* Cambridge, Mass.: Harvard University Press.

Henige, David
1991 *In Search of Columbus: The Sources for the First Voyage.* Tucson: University of Arizona Press.

Henry, P.W.T.
1974 *The Pine Forests of the Bahamas.* Ministry of Overseas Development, Land Resources Study no. 16, Surrey, England.

Herrera y Tordesillas, Antonio de
1601 *Historia General de los Hechos de los Castellanos, en las Islas, y Tierra-Firme de el Mar Oceano.* 4 vols. Madrid.

Hesse, R.C., and K. Orr Hesse
1977 The Conch Industry in the Turks and Caicos Islands. *Underwater Naturalist* 10:4–9.

Hirshleifer, J.
1980 *Price Theory Applications.* 2d ed. Englewood Cliffs, N.J.: Prentice Hall.

Hodder, Ian
1985 Postprocessual Archaeology. In *Advances in Archaeological Method and Theory,* vol. 9, edited by M.B. Schiffer, pp. 1–26. New York: Academic Press.
1991 Post-Processual Archaeology: The Current Debate. In *Processual and Postprocessual Archaeologies: Multiple Ways of Knowing the Past,* edited by R.W. Preucel, pp. 30–41. Center for Archaeological Investigations, Occasional Paper no. 10. Carbondale: Southern Illinois University Press.

Hodder, Ian, and Clive Orton
1976 *Spatial Analysis in Archaeology.* Cambridge: Cambridge University Press.

Hoffman, Charles A., Jr.
  1967   *Bahama Prehistory: Cultural Adaptation to an Island Environment.*
         Ph.D. dissertation, University of Arizona. Ann Arbor: University
         Microfilms.
  1970   The Palmetto Grove Site on San Salvador, Bahamas. *Contributions
         of the Florida State Museum, Social Sciences* 16:1–26. Gainesville.
  1973a Archaeological Investigations on St. Kitts. *Caribbean Journal of
         Science* 13(3–4):237–250.
  1973b Petroglyphs on Crooked Island, Bahamas. In *Proceedings of the
         Fourth International Congress for the Study of the Pre-Columbian
         Cultures of the Lesser Antilles*, pp. 9–12. Castries, St. Lucia.
  1987a Archaeological Investigations at the Long Bay Site, San Salvador,
         Bahamas. In *Proceedings of the First San Salvador Conference Co-
         lumbus and His World*, edited by D.T. Gerace, pp. 237–245. Fort
         Lauderdale: CCFL Bahamian Field Station.
  1987b The Long Bay Site, San Salvador. *American Archaeology* 6:97–102.
Hoffman, Charles A., Jr., ed.
  1987c Current Research, Caribbean. *American Antiquity* 52:191–3.
  1988   Current Research, Caribbean. *American Antiquity* 53:189–2.
Horn, H. S.
  1978   Optimal Tactics of Reproduction and Life-History. In *Behavioral
         Ecology*, edited by J. R. Krebs and N.B. Davies, pp. 411–429. Oxford:
         Blackwell Scientific.
Hudson, C., M. Smith, D. Hally, R. Polhemus, and C.DePratter
  1987   Reply to Boyd and Schroedl. *American Antiquity* 52:845–856.
Hudson, John
  1969   A Location Theory for Rural Settlement. *Annals of the Association
         of American Geographers* 59:365–381.
Iverson, J.B.
  1979   Behavior and Ecology of the Rock Iguana, *Cyclura carinata*. *Bul-
         letin of the Florida State Museum*, no. 24. Gainesville.
Jackson, J.B.C.
  1972   The Ecology of the Mollusks of *Thalassia* Communities, Jamaica,
         West Indies. II. Molluscan Population Variability Along an Envi-
         ronmental Stress Gradient. *Marine Biology* 14:304–337.
  1973   The Ecology of the Mollusks of *Thalassia* Communities, Jamaica,
         West Indies. I. Distribution, Environmental Physiology, and Ecol-
         ogy of Common Shallow-Water Species. *Bulletin of Marine Science*
         23: 313–350.
Johannes, R. E.
  1981   *Words of the Lagoon.* Berkeley: University of California Press.

Johnson, A.
  1975   Time Allocation in a Machiguenga Community. *Ethnology* 14:301–310.
  1980   The Limits of Formalism in Agricultural Decision Research. In *Agricultural Decision Making*, edited by P.F. Barlett, pp. 19–43. New York: Academic Press.
  1982   Reductionism in Cultural Ecology: The Amazon Case. *Current Anthropology* 23:413–418.
  1983   Machiguenga Gardens. In *Adaptive Responses of Native Amazonians*, edited by R.B. Hames and W.T. Vickers, pp. 29–63. New York: Academic Press.

Johnson, A., and M. Baksh
  1987   Ecological and Structural Influences on the Proportions of Wild Foods in the Diets of Two Machiguenga Communities. In *Food and Evolution*, edited by M. Harris and E.B. Ross, pp. 387–406. Philadelphia: Temple University Press.

Johnson, A., and C.A. Behrens
  1982   Nutritional Criteria in Machiguenga Food Production Decisions: A Linear Programming Analysis. *Human Ecology* 10:167–189.

Johnson, A. and Timothy K. Earle
  1987   *The Evolution of Human Society: From Forager Group to Agrarian State.* Stanford, Calif.: Stanford University Press.

Jones, Alick R.
  1985   Diet Change and Human Population at Indian Creek, Antigua. *American Antiquity* 50:518–536

Jones, W.O.
  1959   *Manioc in Africa.* Stanford, Calif.: Stanford University Press.

Joyce, Thomas A.
  1907   Prehistoric Antiquities from the Antilles, in the British Museum. *Journal of the Royal Anthropological Institute* 37:402–419.
  1919   Notes on a Wooden Stool from the Island of Eleuthera, Bahamas. *Man* 19:1–2.

Judge, Joseph
  1986   Where Columbus Found the New World. *National Geographic Magazine* 170:566–599.

Keegan, W.F.
  1982a   A Biological Introduction to the Prehistoric Procurement of the *Strombus gigas*. *Florida Anthropologist* 35:76–88.
  1982b   Lucayan Cave Burials from the Bahamas. *Journal of New World Archaeology* 5:57–65.

1982c   Lucayan Fishing Practices: An Experimental Approach. *Florida Anthropologist* 35:146–161.

1983a   An Archaeological Reconnaissance of Crooked Island and Acklins Island, Bahamas. Report, Department of Anthropology, Florida Museum of Natural History, Gainesville.

1983b   Archaeological Investigations on Mayaguana, Bahamas: A Preliminary Report. Report, Department of Anthropology, Florida Museum of Natural History, Gainesville.

1984a   Columbus and the City of Gold. *Journal of the Bahamas Historical Society* 6:34–39.

1984b   Pattern and Process in *Strombus gigas* Tool Replication. *Journal of New World Archaeology* 6:15–25.

1985   *Dynamic Horticulturalists: Population Expansion in the Prehistoric Bahamas.* Ph.D. dissertation, Department of Anthropology, UCLA. Ann Arbor: University Microfilms.

1986a   The Ecology of Lucayan Arawak Fishing Practices. *American Antiquity* 51:816–825.

1986b   The Optimal Foraging Analysis of Horticultural Production. *American Anthropologist* 88:92–107.

1987   Diffusion of Maize from South America: The Antillean Connection Reconstructed. In *Emergent Horticultural Economies of the Eastern Woodlands*, edited by W.F. Keegan, pp. 329–344. Center for Archaeological Investigations, Occasional Paper no. 7. Carbondale: Southern Illinois University.

1988   Archaeological Investigations on Crooked and Acklins Islands, Bahamas: A Preliminary Report of the 1987 Field Season. *Miscellaneous Project Report Number 36*, Florida State Museum, Gainesville.

1989a   The Columbus Chronicles. *The Sciences*, January–February, pp. 47–55.

1989b   Creating the Guanahatabey (Ciboney): The Modern Genesis of an Extinct Culture. *Antiquity* 63:373–379.

1989c   Stable Isotope Analysis of Prehistoric Diet. In *Reconstruction of Life From the Skeleton*, edited by M.Y. Iscan and K.A.R. Kennedy, pp. 223–236. New York: Alan R. Liss.

1989d   Transition from a Terrestrial to a Maritime Economy: A New View of the Crab/Shell Dichotomy. In *Early Ceramic Population Lifeways and Adaptive Strategies in the Caribbean*, edited by Peter Siegel, pp. 119–128. Oxford: BAR International Series 506.

1991a   Culture Processes and Culture Realities. In *Processual and Postprocessual Archaeologies: Multiple Ways of Knowing the Past*, edited by R. W. Preucel, pp. 183–196. Center for Archaeological Investigations, Occasional Paper no. 10. Carbondale: Southern Illinois University.

1991b   Lucayan Settlement Patterns and Coastal Changes in the Bahamas. In *Paleoshorelines and Prehistoric Settlement*, edited by Lucy Lewis Johnson. Boca Raton, Fla.: CRC Press.

Keegan, W. F., and B. M. Butler

1987   The Microeconomic Logic of Horticultural Intensification in the Eastern Woodlands. In *Emergent Horticultural Economies of the Eastern Woodlands*, edited by W.F. Keegan, pp. 109–127. Center for Archaeological Investigations, Occasional Paper no. 7. Carbondale: Southern Illinois University.

Keegan, W.F., and M.J. DeNiro

1988   Stable Carbon- and Nitrogen-Isotope Ratios of Bone Collagen Used to Study Coral-Reef and Terrestrial Components of Prehistoric Bahamian Diet. *American Antiquity* 53: 320–336.

Keegan, W.F., and J.M. Diamond

1987   Colonization of Islands by Humans: A Biogeographical Perspective. In *Advances in Archaeological Method and Theory*, vol. 10, edited by M.B. Schiffer, pp. 49–92. San Diego: Academic Press.

Keegan, W. F., and M.D. Maclachlan

1989   The Evolution of Avunculocal Chiefdoms: A Reconstruction of Taino Kinship and Politics. *American Anthropologist* 91:613–630.

Keegan, W.F. and S.W. Mitchell

1984a   Archaeological Investigations on Great and Little Exuma, Bahamas. Report, Department of Anthropology, Florida State Museum, Gainesville.

1984b   The Archaeological Survey of Long Island, Bahamas: Final Report. Report, Department of Anthropology, Florida Museum of Natural History, Gainesville.

1986   Possible Allochthonous Lucayan Arawak Artifact Distributions, Bahama Islands. *Journal of Field Archaeology* 13:255–258.

1987   The Archaeology of Christopher Columbus's Voyage Through the Bahamas, 1492. *American Archaeology* 6:102–108.

Keegan, William F., and Neil E. Sealey

1988   A Preliminary Archaeological Survey of the Fehling Site (AN-1), Andros, Bahamas. Florida Museum of Natural History, Department of Anthropology *Miscellaneous Project Report Number 40*, and Bahamas Archaeological Team Project Report no. 2. Gainesville.

Keegan, W., A. Johnson, and T. Earle

1985   Carrying Capacity and Population Regulation: A Comment on Dewar. *American Anthropologist* 87:659–663.

Keegan, William F., Maurice W. Williams, and Grethe Seim
    1990   Archaeological Survey of Grand Turk, B.W.I. *Miscellaneous Project Report Number 43*, Department of Anthropology, Florida Museum of Natural History, Gainesville.

Keene, A.S.
    1982   *Prehistoric Foraging in a Temperate Forest: A Linear Programming Model.* New York: Academic Press.

Keesing, R.M.
    1975   *Kin Groups and Social Structure.* New York: Holt, Rinehart and Winston.

Keith, D.H.
    1987   "The Molasses Reef Wreck." Ph.D. dissertation, Texas A & M University, College Station.

Keith, D.H., J.A. Duff, S.R. James, T.J. Oertling, and J.J. Simmons
    1984   The Molasses Reef Wreck, Turks and Caicos Islands, B.W.I.: A Preliminary Report. *International Journal of Nautical Archaeology and Underwater Exploration* 13:45–63.

Keith, D.H., and J.J. Simmons
    1985   Analysis of Hull Remains, Ballast and Artifact Distribution of a 16th-Century Shipwreck, Molasses Reef, British West Indies. *Journal of Field Archaeology* 12:411–424.

Keith, D.H., and Bruce F. Thompson
    1985   *An Archaeological Survey of La Isabela, Dominican Republic.* INA Exploration and Discovery Research Team Report, Texas A & M University, College Station.

Kelley, James E., Jr.
    1983   In the Wake of Columbus on a Portolan Chart. *Terrae Incognitae* 15:77–111.
    1987   The Navigation of Columbus on his First Voyage to America. In *Proceedings of the First San Salvador Conference, Columbus and His World,* edited by D.T. Gerace, pp. 121–140. Fort Lauderdale: CCFL Bahamian Field Station.
    1988   Preliminary Estimates of Magnetic Variation along Columbus's Route on his Second Voyage to the New World. Manuscript in possession of the author.
    1989   The Map of the Bahamas Implied by Chaves's *Derrotero.* What Is Its Relevance to the First Landfall Question? *Imago Mundi* 42: in press.

Kirby, I.E., and C.I. Martin
    1972   *The Rise and Fall of the Black Caribs of St. Vincent.* St. Vincent.

Kirch, P.V.
  1980   Polynesian Prehistory: Cultural Adaptation in Island Ecosystems.
          American Scientist 68:39–48.
  1982   The Ecology of Marine Exploitation in Prehistoric Hawaii. *Human
          Ecology* 10:455–476.
  1984   *The Evolution of the Polynesian Chiefdoms.* New York: Cambridge
          University Press.

Klingel, Gilbert
  1961   *The Ocean Island (Inagua).* New York: Natural History Press.

Krebs, J.R.
  1978   Optimal Foraging: Decision Rules for Predators. In *Behavioural
          Ecology,* edited by J.R. Krebs and N.B. Davies, pp. 23–63. Oxford:
          Blackwell Scientific.

Krebs, J.R., and N.B. Davies
  1981   *An Introduction to Behavioural Ecology.* Sunderland, Mass: Sinauer
          Associates.

Krieger, Herbert W.
  1937   The Bahama Islands and their Prehistoric Population. In *Explora-
          tions and Fieldwork of the Smithsonian Institution in 1936,* pp.
          93–98. Washington, D.C.: Smithsonian Institution.
  1938   Archaeology of the Virgin Islands. *Explorations and Fieldwork of
          the Smithsonian Institution in 1937,* pp. 95–102. Washington, D.C.:
          Smithsonian Institution.

Lancaster, Kelvin
  1971   *Consumer Demand: A New Approach.* New York: Columbia Uni-
          versity Press.

Larimore, C.C.
  1988   Terrae Recognitae: A Reconstruction of the Verdadera Route of
          Christopher Columbus. Paper presented at the Society for the His-
          tory of Discoveries Meeting, Minneapolis.

Las Casas, B. de
  1951   *Historia de las Indias.* 3 vols. Mexico City: Fondo de Cultura Eco-
          nómica.

Lathrap, D.W.
  1970   *The Upper Amazon.* London: Thames and Hudson.
  1977   Our Father the Cayman, Our Mother the Gourd: Spinden Revis-
          ited, or a Unitary Model for the Emergence of Agriculture in the
          New World. In *Origins of Agriculture,* edited by C.A. Reed, pp.
          713–751. The Hague: Mouton.
  1987   The Introduction of Maize in Prehistoric Eastern North America:

The View from Amazonia and the Santa Elena Peninsula. In *Emergent Horticultural Economies of the Eastern Woodlands*, edited by W.F. Keegan, pp. 345–371. Center for Archaeological Investigations, Occasional Paper no. 7. Carbondale: Southern Illinois University.

Lee, R.B., and E. De Vore, eds.
1968   *Man the Hunter.* Chicago: Aldine.

Levins, Richard
1966   The Strategy of Model Building in Population Biology. *American Scientist* 54:421–431.

Linares, Olga
1976   "Garden Hunting" in the American Tropics. *Human Ecology* 4:331–349.

Link, E.A., and M.C. Link
1958   A New Theory on Columbus's Voyage Through the Bahamas. *Smithsonian Miscellaneous Collections*, vol. 135(4).

Linton, R.
1936   *The Study of Man.* New York: Appleton-Century-Crofts.

Little, B.G., D.K. Buckley, R. Cant, P.W.T. Henry, A. Jefferiss, J.D. Mather, J. Stark, and R.N. Young, eds.
1977   *Land Resources of the Bahamas: A Summary.* Surrey, England: Ministry of Overseas Development, Land Resource Study no. 27.

Loven, S.
1935   *Origins of the Tainan Culture, West Indies.* Göteborg, Sweden: Elanders Boktryckeri Aktiebolag.

Lyon, E.
1986   The Diario of Christopher Columbus, October 10–October 27, 1492. In *A Columbus Casebook*, pp. 5–45. Washington, D.C.: National Geographic Society.
1989   Niña, Ship of Discovery. In *First Encounters: Spanish Explorations in the Caribbean and the United States, 1492–1570*, edited by J.T. Milanich and S. Milbrath, pp. 55–65. Gainesville: University Presses of Florida.

McArthur, Norma, I.W. Saunders, and R.L. Tweedie
1976   Small Population Isolates: A Micro-simulation Study. *The Journal of the Polynesian Society* 85:307–326.

MacArthur, R.H.
1972   *Geographical Ecology.* Princeton, N.J.: Princeton University Press.

MacArthur, R.H., and E.O. Wilson
1967   *The Theory of Island Biogeography.* Princeton, N.J.: Princeton University Press.

McGhee, R.
  1984 Contact Between Native North Americans and the Medieval Norse: A Review of the Evidence. *American Antiquity* 49:4–26.

McGuirk, Don, Jr.
  1989 The Juan de la Cosa Theory of Columbus's First Landfall. Manuscript in possession of the author..

McKinnen, Daniel
  1804 *Tour Through the British West Indies, in the Years 1802 and 1803 Giving a Particular Account of the Bahama Islands.* London: R. Taylor.

McKusick, Marshall
  1960 Aboriginal Canoes in the West Indies. *Yale University Publications in Anthropology,* no. 63. New Haven: Yale University Press.

Maclachlan, Morgan D., and William F. Keegan
  1990 Archeology and the Ethno-Tyrannies. *American Anthropologist* 92: 1011–1013.

MacLaury, J.C.
  1968 *Archaeological Investigations on Cat Island, Bahamas.* Master's thesis, Department of Anthropology, Florida Atlantic University, Boca Raton.
  1970 Archaeological Investigations on Cat Island, Bahamas. *Contributions of the Florida State Museum, Social Sciences* 16:27–50. Gainesville.

Malinowski, B.
  1978 *Coral Gardens and Their Magic.* New York: Dover.

Malthus, Thomas
  1959 *Population: The First Essay* [1798]. Ann Arbor: University of Michigan Press.

Mann, C.J.
  1986 Composition and Origin of Material in Pre-Columbian Pottery, San Salvador Island, Bahamas. *Geoarchaeology* 1:183–194.

Mansfield, Edwin
  1982 *Microeconomics: Theory and Applications.* 4th ed. New York: W.W. Norton.

Marcus, George E., and M.M.J. Fischer
  1986 *Anthropology as Cultural Critique.* Chicago: University of Chicago Press.

Marden, Luis
  1986 The First Landfall of Columbus. *National Geographic Magazine* 170:572–577.

Marquardt, W.H.
   1987   South Florida Contacts with the Bahamas: A Review and Some
          Speculations. Paper presented at the conference "Bahamas 1492: Its
          People and Environment," Freeport, Bahamas.

Martin, John F.
   1983   Optimal Foraging Theory: A Review of Some Models and Their
          Applications. *American Anthropologist* 85:612–629.
   1985   More Optimal Foraging Theory. *American Anthropologist* 87:649–
          650.

Martyr [D'Anghiera], P.
   1970   *De Orbe Novo* [1493–1525]. Translated by F.A. MacNutt. New York:
          Burt Franklin.

Marvel, Josiah, and Robert H. Power
   1991   The Quest of Where America Began: The Case for Grand Turk.
          American History Illustrated 25(6): 48–69.

Mason, Otis T.
   1877   Jadeite Celts from Turks and Caicos Islands, also Two Low Wooden
          Stools. *American Naturalist* 11:626.

Maybury-Lewis, David
   1974   *Akwe-Shavante Society.* Oxford: Oxford University Press.

Maynard, Charles Johnson
   1890   Some Inscriptions Found in Hartford Cave, Rum Cay, Bahamas.
          Contributions to Science 1:167–171.
   1893   Traces of the Lucayan Indian in the Bahamas. *Contributions to
          Science* 2:23–34.
   1915   Some Traces of Lucayan Indians in the Bahamas. *Records of Walks
          and Talks with Nature* 7:196–200.

Maynard Smith, John
   1988   *Did Darwin Get it Right?* New York: Chapman and Hall.

Meehan, Betty
   1977   Man Does Not Live by Calories Alone: The Role of Shellfish in a
          Coastal Cuisine. In *Sunda and Sahul*, edited by J. Allen, J. Golson,
          and R. Jones. New York: Academic Press.

Meggers, B.J.
   1954   Environmental Limitation on the Development of Culture. *Ameri-
          can Anthropologist* 56:801–824.
   1971   *Man and Culture in a Counterfeit Paradise.* Chicago: Aldine.

Meggers, B.J. and C. Evans, Jr.
   1957   *Archaeological Investigations at the Mouth of the Amazon.* Bul-

letin of American Ethnology 167. Washington, D.C.: Smithsonian Institution.

1983   Lowland South America and the Antilles. In *Ancient South Americans*, edited by J.D. Jennings, pp. 287–335. San Francisco: W. H. Freeman.

Meylan, Anne
1981a   Behavioral Ecology of the West Caribbean Green Turtle (*Chelonia mydas*) in the Internesting Habitat. In *Biology and Conservation of Sea Turtles*, Proceedings of the World Conference on Sea Turtle Conservation, edited by K.A. Bjorndal, pp. 67–80. Washington, D.C.: Smithsonian Institution Press.

1981b   Estimation of Population Size in Sea Turtles. In *Biology and Conservation of Sea Turtles*, Proceedings of the World Conference on Sea Turtle Conservation, edited by K.A. Bjorndal, pp. 135–138. Washington, D.C.: Smithsonian Institution Press.

Michener, James
1988   *Caribbean.* New York: Knopf.

Milanich, Jerald T., and Susan Milbrath, eds.
1989   *First Encounters: Spanish Explorations in the Caribbean and the United States, 1492–1570.* Gainesville: University Presses of Florida.

Milbrath, Susan
1989   Old World Meets New: Views Across the Atlantic. In *First Encounters: Spanish Explorations in the Caribbean and the United States, 1492–1570*, edited by J.T. Milanich and S. Milbrath, pp. 183–210. Gainesville: University Presses of Florida.

Miller, W.H.
1945   The Colonization of the Bahamas, 1647–1670. *William and Mary Quarterly* 2:33–46.

Minagawa, M., and E. Wada
1984   Stepwise Enrichment of ^{15}N along Food Chains: Further Evidence and the Relation between d^{15}N and Animal Age. *Geochimica et Cosmochimica Acta* 48:1135–1140.

Mitchell, S.W.
1984   Late Holocene Tidal Creek-Lake Transitions, Long Island, Bahamas. Addendum to *Proceedings of the Second Symposium on the Geology of the Bahamas*, edited by J.W. Teeter, pp. 1–28. Fort Lauderdale: CCFL Bahamian Field Station.

Mitchell, S.W., and W.F. Keegan
1987   Reconstruction of the Coastlines of the Bahama Islands in 1492. *American Archaeology* 6:88–96.

Miyake, Y., and E. Wada
    1967   The Abundance Ratio of ¹⁵N/¹⁴N in Marine Environments. *Recent Oceanographic Works in Japan* 9:32–53.

Molander, Arne
    1982   The Search for San Salvador. *Journal of the Bahamas Historical Society* 4:3–8.
    1983   A New Approach to the Columbus Landfall. *Terrae Incognitae* 15:113–149.
    1984   Ponce de León Belongs to the Bahamas. *Journal of the Bahamas Historical Society* 6:40–47.

Morison, Samuel Eliot
    1942   *Admiral of the Ocean Sea.* 2 vols. Boston: Little, Brown and Company.
    1974   *The European Discovery of America: The Southern Voyages.* New York: Oxford University Press.

Moscoso, Francisco
    1981   *The Development of Tribal Society in the Caribbean.* Ph.D. diss., SUNY-Binghamton. Ann Arbor: University Microfilms.
    1983   Parentesco y Clase en los Cacicazgos Tainos: Es Caso de los Naborias. In *Proceedings of the Ninth International Congress for the Study of the Pre-Columbian Cultures of the Lesser Antilles,* pp. 485–494. Montreal: Centre de Recherches Caraibes.
    1987   Etapas Históricas de la Sociedad Tribal en las Antillas. *Dedalo* 25:99–136.

Murdock, G.P.
    1949   *Social Structure.* New York: Macmillan.

Murphy, Yolanda, and Robert F. Murphy
    1974   *Women of the Forest.* New York: Columbia University Press.

Myers, Robert A.
    1984   Island Carib Cannibalism. *Nieuwe West-Indische Gids* 158:147–184.

Nardi, Bonnie Anna
    1981   Modes of Explanation in Anthropological Population Theory. *American Anthropologist* 83:28–56.

Narganes Storde, Yvonne M.
    1991   Secuencia Cronológica de Dos Sitios Arqueológicos de Puerto Rico (Sorcé, Vieques y Tecla, Guayanilla). *Proceedings of the Thirteenth International Congress for Caribbean Archaeology,* edited by E.N. Ayubi and J.B. Haviser, pp. 628–646. Reports of the Archaeological-Anthropological Institute of the Netherlands Antilles, no. 9. Curacao.

Nicholson, Desmond V.
  1976   Pre-Columbian Seafaring Capabilities in the Lesser Antilles. In *Proceedings of the Sixth International Congress for the Study of the Pre-Columbian Cultures of the Lesser Antilles*, pp. 98–105. Guadeloupe.

Nietschmann, Bernard
  1981   The Cultural Context of Sea Turtle Hunting in the Caribbean and Problems Caused by Commercial Exploitation. In *Biology and Conservation of Sea Turtles*, Proceedings of the World Conference on Sea Turtle Conservation, edited by K.A. Bjorndal, pp. 67–80. Washington, D.C.: Smithsonian Institution Press.

Nordstrom, Sharon
  1979   *A Limnological Study of the Ponds on Pine Cay, Turks and Caicos Islands, B.W.I.* Master's thesis, University of New Haven.

Northfelt, D.W., M.J. DeNiro, and S. Epstein
  1981   Hydrogen and Carbon Isotopic Ratios of Cellulose Nitrate and Saponifiable Lipid Fractions Prepared from Annual Growth Rings of a California Redwood. *Geochimica et Cosmochimica Acta* 45:1895–1898.

Obregón, M.
  1987   Columbus's First Landfall: San Salvador. In *Proceedings of the First San Salvador Conference, Columbus and His World*, edited by D.T. Gerace, pp. 185–195. Fort Lauderdale: CCFL Bahamian Field Station.

Orians, G.H.
  1980   *Some Adaptations of Marsh-Nesting Blackbirds.* Princeton, N.J.: Princeton University Press.

Osgood, C.
  1942   The Ciboney Culture of Cayo Redondo, Cuba. *Yale University Publications in Anthropology*, no. 25. New Haven: Yale University Press.

Ostrander, Gary K.
  1982   Discovery of an Isolated Colony of Rock Iguanas. *Bahamas Naturalist* 6:22–24.

Oviedo, Gonzalo Fernández de
  1959   *Natural History of the West Indies.* Translated and edited by Sterling A. Stoudemire. University of North Carolina Studies in the Romance Languages and Literature, no. 32. Chapel Hill: University of North Carolina Press.

Palmer, Robert
  1989   *Deep into Blue Holes.* London: Unwin Hyman.

Parker, J.
  1983   The Columbus Landfall Problem: A Historical Perspective. *Terrae Incognitae* 15:1–28.

Patterson, Jack, and George Stevenson
  1977   *Native Trees of the Bahamas*. Abaco, Bahamas: Private printing.

Petersen, G.
  1982   Ponapean Matriliny: Production, Exchange, and the Ties that Bind. *American Ethnologist* 9:129–144.

Peterson, M.L.
  1974   Exploration of a 16th-century Bahaman Shipwreck. *National Geographic Society Research Reports, 1967 Projects*, pp. 231–242. Washington, D.C.

Petitjean-Roget, Henry
  1978   L'art des Arawak et des Caraibes des Petites Antilles. Analyse de la Décoration des Céramiques. Les Cahiers du Ceraq. *Centre d'Etudes Régionales Antilles-Guyane*, no. 35.

Pianka, E.R.
  1974   *Evolutionary Ecology*. New York: Harper and Row.

Pinder, D.A., and M.E. Witherick
  1972   Nearest-Neighbor Analysis of Linear Point Patterns. *Tijdschrift voor Economische en Sociale Geografie* 64:160–163.
  1975   A Modification of Nearest-Neighbor Analysis for Use in Linear Situations. *Geography* 60:16–23.

Pohl, Frederick J.
  1966   *Amerigo Vespucci, Pilot Major*. New York: Octagon Books.

Powell, H.A.
  1960   Competitive Leadership in Trobriand Political Organization. *Journal of the Royal Anthropological Institute* 90:118–148.

Pratt, Marjorie K.
  1974a   *Preliminary Report 1973: Prehistoric Archaeology of San Salvador, Bahamas*. Corning, N.Y.: CCFL Publications.
  1974b   *Preliminary Report 1974: Prehistoric Archaeology of San Salvador, Bahamas*. Corning, N.Y.: CCFL Publications.

Preucel, Robert W.
  1982   "Settlement Pattern Succession on the Pajarito Plateau." Master's paper, Archaeology Program, UCLA.
  1985   Settlement Pattern Succession on the Pajarito Plateau: Hudson's Model Revisited. Paper presented at the 50th Annual Meeting of the Society for American Archaeology, Denver.

1991 Mapping the Terrain of Philosophy in Archaeology. In *Processual and Postprocessual Archaeologies: Multiple Ways of Knowing the Past*, edited by R.W. Preucel, pp. 17–29. Center for Archaeological Investigations, Occasional Paper no. 10. Carbondale: Southern Illinois University Press.

Rainey, Froelich G.
1934 Diary Beginning January 22, 1934, Upon Arrival in Port-au-Prince, Haiti. Manuscript, Yale Peabody Museum, New Haven, Conn.

Ramenofsky, Ann
1987 *Vectors of Death*. Albuquerque: University of New Mexico Press.

Randall, John E.
1965 Grazing Effects on Sea Grasses by Herbivorous Reef Fishes in the West Indies. *Ecology* 46:255–260.
1967 Food Habits of Reef Fishes of the West Indies. In *Studies in Tropical Oceanography Miami* 5:665–847.
1968 *Caribbean Reef Fishes*. Jersey City, N.J.: TFH Publications.

Rathje, William L.
1971 The Origin and Development of Lowland Classic Maya Civilization. *American Antiquity* 43:203–222.

Reidhead, V.A.
1980 The Economics of Subsistence Change: A Test of an Optimization Model. In *Modeling Change in Prehistoric Subsistence Economies*, edited by T.K. Earle and A.L. Christenson, pp. 141–186. New York: Academic Press.

Rice, Prudence M.
1987 *Pottery Analysis: A Sourcebook*. Chicago: University of Chicago Press.

Richards, Douglas G.
1988 Archaeological Anomalies in the Bahamas. *Journal of Scientific Exploration* 2:181–201.

Richardson, Philip L., and Roger A. Goldsmith
1987 The Columbus Landfall: Voyage Track Corrected for Winds and Currents. *Oceanus* 30(3):2–10.

Riley, Sandra
1983 *Homeward Bound*. Miami: Island Research.

Rindos, D.
1984 *The Origins of Agriculture*. New York: Academic Press.

Roe, Peter G.
1989 A Grammatical Analysis of Cedrosan Saladoid Vessel Form Catego-

ries and Surface Decoration: Aesthetic and Technical Styles in
Early Antillean Ceramics. In *Early Ceramic Population Lifeways
and Adaptive Strategies in the Caribbean*, edited by P. Siegel, pp.
267–382. Oxford: British Archaeological Reports, International Series 506.

Roosevelt, A. C.
  1980   *Parmana: Prehistoric Maize and Manioc Subsistence Along the
          Amazon and Orinoco.* New York: Academic Press.
  1990   Holistic Archaeology in Amazonia. Paper presented at the 55th
          Annual Meeting of the Society for American Archaeology, Las
          Vegas.

Rose, Richard
  1982   The Pigeon Creek Site, San Salvador, Bahamas. *Florida Anthro-
          pologist* 35:129–145.
  1987   Lucayan Lifeways at the Time of Columbus. In *Proceedings of the
          First San Salvador Conference, Columbus and His World*, edited by
          D.T. Gerace, pp. 321–339. Fort Lauderdale: CCFL Bahamian Field
          Station.

Rosenblat, Angel
  1954   *La Población de America en 1492. Viejos y Nuevos Cálculos.* Mex-
          ico City.
  1976   The Population of Hispaniola at the Time of Columbus. In *The
          Native Population of the Americas in 1492*, edited by W.M. Dene-
          van, pp. 43–66. Madison: University of Wisconsin Press.

Ross, Eric B.
  1978   Food Taboos, Diet, and Hunting Strategy: The Adaptation to Ani-
          mals in Amazon Cultural Ecology. *Current Anthropology* 19:1–36.

Rouse, I.
  1939   Prehistory in Haiti: A Study in Method. *Yale University Publica-
          tions in Anthropology*, no. 21. New Haven: Yale University Press.
  1941   Culture of the Ft. Liberté Region, Haiti. *Yale University Publica-
          tions in Anthropology*, nos. 23 and 24. New Haven: Yale University
          Press.
  1948   The West Indies. In *Handbook of South American Indians*. Vol. 4,
          The Circum-Caribbean Tribes, edited by J. H. Steward. Bureau of
          American Ethnology Bulletin 143(4):497–565. Washington, D.C.
  1949   Petroglyphs. In *Handbook of South American Indians*, vol. 5, edited
          by J. Steward. Bureau of American Ethnology Bulletin. 143:493–502.
          Washington, D.C.
  1972   *Introduction to Prehistory: A Systematic Approach.* New York:
          McGraw–Hill.

1977   Pattern and Process in West Indian Archaeology. *World Archaeology* 9(1):1–11.

1980   The Concept of Series in Bahamian Archaeology. *Florida Anthropologist* 33(3):94–98.

1982   Ceramic and Religious Development in the Greater Antilles. *Journal of New World Archaeology* 5(2):45–55.

1986   *Migrations in Prehistory: Inferring Population Movements from Cultural Remains.* New Haven: Yale University Press.

1987   Whom Did Columbus Discover in the West Indies? *American Archaeology* 6:85–88.

1989a   Peoples and Cultures of the Saladoid Frontier in the Greater Antilles. In *Early Ceramic Population Lifeways and Adaptive Strategies in the Caribbean,* edited by P.E. Siegel, Oxford: BAR International Series no. 506.

1989b   Peopling and Repeopling of the West Indies. In *Biogeography of the West Indies, Past, Present and Future,* edited by C.A. Woods. Gainesville: Sandhill Crane Press.

Rouse, I., and L. Allaire
  1978   Caribbean. In *Chronologies in New World Archaeology,* edited by R.E. Taylor and C. Meighan, pp. 431–481. New York: Academic Press.

Rouse, I., and José Cruxent
  1959   Venezuelan Archaeology. *Caribbean Series,* no. 6. New Haven: Yale University Press.

Rouse, Irving, and Clark Moore
  1985   Cultural Sequence in Southwestern Haiti. In *Proceedings of the Tenth International Congress for the Study of the Pre-Columbian Cultures of the Lesser Antilles,* pp. 3–21. Montreal: Centre de Recherches Caraibes.

Rubel, Paula, and Abraham Rosman
  1983   The Evolution of Exchange Structures and Ranking: Some Northwest Coast and Athapaskan Examples. *Journal of Anthropological Research* 39:1–25.

Ruddle, Kenneth
  1974   The Yupka Cultivation System: A Study of Shifting Cultivation in Colombia and Venezuela. *Ibero-Americana,* no. 52. Los Angeles: University of California Press.

Sadler, H.E.
  1972   *Turks Island Landfall.* Grand Turk: Private printing.

Sahlins, M.D.
  1961   The Segmentary Lineage: An Organization of Predatory Expansion.
          American Anthropologist 63:322–343.
  1985   *Islands of History.* Chicago: University of Chicago Press.
Sale, Kirkpatrick
  1990   *The Conquest of Paradise.* New York: Penguin.
Sanders, W.T., J.R. Parsons, and R.S. Santley
  1979   *The Basin of Mexico: Ecological Processes in the Evolution of a
          Civilization.* New York: Academic Press.
Sanoja, M., and I. Vargas
  1983   New Light on the Prehistory of Eastern Venezuela. *Advances in
          World Archaeology* 2:205–244.
Sauer, C.O.
  1966   *The Early Spanish Main.* Berkeley: University of California Press.
Saunders, D. Gail
  1983   *The Bahamian Loyalists and Their Slaves.* London: Macmillan.
  1985   *Slavery in the Bahamas 1648–1838.* Nassau: *The Nassau Guardian.*
Schimmelmann, A.
  1985   *Stable Isotopic Studies on Chitin.* Ph.D. dissertation, University of
          California, Los Angeles. Ann Arbor: University Microfilms.
Schneider, D.M.
  1961   The Distinctive Features of Matrilineal Descent Groups. In *Matri-
          lineal Kinship,* edited by D.M. Schneider and K. Gough, pp. 1–29.
          Berkeley: University of California Press.
Schneider, D.M., and K. Gough, eds.
  1961   *Matrilineal Kinship.* Berkeley: University of California Press.
Schoeninger, M.J., and M.J. DeNiro
  1984   Nitrogen and Carbon Isotopic Composition of Bone Collagen from
          Marine and Terrestrial Animals. *Geochimica et Cosmochimica
          Acta* 48:625–639.
Schoeninger, M.J., M.J. DeNiro, and H. Tauber
  1983   Stable Nitrogen Isotope Ratios of Bone Collagen Reflect Marine
          and Terrestrial Components of Prehistoric Human Diet. *Science*
          220:1381–1383.
Schultz, T.P.
  1981   *Economics of Population.* Reading, Mass.: Addison-Wesley.
Sealey, J.C., and N.J. van der Merwe
  1985   Isotope Assessment of Holocene Human Diets in Southwestern
          Cape, South Africa. *Nature* 315:138–140.

Sealey, N.E.

1985   *Bahamian Landscapes: An Introduction to the Geography of the Bahamas.* London: Collins Caribbean.

1987   New Developments on the Columbus Landfall Issue. *Journal of the Bahamas Historical Society* 9:5–13.

Sears, W.H.

1975   Cruising with a Purpose. *Yachting*, November, pp. 44–46.

1976   Columbus and the Arawaks. *Yachting*, November, pp. 62–63.

Sears, W.H., and S.D. Sullivan

1978   Bahamas Prehistory. *American Antiquity* 43(1):3–25.

Severin, T.

1978   *The Brendan Voyage.* New York: McGraw-Hill.

Sibley, R.M.

1983   Optimal Group Size Is Unstable. *Animal Behavior* 31:947–948.

Siegel, Peter E.

1991   Migration Research in Saladoid Archaeology: A Review. *Florida Anthropologist* 44(1):in press.

Siegel, Peter E., ed.

1989   *Early Ceramic Population Lifeways and Adaptive Strategies in the Caribbean.* Oxford: BAR International Series no. 506.

Sillen, A., J.C. Sealey, and N.J. van der Merwe

1989   Chemistry and Paleodietary Research: No More Easy Answers. *American Antiquity* 54:504–512.

Sleight, Frederick W.

1965   Certain Environmental Considerations in West Indian Archaeology. *American Antiquity* 31(2):226–231.

Smith, B.N., and S.Epstein

1971   Two Categories of $^{13}C/^{12}C$ Ratios of Higher Plants. *Plant Physiology* 47:80–84.

Smith, E.A.

1981   The Application of Optimal Foraging Theory to the Analysis of Hunter-Gatherer Group Size. In *Hunter-Gatherer Foraging Strategies,* edited by B. Winterhalder and E.A. Smith, pp. 36–65. Chicago: University of Chicago Press.

1983   Anthropological Applications of Optimal Foraging Theory: A Critical Evaluation. *Current Anthropology* 24:625–651.

Smith, E.A., and B. Winterhalder

1985   On the Logic and Application of Optimal Foraging Theory: A Brief Reply to Martin. *American Anthropologist* 87:645–648.

Smith, R.C.
   1986   *Early Modern European Ship-Types 1450-1650.* The Newberry Library Slide Set Number 6. Chicago: The Newberry Library.
   1987   The Search for the Lost Caravels. *American Archaeology* 6:109-114.

Smith, R.C., D.H. Keith, and D. Lakey
   1985   The Highborn Cay Wreck: Further Exploration of a 16th-Century Bahaman Shipwreck. *International Journal of Nautical Archaeology and Underwater Exploration* 14:63-72.

Smith, R., D. Lakey, T. Oertling, B. Thompson, and R. Woodward
   1982   *Sevilla la Nueva: A Site Survey and Historical Assessment of Jamaica's First European Town.* Project report, Institute of Nautical Archaeology, Texas A & M University, College Station.

Smole, William J.
   1976   *The Yanoama Indians: A Cultural Geography.* Austin: University of Texas Press.

Stevens-Arroyo, Antonio M.
   1988   *Cave of the Jagua: The Mythological World of the Tainos.* Albuquerque: University of New Mexico Press.

Steward, J.H.
   1947   American Culture History in the Light of South America. *Southwestern Journal of Anthropology* 3(2):85-107.

Steward, J.H., and L.C. Faron
   1959   *Native Peoples of South America.* New York: McGraw-Hill.

Stuiver, M., and P.J. Reimer
   1986   A Computer Program for Radiocarbon Age Calibration. *Radiocarbon* 28:1022-1030.

Stump, R.K., and J.W. Frazer
   1973   Simultaneous Determination of Carbon, Hydrogen and Nitrogen in Organic Compounds. *Nuclear Science Abstracts* 28:746.

Sturtevant, W.C.
   1961   Taino Agriculture (in The Evolution of Horticultural Systems in Native South America: Causes and Consequences—A Symposium). *Anthropologica* (Suppl. 2):69-73.
   1966   History and Ethnography of Some West Indian Starches. In *The Domestication and Exploitation of Plants and Animals,* edited by P.J. Ucko and G.W. Dimbleby, pp. 177-197. Chicago: Aldine.
   1969   History and Ethnography of Some West Indian Starches. In *The Domestication and Exploitation of Plants and Animals,* edited by P.J. Ucko and G.W. Dimbleby, pp. 177-179. Chicago: Aldine.

Sued-Badillo, Jalil
  1978   *Los Caribes: Realidad o Fabula.* Río Piedras, P.R.: Editorial Antillana.
  1979   *La Mujer Indígena y su Sociedad.* 2d ed. Río Piedras, P.R. Editorial Antillana.
Sullivan, S.D.
  1974   *Archaeological Reconnaissance of Eleuthera, Bahamas.* Master's thesis, Florida Atlantic University, Boca Raton.
  1976   *Archaeological Reconnaissance of the Turks and Caicos Islands, British West Indies.* Report submitted to the government of the Turks and Caicos.
  1980   An Overview of the 1976 to 1978 Archaeological Investigations in the Caicos Islands. *Florida Anthropologist* 33:94–98.
  1981   *Prehistoric Patterns of Exploitation and Colonization in the Turks and Caicos Islands.* Ph.D. dissertation, University of Illinois. Ann Arbor: University Microfilms.
Swanton, John R.
  1946   *The Indians of the Southeastern United States.* Washington, D.C.: Smithsonian Institution Press.
Tabio, E., and E. Rey
  1979   *Prehistoria de Cuba.* 2d ed. Havana: Editorial de Ciencias Sociales.
Tannenbaum, Nicola
  1984   The Misuse of Chayanov: "Chayanov's Rule" and Empiricist Bias in Anthropology. *American Anthropologist* 86:927–942.
Tauber, H.
  1981 ^{13}C Evidence for Dietary Habits of Prehistoric Man in Denmark. *Nature* 292:332–333.
Taviani, P.E.
  1985   *Christopher Columbus: The Grand Design.* London: Orbis.
  1987   Why We are Favorable for the Watling-San Salvador Landfall. In *Proceedings of the First San Salvador Conference, Columbus and His World,* edited by D.T. Gerace, pp. 197–228. Fort Lauderdale: CCFL Bahamian Field Station.
Taylor, D., and I. Rouse
  1955   Linguistic and Archaeological Time Depth in the West Indies. *International Journal of American Linguistics,* 21(2):105–115.
Terrell, J.
  1986   *Prehistory in the Pacific Islands.* New York: Cambridge University Press.

1990   Storytelling in Prehistory. In *Archaeological Method and Theory*, vol. 2, edited by M.B. Schiffer, pp. 1–27. Tucson: University of Arizona Press.

Textor, R.B.
1967   *A Cross-Cultural Summary*. New Haven: HRAF Press.

Vandermeer, John
1981   *Elementary Mathematical Ecology*. New York: John Wiley and Sons.

van der Merwe, N.J.
1982   Carbon Isotopes, Photosynthesis and Archaeology. *American Scientist* 70:596–606.

van der Merwe, N.J., A.C. Roosevelt, and J.C. Vogel
1981   Isotopic Evidence for Prehistoric Subsistence Change at Parmana, Venezuela. *Nature* 292:536–538.

Varela, C.
1984   *Cristóbal Colón, Textos y Documentos Completos*. 2d ed. Madrid: Editorial Alianza.
1987   Florentine's Friendship and Kinship with Christopher Columbus. In *Proceedings of the First San Salvador Conference, Columbus and His World*, edited by D.T. Gerace, pp. 33–43. Fort Lauderdale: CCFL Bahamian Field Station.

Veloz Maggiolo, Marcio, and Bernardo Vega
1982   The Antillean Preceramic: A New Approximation. *Journal of New World Archaeology* 5(2):33–44.

Veloz Maggiolo, M., E. Ortega, and A. Caba Fuentes
1981   *Los Modos de Vida Meillacoides y sus Posibles Origenes*. Santo Domingo: Museo del Hombre Dominicano.

Veloz Maggiolo, M., I. Vargas, M. Sanoja, and F. Luna Calderón
1976   *Arqueología de Yuma (República Dominicana)*. Santo Domingo: Taller.

Vignaud, H.
1905   *Études Critiques sur la Vie de Colomb Vant ses Découvertes*. Paris: H. Welter.

Vogel J.C., and J. van der Merwe
1977   Isotopic Evidence for Early Maize Cultivation in New York State. *American Antiquity* 42:238–242.

Watters, D.R.
1980   *Transect Surveying and Prehistoric Site Locations on Barbuda and Montserrat, Leeward Islands, West Indies*. Ph.D. dissertation, University of Pittsburgh. Ann Arbor: University Microfilms.

1982   Relating Oceanography to Antillean Archaeology: Implications
        from Oceania. *Journal of New World Archaeology* 5(2):3–12.

Webster, C.C., and P.N. Wilson
1966   *Agriculture in the Tropics.* London: Longman Group.

Weiner, A.B.
1976   *Women of Value, Men of Reknown.* Austin: University of Texas
        Press.

Werner, Dennis
1983   Why Do the Mekranoti Trek? In *Adaptive Responses of Native
        Amazonians,* edited by R.B. Hames and W.T. Vickers, pp. 225–238.
        New York: Academic Press.

White, Peter J., and James F. O'Connell
1982   *A Prehistory of Australia, New Guinea and Sahul.* New York: Aca-
        demic Press.

Whittaker, Robert H.
1975   *Communities and Ecosystems.* New York: Macmillan.

Wilbert, Johannes
1977   Navigators of the Winter Sun. In *The Sea in the Pre-Columbian
        World,* edited by E.P. Benson, pp. 17–46. Washington, D.C.: Dum-
        barton Oaks.

Willey, Gordon R.
1953   *Prehistoric Settlement Patterns in the Virú Valley, Peru.* Bureau of
        American Ethnology, Bulletin 155, Washington, D.C.

Wilson, C.L., W.E. Loomis, and T.A. Steeves
1971   *Botany.* 5th ed. New York: Holt, Rinehart and Winston.

Wilson, Samuel M.
1990a   *Hispaniola: The Chiefdoms of the Caribbean in the Early Years of
        European Contact.* Tuscaloosa: University of Alabama Press.
1990b   Taíno and Carib Strategies for Survival. Paper presented at the con-
        ference "Non-Imperial Polities in the Lands Visited by Christopher
        Columbus During His Four Voyages to the New World." Panama:
        Smithsonian Tropical Research Institute.

Wing, Elizabeth S.
1969   Vertebrate Remains Excavated from San Salvador Island, Bahamas.
        Journal of Caribbean Science 9(1–2):25–29.
1987   The Versatile Lucayans. Paper presented at the conference "Baha-
        mas 1492: Its People and Environment," Freeport, Bahamas.

Wing, Elizabeth S., and Antoinette Brown
1979   *Paleonutrition.* New York: Academic Press.

Wing, Elizabeth S., and Elizabeth J. Reitz
  1982   Prehistoric Fishing Communities of the Caribbean. *Journal of New World Archaeology* 5:13–32.
Wing, Elizabeth S., and Sylvia J. Scudder
  1980   Use of Animals by Prehistoric Inhabitants of St. Kitts, West Indies. In *Proceedings of the Eighth International Congress for the Study of the Pre-Columbian Cultures of the Lesser Antilles*, pp. 237–245. Arizona State University, Anthropological Research Papers no. 22.
  1983   Animal Exploitation by Prehistoric People Living on a Tropical Marine Edge. In *Animals and Archaeology*. Vol. 2. *Shell Middens, Fishes and Birds*, edited by C. Grigson and J. Clutton-Brock, pp. 197–210. Oxford: B.A.R. International Series no. 183.
Winslow, John H.
  1991   Far North by Far West: Columbus's First Landfalls in the Bahamas and the North Coast of Cuba. *HRD News* 2(5, 6):1–10.
Winter, J.
  1978a The Clifton Pier Rockshelter, New Providence, Bahamas. *Journal of the Virgin Islands Archaeological Society* 6:45–48.
  1978b A Note on Bahamian Griddles. In *Proceedings of the Seventh International Congress for the Study of the Pre-Columbian Cultures of the Lesser Antilles*, pp. 231–236. Montreal: Centre de Recherches Caraibes.
  1978c Preliminary Work from the McKay Site on Crooked Island. In *Proceedings of the Seventh International Congress for the Study of the Pre-Columbian Cultures of the Lesser Antilles*, pp. 237–242. Montreal: Centre de Recherches Caraibes.
  1980   A Preliminary Archaeological Survey of San Salvador, Bahamas. *Bahamas Archaeological Project, Reports and Papers for 1980*. San Salvador: CCFL Bahamian Field Station.
  1981   Archaeological Reconnaissance on San Salvador, Cat Island and Rum Cay. *Bahamas Archaeological Project, Reports and Papers for 1981*. San Salvador: CCFL Bahamian Field Station.
  1982   Archaeological Reconnaissance on San Salvador, New Providence, Abaco and Rum Cay. *Bahamas Archaeological Project, Reports and Papers for 1982*. San Salvador: CCFL Bahamian Field Station.
Winter, J., J. Granberry, and A. Leibold
  1985   Archaeological Investigations within the Bahamas. In *Proceedings of the Tenth International Congress for the Study of the Pre-Columbian Cultures of the Lesser Antilles*, pp. 83–92. Montreal: Centre de Recherches Caraibes.

Winter, J., and J. Stipp
    1983   Preliminary Investigations of the Minnis/Ward Site, San Salvador,
            Bahamas. In *Proceedings of the Ninth International Congress for
            the Study of the Pre-Columbian Cultures of the Lesser Antilles*, pp.
            155–162. Montreal: Centre de Recherches Caraibes.

Winter, Marcus
    1976   The Archaeological Household Cluster in the Valley of Oaxaca. In
            The Early Mesoamerican Village, edited by K.V. Flannery, pp. 25–31.
            New York: Academic Press.

Winterhalder, B.
    1981   Optimal Foraging Strategies and Hunter-Gatherer Research in An-
            thropology: Theory and Models. In *Hunter-Gatherer Foraging Strat-
            egies*, edited by B. Winterhalder and E.A. Smith, pp. 13–25. Chicago:
            University of Chicago Press.

Winterhalder, B., and E.A. Smith, eds.
    1981   *Hunter-Gatherer Foraging Strategies*. Chicago: University of Chi-
            cago Press.

Wright, George
    1984   *Behavioral Decision Theory*. Beverly Hills, Calif.: Sage.

Wylie, Alison
    1990   "An Unexamined Life is not Worth Living": Forthright Realism and
            Scientific Practice in Archaeology. Paper presented at the 55th An-
            nual Meeting of the Society for American Archaeology, Las Vegas.

Zambardino, R.A.
    1978   Critique of David Henige's "On the Contact Population of Hispan-
            iola: History as Higher Mathematics." *Hispanic American Histori-
            cal Review* 58:700–708.

Zucchi, A., K. Tarble, and J.E. Vaz
    1984   The Ceramic Sequence and New TL and C^{14} Dates for the Aguerito
            Site of the Middle Orinoco. *Journal of Field Archaeology* 11:155–180.

INDEX

Library of Congress Cataloging-in-Publication Data

Keegan, William F.
    The people who discovered Columbus: the prehistory of the Bahamas
/ William F. Keegan.
        p.   cm. — (The Ripley P. Bullen series / Florida Museum of
Natural History)
    Includes bibliographical references and index.
    ISBN 0-8130-1137-X
    1. Lucayan Indians—Antiquities.   2. Lucayan Indians—History.
3. Indians of the West Indies—Bahamas—Antiquities.   4. Bahamas—
Antiquities.   I. Title.   II. Series: The Ripley P. Bullen series.
F1655.K44   1992   92-3773
972.96—dc20   CIP

St. Louis Community College
at Meramec
LIBRARY

St. Louis Community College
at Meramec
Library